AMERICA'S MOST WANTED RECIPES

AMERICA'S MOST WANTED RECIPES

DELICIOUS RECIPES FROM YOUR FAMILY'S

FAVORITE RESTAURANTS

RON DOUGLAS

ATRIA PAPERBACK
New York London Toronto Sydney

ATRIA PAPERBACK
A Division of Simon & Schuster, Inc.
1230 Avenue of the Americas
New York, NY 10020

Copyright © 2009 by Verity Associates LLC

First Atria Paperback edition July 2009

ATRIA PAPERBACK and colophon are trademarks of Simon & Schuster, Inc.

For information about special discounts for bulk purchases, please contact Simon & Schuster Special Sales at 1-866-509-1949 or business@simonandschuster.com.

The Simon & Schuster Speakers Bureau can bring authors to your live event. For more information or to book an event, contact the Simon & Schuster Speakers Bureau at 1-866-248-3049 or visit our Web site at www.simonspeakers.com.

Designed by Davina Mock-Maniscalco

Manufactured in the United States of America

20 19 18 17 16 15 14

Library of Congress Cataloging-in-Publication Data is available.

ISBN 978-1-4391-4706-1
ISBN 978-1-4391-5572-1 (ebook)

Thank you ...

Nilaja Duckett (Sweetie), Nia Duckett (Baby Girl), Ryan Duckett (Little Man), Tom Grossmann (Chef Tom), Marygrace Wilfrom (Kitchen Witch), Charles Yates (Festo), Sharon Duckett, Sharonda Duckett, Maston Murphy (Pop), Rose Murphy, Marcia Ferguson, Bill and Jeanette Duckett, Adam Weiss Public Relations, Gloria Pitzer, Mike Filsaime .com Inc. staff, the Warrior Forum, Fox Business, the Secret Recipe Forum.

CONTENTS

Preface	xi
About *America's Most Wanted Recipes*	xvii
Helpful Cooking Tips	xix
Cooking Terms	xxiii
Guidelines for Buying Fresh Vegetables	xxv
Guidelines for Buying Fresh Fruits	xxvi
Herbs and Spices	xxvii
Are Your Herbs and Spices Fresh?	xxix
Guide to Symbols in Recipes	xxx

APPLEBEE'S™

Baby Back Ribs	1
Bacon–Green Onion Mashed Potatoes	3
Chicken Quesadilla Grande	4
Crispy Orange Chicken Skillet	5
Fiesta Lime Chicken	7
Garlic Mashed Potatoes	8
Low-Fat Grilled Tilapia with Mango Salsa	9
Santa Fe Chicken	10
Spinach Pizza	12
Tomato-Basil Soup	14
Walnut Blondie with Maple Butter Sauce	15

ARBY'S™

Apple Turnovers	16
Barbecue Sauce	18

ARTHUR TREACHER'S™

Fried Fish	19

BAHAMA BREEZE™

Jamaican Jerk Grilled Chicken Wings	21

BASKIN-ROBBINS™

Cheesecake Ice Cream	23

BENIHANA™

Hibachi Steak	24
Japanese Fried Rice	25

BENNIGAN'S™

Broccoli Bites	26
Honey Mustard Dressing	27
Hot Bacon Dressing	28
Linguine Diablo	29
Onion Soup	31

BOSTON MARKET™

Creamed Spinach	32
Cucumber Salad	34
Dill Potato Wedges	35
Macaroni and Cheese	36
Meat Loaf	37
Spicy Rice	38
Squash Casserole	39
Stuffing	40

BROOKLYN CAFE™

Sun-Dried Tomato Seared Scallops	41

BULLFISH GRILL™

Shrimp and Cheese Grits	43

CALIFORNIA PIZZA KITCHEN™

BBQ Chicken Pizza	45
Chicken-Tequila Fettuccine	46

CARRABBA'S ITALIAN GRILL™

Italian Butter	47
Meatballs	48

THE CHEESECAKE FACTORY™

Avocado Egg Rolls	49
Banana Cream Cheesecake	51
Cajun Jambalaya Pasta	52

Contents

Chicken Fettuccine 53
Crab Cakes 54
Oreo Cheesecake 56
Pumpkin Cheesecake 58

CHI-CHI'S™
Baked Chicken Chimichangas 60
Pork Tenderloin with Bourbon Sauce 61
Salsa Verde Chicken Kabobs 62
Steak and Mushroom Quesadillas 63

CHILI'S™
Baby Back Ribs 65
Beef Fajitas 66
Chicken Enchilada Soup 67
Chocolate Chip Paradise Pie 68
Margarita Grilled Chicken 69
Salsa 70
Southwestern Chicken Chili 71
Southwestern Egg Rolls 72
Southwestern Vegetable Soup 74

CHURCH'S™
Fried Chicken 75

CRACKER BARREL™
Baby Limas 77
Banana Pudding 78
Cherry-Chocolate Cobbler 79
Fried Apples 80

DAIRY QUEEN™
Heath Blizzard 81
Ice Cream 82
Onion Rings 83

DENNY'S™
Country Fried Steak 84
Country Gravy 85

DOLLYWOOD™
Dipped Chocolate Chip Cookies 86

EL POLLO LOCO™
Beans 87
Pollo Asada 88

HARD ROCK CAFE™
Baked Potato Soup 89
BBQ Beans 91
BBQ Ribs 92
Homemade Chicken Noodle Soup 93
Pulled Pork 94
Shrimp Fajitas 95

HARDEE'S™
Cinnamon "Flake" Biscuits 96

HOOTERS™
Buffalo Shrimp 98
Buffalo Wings 100

HOUSTON'S™
Buttermilk-Garlic Dressing 101
Spinach and Artichoke Dip 102

IHOP™
Banana-Nut Pancakes 103
Colorado Omelet 105
Cream of Wheat Pancakes 106
Pancakes 107
Swedish Pancakes 108

JOE'S CRAB SHACK™
Crab Cakes 109
Étouffée 110
Rice Pilaf 111
Seafood-Stuffed Mushrooms 112
Seafood Stuffing 113
Stuffed Shrimp en Brochette 114

JOHNNY CARINO'S™
Five-Cheese Chicken Fettuccine 115

JUNIOR'S™
Famous No. 1 Cheesecake 116

KFC™
Buttermilk Biscuits 118
Honey Barbecue Wings 119
Original Recipe Fried Chicken 120

Contents

LUBY'S™ CAFETERIA
Spaghetti Salad — 122

MACARONI GRILL™
Chocolate Cake with Fudge
Sauce — 123
Focaccia — 125
Insalata Florentine — 126
Pasta Gamberetti e Pinoli — 127
Reese's Peanut Butter Cake — 129
Roasted Garlic–Lemon
Vinaigrette — 131
Sesame Shrimp — 132
Shrimp Portofino — 133

OLIVE GARDEN™
Angel Hair and Three-Onion
Soup — 134
Beef Fillets in Balsamic Sauce — 135
Bread Sticks — 136
Bruschetta al Pomodoro — 137
Chicken Crostina — 138
Chicken San Marco — 140
Chocolate Lasagna — 142
Fettuccine Alfredo — 144
Fettuccine Assortito — 145
Five-Cheese Lasagna — 146
Fried Mozzarella — 148
Lemon Cream Cake — 149
Oven-Roasted Potatoes — 151
Pasta e Fagioli — 152
Pizza Bianco — 153
Pork Filettino — 154
Salad Dressing — 155
Sangria — 156
Tiramisù — 157
Tuscan Tea — 158
Zuppa Toscana — 159

OUTBACK STEAKHOUSE™
Cyclone Pasta — 160
Honey-Wheat Bushman Bread — 161
Key Lime Pie — 162
Marinated Steak — 163
Walkabout Soup — 164

PANDA EXPRESS™
Orange-Flavored Chicken — 165

PANERA BREAD™
Asian Sesame-Chicken Salad — 167
Broccoli-Cheese Soup — 168

PAT'S KING OF STEAKS™
Philly Cheesesteak — 169

PERKINS RESTAURANT AND BAKERY™
Pancakes — 171

P.F. CHANG'S™
Chicken-Lettuce Wrap — 172
Chicken with Black Bean Sauce — 174
Sichuan Chicken Chow Fun — 175

PIZZA HUT™
Cavatini — 176

PLANET HOLLYWOOD™
Cap'n Crunch Chicken — 177

POPEYES™
Cajun Rice — 178
Dirty Rice — 179

RAINFOREST CAFE™
Blue Mountain Grilled Chicken
Sandwich — 180
Crab Cakes — 181
Safari Sauce — 182

RED LOBSTER™
Batter-Fried Shrimp — 183
Caesar Dressing — 184
Cajun Shrimp Linguine — 185
Cheddar Biscuits — 186
Clam Chowder — 187
Deep-Fried Catfish — 188
Dungeness Crab Bisque — 189
Fried Chicken Tenders — 190
Grouper Siciliano — 192
Hush Puppies — 193

Contents

Lobster Fondue 194

Shrimp Diablo 195

South Beach Seafood Paella 196

Trout Veracruz 198

ROADHOUSE GRILL™

Roast Beef and Mashed Potatoes 199

RUBY TUESDAY™

Chicken Quesadillas 201

Shrimp Pasta Parmesan 203

Sonoran Chicken Pasta 205

Super Salad Bar Pasta 207

RUTH'S CHRIS™ STEAK HOUSE

Barbecued Shrimp 208

SHONEY'S™

Marinated Mushrooms 209

Pot Roast 210

Tomato Florentine Soup 211

THE SOUP NAZI™

Crab Bisque 212

Cream of Sweet Potato Soup 214

Indian Mulligatawny Soup 215

Mexican Chicken Chili 216

STARBUCKS™

Chocolate Fudge Squares with
Mocha Glaze 217

Gingerbread Loaf 219

SUBWAY™

Sweet Onion Sauce 220

TACO BELL™

Beef Chalupa Supreme 221

Burrito Supreme 223

Enchirito 225

Mexican Pizza 226

T.G.I. FRIDAY'S™

Baked Potato Skins 227

Broccoli-Cheese Soup 228

Honey Mustard Dressing 229

Jack Daniel's Dipping Sauce 230

Orange Cream 231

Shrimp Marinara 232

Sizzling Chicken and Cheese 233

UNION PACIFIC™

Apple Pancakes 234

Grilled White Pekin Duck Breast 235

Measurements 237

Recipes by Category 239

Trademarks 245

Restaurant Web Sites 249

Index 251

PREFACE

This cookbook is a compilation of the most beloved restaurant dishes in America based on research and consumer surveys. These recipes generate billions of dollars for the restaurant industry every year. But while everyone enjoys eating out, there's nothing like a home-cooked meal made from scratch. Why not have the best of both worlds? With these "secret recipes," you can enjoy your favorite restaurant dishes at home and save money in the process!

To give you a little background, I grew up in a family of people with southern roots who loved to cook. As a kid, I used to be my grandmother's "personal assistant," helping her at the grocery store and in the kitchen as we prepared dinner for the family. The best feeling came from the smiles on their faces and the quiet in the room as they enjoyed the meal.

It is no wonder that I'm a foodie today. But it wasn't until my wife challenged me to make KFC's famous fried chicken for her that I became hooked on the idea of re-creating restaurant recipes that tasted just like the originals. The first place I went to research recipes was the Internet, which was a frustrating experience at the time. I found lots of recipes that were either incomplete or not even close to the originals. But I also discovered that there were thousands of people who were into "recipe cloning" and were searching the Internet every day for new secret recipes to try at home. Having been in e-commerce at the time, I thought it would be a great idea to set up a community Web site where these people could share their results and work together to create accurate clone recipes. The Secret Recipe Forum was launched and became the research hub and "virtual think tank" that inspired this cookbook. Today, RecipeSecrets.net has more than 70,000 recipe cloners and over 179,000 newsletter subscribers.

Each week, I would try to clone a new restaurant recipe and share the results with my members. Needless to say, I became a regular at many of the restaurants and was on a first-name basis with a lot of the servers.

Members of the Web site would also try the recipes and add their feedback and recommendations. As the Web site grew, it became more than just a hobby. Cooking experts and even professional chefs began getting involved with our recipe-cloning movement.

For many people, re-creating restaurant recipes at home was not just a fun way to impress their family and dinner guests, it was also a great way to save money.

HOW MUCH MONEY CAN YOU SAVE?

Studies show that nearly half of all U.S. adults are eating out each day. According to Nielsen Consumer Research:

The restaurant industry in the U.S. is projected to top $558 billion in food and drink sales in 2008, an average of over $1.5 billion a day. Approximately 133 million Americans are food-service patrons on any given day, making the average check size nearly $12 per person. This level of spending is a 13-fold increase in sales since 1970 and today accounts for about 4% of total U.S. GDP. There are nearly 950 thousand places to eat in the U.S., employing over 13 million people. Nearly one in five persons (18%) visits quick-serve restaurants ten or more times per month, and 19% visit sit-down restaurants six or more times per month.

Eating out is typically more expensive than preparing a home-cooked meal because restaurants have to price their food to pay high overhead expenses such as salaries to chefs, managers, and servers, and rent and advertising. By making these dishes at home, you can cut out all the excess costs and prepare each meal to your liking.

The table shows the potential savings per serving for a sampling of ten restaurant dishes featured in this cookbook.

Dish	Restaurant Price (1 serving)	At-Home Cost (1 serving)	You Save
Applebee's™ Fiesta Lime Chicken	$10.99	$6.62	$4.37
Benihana™ Hibachi Steak	$21.99	$11.46	$10.53
The Cheesecake Factory™ Cajun Jambalaya Pasta	$14.95	$9.79	$5.16
Chili's™ Beef Fajitas	$12.99	$5.43	$7.56
IHOP™ Banana-Nut Pancakes	$7.99	$3.49	$4.50
Olive Garden™ Fettuccine Alfredo	$11.95	$4.28	$7.67
Outback Steakhouse™ Marinated Steak	$17.99	$9.31	$8.68
P.F. Chang's™ Chicken-Lettuce Wrap	$8.00	$4.68	$3.32
Red Lobster™ Maine Lobster with Crabmeat Stuffing	$29.99	$14.74	$15.25
Ruby Tuesday™ Sonoran Chicken Pasta	$14.99	$7.54	$7.45

Let's consider the following example of how much you can save over time (assuming an average restaurant bill of $25 and an average at-home cost of $10) if you prepare these dishes at home instead of eating out three times per week:

Approximate savings per week = $45
Approximate savings per month = $180
Approximate savings per year = $2,160

Of course, preparing these dishes at home isn't a substitute for the restaurant dining experience, but for those looking to save a few bucks, it's well worth it.

A HEALTHIER ALTERNATIVE

If you need another reason for making these dishes at home, consider the fact that the foods many people eat when dining out are much higher in calories than foods prepared at home. And children in particular consume substantially more calories when eating a restaurant meal than when eating a meal at home.

The higher caloric density of restaurant food was much less of a factor for obesity when Americans ate out less. Today, though, with nearly half of all persons eating out each day, high-calorie restaurant meals are making much more of an impact.

A University of Minnesota study found that children who never eat at quick-serve restaurants during the week average 1,952 calories per day, while those who average one or two visits per week average 2,192. Children who frequent quick-serve restaurants three or more times per week average 2,752 calories per day, over 40 percent more than those who never eat there. This level of consumption, combined with falling levels of physical activity among children, has helped to drive the doubling obesity rate seen for children in the past twenty years. And teens have seen a tripling of the rate over the same period.

With this cookbook, you can replicate your favorite restaurant recipes at home, and you have complete control over the serving sizes and the ingredients you use.

Here are some suggested ingredient substitutes that will serve as healthier alternatives for you and your family:

If the recipe calls for:	Try substituting:
All-purpose flour in baked goods	Whole wheat flour for half the all-purpose flour
Butter, margarine, shortening, or oil in baked goods	Applesauce or prune puree for half the butter, margarine, shortening, or oil
Butter, margarine, shortening, or oil to prevent sticking	Cooking spray or using nonstick pans

Eggs	Two egg whites or ¼ cup egg substitute for each whole egg
Enriched pasta	Whole wheat pasta
Full-fat sour cream	Fat-free or low-fat sour cream or plain fat-free or low-fat yogurt
Ground beef	Extra-lean or lean ground beef, or ground chicken or turkey breast
Mayonnaise	Reduced-fat mayonnaise
Salad dressing	Fat-free or reduced-calorie dressing or flavored vinegars
Salt	Herbs, spices, or salt-free seasoning mixes or herb blends
White bread	Whole wheat bread
White rice	Brown rice, wild rice, bulgur, or pearl barley
Whole milk	Reduced-fat or fat-free milk

ABOUT *AMERICA'S MOST WANTED RECIPES*

Each recipe in *America's Most Wanted Recipes* has been tested and tweaked to taste just like the original. Although I can claim to offer only "clones" of these famous dishes, I am confident that if you follow the instructions, you won't be able to tell the difference.

There are tips throughout the book in which I share my personal experience and suggestions for making these dishes as well as tips for saving money, saving time, and preparing healthier alternatives.

I encourage you to put the book to good use and make these famous dishes yourself. Once you've tried the recipes, you'll see what makes them so special and why I have so many satisfied customers.

I hope this cookbook brings enjoyment to you and your family and friends for years to come.

Ron Douglas

HELPFUL COOKING TIPS

- Always chill juices and sodas before adding to beverage recipes.
- Store ground coffee in the refrigerator or freezer to keep it fresh.
- Seeds and nuts, both shelled and unshelled, keep best and longest when stored in the freezer. Unshelled nuts crack more easily when frozen. Nuts and seeds can be used directly from the freezer.
- To prevent cheese from sticking to a grater, spray the grater with cooking spray.
- Fresh lemon juice will remove the scent of onion from hands.
- Instant potatoes are a good stew thickener.
- Three large ribs of celery, chopped and added to about 2 cups of cooked dried beans (navy, brown, pinto), will make the beans easier to digest.
- When cooking vegetables that grow aboveground, the rule of thumb is to boil them without a cover.
- A tablespoon of sugar added to the water when cooking greens helps the vegetables retain their fresh color.
- Never soak vegetables after slicing them; they will lose much of their nutritional value.
- To cut down on odors when cooking cabbage, cauliflower, and other crucifers, add a little vinegar to the cooking water.
- Perk up soggy lettuce by soaking it in a mixture of lemon juice and cold water.
- Eggshells can easily be removed from hard-boiled eggs if the eggs are quickly rinsed in cold water after they are boiled.
- Keep bean sprouts and jicama fresh and crisp up to 5 days by submerging them in a container of water and then refrigerating them.
- When trying to reduce your fat intake, buy the leanest cuts of meat you can find. Fat can show up as an opaque white coating or can be evenly distributed throughout the meat, as marbling. Stay away from well-marbled cuts of meat.

- Pound meat lightly with a mallet or rolling pin, pierce with a fork, sprinkle lightly with meat tenderizer, and cover in a marinade. Refrigerate for about 20 minutes, and you'll have tender meat.
- Marinating is easy if you use a resealable plastic bag. The meat stays covered in the marinade and it's easy to turn and rearrange.
- It's easier to thinly slice meat if it's partially frozen.
- Tomatoes added to roasts will help to naturally tenderize them.
- Cut meats across the grain; they will be easier to eat and have a better appearance.
- When frying meat, sprinkle paprika over it to turn it golden brown.
- Always thaw all meats in the refrigerator for maximum safety.
- Refrigerate poultry promptly after purchasing. Keep it in the coldest section of your refrigerator for up to 2 days. Freeze poultry for longer storage. Never leave poultry at room temperature for more than 2 hours.
- If you're microwaving skinless chicken, cover the baking dish with vented plastic wrap to keep the chicken moist.
- Lemon juice rubbed on fish before cooking will enhance the flavor and help maintain a good color.
- Scaling a fish is easier if vinegar is rubbed on the scales first.
- Overripe bananas can be peeled and frozen in a plastic container until it's time to bake bread or cake.
- When baking bread, a small ovenproof dish of water in the oven will help keep the crust from getting too hard or too brown.
- Use vegetable shortening to grease pans, as margarine and oil absorb more readily into the dough or batter (especially bread).
- To make self-rising flour, mix together 4 cups all-purpose flour, 2 teaspoons salt, and 2 tablespoons baking powder, and store in a tightly covered container.
- Hot water kills yeast. One way to tell the correct temperature is to test a few drops of water on your forearm. If you cannot feel either hot or cold, the temperature is just right.
- When in doubt, always sift flour before measuring.
- When using a glass baking pan, reduce the oven temperature by 25°F.

- When baking bread, you get a finer texture if you use milk in the recipe. Water makes a coarser bread.
- To make bread crumbs, toast the heels of bread loaves and chop in a blender or food processor.
- Cracked eggs should not be used, as they may contain bacteria.
- The freshness of eggs can be tested by placing them in a large bowl of cold water; if they float, do not use them.
- Dust baking pans and work surfaces with flour by using a saltshaker filled with flour.
- To keep cauliflower white while cooking, add a little milk to the water.
- A roast with the bone in will cook faster than a boneless roast. The bone carries the heat to the inside more quickly.
- For a juicier hamburger, add a little cold water to the beef before grilling.
- To store cooked meatballs, freeze them on a cookie sheet, then transfer to resealable plastic bags and return to the freezer.
- When boiling corn, add sugar to the water instead of salt. Salt toughens the corn.
- To ripen tomatoes, put them in a brown paper bag in a dark pantry.
- To keep celery crisp, stand it upright in a pitcher of cold, salted water and refrigerate.
- When cooking cabbage, place a small glass or can half-full of vinegar on the stove near the cabbage. It will absorb the odor.
- Potatoes soaked in salt water for 20 minutes before baking will bake more rapidly.
- Let cut-up raw potatoes soak in cold water for at least a half hour before frying in order to improve the crispness of French fries. Be sure to dry the potatoes completely before adding to the oil.
- A few drops of lemon juice in the cooking water will whiten boiled potatoes.
- Buy mushrooms before they "open." When stems and caps are attached firmly, they are fresh.
- Do not use metal bowls when mixing salads. Use wood or glass.
- Lettuce keeps better if you store it in the refrigerator without washing it. Keep the leaves dry. Wash the lettuce before using.

- Never use baking soda when cooking to keep vegetables green. It destroys the vitamin C.
- If you oversalt your gravy, stir in some instant mashed potatoes to repair the damage. Add a little more liquid if necessary.
- After stewing chicken, let it cool in its broth before cutting, to add more flavor.

COOKING TERMS

Au gratin: Covered with bread crumbs and/or grated cheese and browned in the oven or under the broiler.

Au jus: Served in its own juices.

Baste: To moisten food at intervals during cooking with pan drippings or sauce in order to add flavor and prevent drying.

Bisque: A thick cream soup.

Blanch: To immerse in rapidly boiling water and allow to cook slightly.

Cream: To soften a fat, like butter, by beating it at room temperature. Butter and sugar are often creamed together.

Crimp: To seal the edges of a two-crust pie by pinching them at intervals with either the fingers or a fork.

Crudités: An assortment of raw vegetables that is served as an hors d'oeuvre, often with a dip.

Degrease: To remove the fat from the surface of stews and soups.

Dredge: To coat lightly with flour, cornmeal, or bread crumbs.

Entrée: The main course.

Fold: To incorporate a delicate ingredient into a mixture without releasing air bubbles.

Glaze: To cover with a glossy coating, such as melted and diluted jelly for fruit desserts.

Julienne: To cut vegetables, fruits, or cheeses into thin strips the size of matchsticks.

Marinate: To soak food in a savory, usually acidic sauce in order to tenderize or to enrich flavor.

Mince: To chop food into very small pieces.

Parboil: To boil until partially cooked; to blanch.

Pare: To remove the outer skin of a fruit or vegetable.

Poach: To cook gently in hot liquid kept just below the boiling point.

Sauté: To cook food in a small amount of butter or oil.

Simmer: To cook in liquid just below the boiling point.

Steep: To let food stand in hot liquid in order to extract or enhance flavor.

Toss: To combine ingredients with a repeated lifting motion.

Whip: To beat rapidly in order to incorporate air and produce expansion.

GUIDELINES FOR BUYING FRESH VEGETABLES

Artichokes: Look for compact, tightly closed heads with green, clean-looking leaves. Avoid those with leaves that are brown or separated.

Asparagus: Stalks should be tender and firm; tips should be closed and compact. Choose stalks with very little white; they are more tender. Use asparagus soon after purchasing because it toughens rapidly.

Beans: Those with small seeds inside the pods are best. Avoid beans with dry-looking pods.

Broccoli, brussels sprouts, cauliflower: Flower clusters on broccoli and cauliflower should be tight and close together. Brussels sprouts should be firm and compact. Smudgy, dirty spots may indicate pests or disease.

Cabbage and head lettuce: Choose heads that are heavy for their size. Avoid cabbage with wormholes and lettuce with discoloration or soft rot.

Cucumbers: Choose long, slender cucumbers for best quality. Avoid yellow ones.

Mushrooms: Caps should be closed around the stems. Avoid black or brown gills.

Peas and lima beans: Select pods that are well filled but not bulging. Avoid dried, spotted, yellow, or flabby pods.

GUIDELINES FOR BUYING FRESH FRUITS

Bananas: Skins should be free of bruises and black or brown spots. Purchase green and allow them to ripen at home at room temperature.

Berries: Select plump, solid berries with good color. Avoid stained containers, which indicate wet or leaky berries. Blackberries and raspberries with stems may be unripe. Strawberries without caps may be overripe.

Melons: In cantaloupes, thick, close netting on the rind indicates best quality. Cantaloupes are ripe when the stem scar is smooth and the space between the netting is yellow or yellow-green. They are best when fully ripe with a fruity odor.

Honeydews are ripe when the rind has a creamy to yellowish color and a velvety texture. Immature honeydews are whitish green.

Ripe watermelons have some yellow color on one side. If melons are white or pale green on one side, they are not ripe.

Oranges, grapefruit, and lemons: Choose those heavy for their size. Smoother, thinner skins usually indicate more juice. Most skin markings do not affect quality. Oranges with a slight greenish tinge may be just as ripe as fully colored ones. Light or greenish yellow lemons are more tart than deep yellow ones. Avoid citrus fruits showing withered, sunken, or soft areas.

HERBS AND SPICES

Basil: Aromatic with a sweet, warm flavor. Use whole fresh or ground dried. Good with lamb, fish, roasts, stews, ground beef, vegetables, and dressings.

Bay leaves: Pungent flavor. Use whole leaf, but remove before serving. Good in vegetable and seafood dishes, stews, and pickles.

Caraway: Aromatic with a spicy flavor. Use in cakes, breads, soups, cheese, and sauerkraut.

Chives: Sweet, mild flavor like that of onions. Excellent in salads. Use to flavor fish, soups, and potatoes.

Cilantro: Use fresh to flavor fish, chicken, rice, beans, and Mexican dishes. Great in salads and salsa.

Curry powder: Several pungent ground spices are combined in the proper proportions to give a distinct flavor to meat, poultry, fish, and vegetables.

Dill: Both seeds and leaves are flavorful. Leaves may be used as a garnish or cooked with fish, soup, dressings, potatoes, and beans. Leaves or the whole plant may be used to flavor pickles.

Fennel: Sweet, hot flavor. Both seeds and leaves are used. Use in small quantities in pies and baked goods. Leaves can be boiled with fish.

Ginger: A pungent root, this aromatic spice is sold fresh, dried, or ground. Use in pickles, preserves, cakes, cookies, and meat dishes.

Marjoram: May be used both dried and fresh. Use to flavor fish, poultry, omelets, lamb, stew, stuffing, and tomato juice.

Mint: Aromatic with a cool, fresh flavor. Excellent in beverages. Use to flavor fish, lamb, cheese, soup, peas, carrots, and fruit desserts.

Oregano: Strong aromatic. Use whole or ground to flavor tomato juice, fish, eggs, pizza, chili, poultry, and vegetables.

Paprika: A bright red ground pepper, this mild spice is used to flavor meat, vegetables, and soups or as a garnish for potatoes, salads, and eggs.

Parsley: Best when used fresh, but can be used dried (labeled "parsley flakes"). Use to flavor fish, omelets, soup, meat, and mixed greens.

Rosemary: Strong aromatic. Can be used fresh or dried. Use to flavor fish, stuffing, beef, lamb, poultry, onions, and potatoes.

Saffron: This orange-yellow spice is used to flavor or color foods such as soup, chicken, rice, and breads.

Sage: Use fresh or dried to flavor fish, beef, poultry, cheese spreads, and breads. The flowers are sometimes used in salads.

Tarragon: Leaves have a pungent, hot taste. Use to flavor sauces, salads, fish, poultry, tomatoes, eggs, green beans, and dressings.

Thyme: Sprinkle leaves on fish or poultry before broiling or baking. Place a few sprigs directly on the coals shortly before meat is finished grilling.

ARE YOUR HERBS AND SPICES FRESH?

Ingredient Shelf Life

- Ground spices: 2 to 3 years
- Whole spices: 3 to 4 years
- Seasoning blends: 1 to 2 years
- Herbs: 1 to 3 years
- Extracts: 4 years, except pure vanilla, which lasts forever

Still not sure? Then use these guidelines:

Check to see that the color of your spices and herbs is vibrant. If the color has faded, chances are so has the flavor.

Rub or crush the spice or herb between your fingers. If the aroma is faint and the flavor is not apparent, it's time to replace it.

Store herbs and spices in tightly capped containers, and keep away from heat, moisture, and direct sunlight. Replace bottle lids tightly immediately after use.

To minimize moisture and caking, avoid sprinkling directly into a steaming pot and use a dry measuring spoon.

Check the freshness date on the container.

Guide to Symbols in Recipes

Follow this key for helpful suggestions and fun facts.

SAVE MONEY
Watch your wallet without giving up restaurant-quality food with these tips on smart shopping and cost-effective preparation and storage.

SAVE TIME
These time-saving shortcuts will have dinner on the table in a fraction of the time.

HEALTHY CHOICE
Low-fat alternatives and waist-slimming suggestions make these dishes nutritious—and still delicious.

FOOD FOR THOUGHT
Test your culinary knowledge with these fun facts on rare ingredients and the art of cooking.

Secret Recipe Tip
Get the inside scoop and carefully guarded cooking tricks from top chefs across the country.

Kids' Choice
Your kids will love these dishes—and you can feel good about serving them! They are healthy, delicious, and kid-approved.

Restaurant History
Discover where it all began with these fascinating and fun accounts of how America's favorite restaurants rose to the top.

America's Most Wanted Recipes

APPLEBEE'S
baby back ribs

BABY BACK RIBS BASTED IN A SWEET BARBECUE SAUCE. TYPICALLY SERVED WITH
BAKED BEANS, FRIES, AND COLESLAW.

Three 1-pound racks pork baby
back ribs, cut in half
1 cup ketchup
¼ cup apple cider vinegar
3 tablespoons dark brown sugar

3 tablespoons Worcestershire
sauce
1 teaspoon liquid smoke
½ teaspoon salt

1. Place the ribs in a large pot and fill the pot with enough water to cover the ribs.
2. Bring the water to a boil, reduce the heat, cover, and simmer for 1 hour or until the ribs are fork-tender.
3. While the ribs are boiling, combine the remaining ingredients in a medium saucepan and bring to a boil.
4. Reduce the heat and simmer, uncovered, stirring often, for 30 minutes or until the sauce mixture is slightly thickened.
5. Preheat the broiler.
6. Place the boiled ribs, meat side down, on a broiler pan.
7. Brush with half the sauce and broil 4 to 5 inches from the heat source for 6 to 7 minutes, or until the edges are slightly charred.
8. Turn the ribs over, brush with the remaining sauce, and broil for an additional 6 to 7 minutes, or until the edges are slightly charred.

Serves 3

You can make your own ribs at home for half the price that you would be paying to eat out.

It's easy to purchase slabs of ribs when on sale and freeze for later use.

If you like your ribs falling off the bone, add 1 cup apple cider vinegar to the water before placing the ribs in to boil.

Remove the silver skin from the back of the ribs if you do not want to boil the ribs first and just bake at 350°F for 1½ to 2 hours, basting with the sauce during the last half hour.

Applebee's™ was founded in Atlanta, Georgia, by Bill Palmer and T. I. Palmer. They envisioned a restaurant that would provide full service, consistently good food, reasonable prices, and quality service in a neighborhood setting. Their first restaurant, T.J. Applebee's Rx for Edibles & Elixirs™, opened in November 1980.

APPLEBEE'S
bacon—green onion mashed potatoes

CREAMY MASHED POTATOES INFUSED WITH CRISP BACON AND GREEN ONIONS.

2 pounds potatoes, peeled and cut into 1-inch cubes

4 cloves garlic, peeled

5 slices bacon, cut into ½-inch pieces

1 cup thinly sliced green onions

½ cup low-fat milk, warmed

½ cup low-fat sour cream

1 teaspoon salt

¼ teaspoon pepper

1. In a large pot, immerse the potatoes and garlic in water.
2. Boil until the potatoes are fork-tender, about 30 minutes.
3. Fry the bacon in a skillet until crisp; drain on paper towels.
4. Pour out all but 1 teaspoon of the bacon drippings from the pan.
5. Add the green onions to the drippings, and sauté until soft but not brown. Return the bacon to the skillet and stir to combine.
6. Drain the potatoes and garlic and return to the pot.
7. Mash the potatoes with the milk, sour cream, salt, and pepper. Stir in the bacon and green onions.
8. Reheat, if necessary, before serving.

Serves 4

You can make this dish using instant potato flakes or buds.

Sauté the green onions in a bit of butter in place of the bacon drippings.

APPLEBEE'S
chicken quesadilla grande

TWO LARGE FLOUR TORTILLAS STUFFED WITH GRILLED CHICKEN, MELTED CHEESE, CRISP BACON, PICO DE GALLO (SALSA), AND A HINT OF CHIPOTLE PEPPER.

Two 12-inch flour tortillas
1 tablespoon vegetable oil
2 tablespoons chipotle sauce
4 ounces grilled chicken breast, sliced

Quesa Filling (use as desired)
Shredded Jack and Cheddar cheeses
Diced jalapeño pepper

Diced tomato
Diced onion
Minced fresh cilantro
Crumbled cooked bacon
Shredded lettuce
Sour cream
Chopped green onion
Salsa
Crumbled cooked bacon (optional)

1. Brush one side of each tortilla with oil.
2. Place one tortilla, oiled side down, on a work surface. Spread the chipotle sauce over the tortilla.
3. Spread the chicken evenly on top of the sauce on the tortilla.
4. Evenly spread the quesa filling over the chicken. Cover with the other tortilla, oiled side up.
5. Brown evenly on both sides in a nonstick pan until the filling is heated thoroughly.
6. Serve with lettuce, sour cream, green onion, and salsa as accompaniments. Sprinkle crumbled bacon on top, if using.

Serves 1

Serve with Spanish rice and fresh guacamole.

APPLEBEE'S
crispy orange chicken skillet

DELICATELY SEASONED BREADED CHICKEN COVERED IN A SPICY-SWEET ORANGE GLAZE. IT IS PERFECT OVER ALMOND RICE PILAF AND A TASTY MIX OF MUSH-ROOMS, BROCCOLI, RED PEPPERS, SUGAR SNAP PEAS, AND SHREDDED CARROTS. TOP WITH TOASTED ALMONDS AND CRISPY NOODLES.

2 pounds boneless, skinless chicken breasts
1 egg, beaten
1½ teaspoons salt
¼ teaspoon black pepper
1 tablespoon vegetable oil
1 cup all-purpose flour plus
  1 tablespoon cornstarch
Oil, for frying

Glaze
1 teaspoon minced garlic
1½ teaspoons grated orange zest
1 cup orange juice
½ cup hoisin sauce
Pinch of cayenne pepper
¼ cup sugar
Salt and black pepper, to taste

1. Cut the chicken into 2-inch pieces and place in a large bowl. Add the egg, salt, pepper, and the 1 tablespoon vegetable oil. Mix well and set aside.
2. Stir the flour and cornstarch together in another large bowl until mixed well. Add the chicken to the flour mixture, and coat each piece well.
3. Pour about ½ inch of oil into a heavy skillet and set over high heat. When the temperature reaches 375°F, carefully add the chicken pieces in small batches and fry for 3 to 4 minutes, until browned and crunchy.
4. Carefully remove the chicken from the oil with a slotted spoon and drain on paper towels. Continue frying the chicken until all the pieces are nicely browned and crisp. Set aside.
5. To make the glaze, allow the oil in the skillet to cool slightly, then remove all but 2 tablespoons of the oil and put the skillet over medium heat. Sauté the garlic for 1 minute; do not burn.
6. Add the remaining ingredients and bring to a boil. Cook, stirring, for

3 minutes. Reduce the heat and simmer until the sauce thickens. Arrange the chicken on a platter, pour the glaze over the chicken, and serve.

Serves 4

Hoisin sauce is made from soybean paste and flavored with garlic, sugar, chiles, and other spices and ingredients.

Hoisin sauce is the "secret ingredient" in many Chinese barbecue sauces.

APPLEBEE'S
fiesta lime chicken

GRILLED BONELESS CHICKEN BREAST MARINATED IN LIME JUICE AND TEQUILA FLAVORS. SERVE WITH APPLEBEE'S GARLIC MASHED POTATOES (PAGE 8) AND MIXED VEGETABLES.

1 cup water	**Dressing**
⅓ cup teriyaki sauce	¼ cup mayonnaise
½ cup lime juice	¼ cup sour cream
3 cloves garlic, minced	2 tablespoons spicy, chunky salsa
1 teaspoon tequila	1 tablespoon milk
1 teaspoon liquid smoke	1 teaspoon Cajun blackening spice
½ teaspoon salt	¼ teaspoon parsley flakes
¼ teaspoon ground ginger	¼ teaspoon Tabasco sauce
1 pound boneless, skinless chicken breasts	⅛ teaspoon dried dill weed
	⅛ teaspoon ground cumin
	1 cup shredded Colby Jack cheese
	2 cups crumbled corn chips

1. Whisk together the water, teriyaki, lime juice, garlic, tequila, liquid smoke, salt, and ginger. Coat the chicken in the mixture, and marinate in the refrigerator for at least 2 hours.
2. To prepare the dressing, whisk together the mayonnaise, sour cream, salsa, milk, Cajun spice, parsley, Tabasco, dill weed, and cumin. Cover, and refrigerate until needed.
3. Preheat the broiler. Grill the marinated chicken breasts for 3 to 5 minutes per side, until cooked through. Discard the marinade.
4. Brush the grilled chicken with the chilled dressing, sprinkle with the cheese, and broil until the cheese has melted.
5. Serve the chicken over a bed of the crumbled chips.

Serves 4

Two chicken breasts will cost you under $2 when on sale!

APPLEBEE'S
garlic mashed potatoes

CREAMY MASHED POTATOES WITH A KICK OF GARLIC.

1 garlic bulb, unpeeled	¼ cup heavy cream
2 pounds red potatoes	3 tablespoons butter
½ cup milk	Salt and pepper, to taste

1. Place the garlic on a sheet of aluminum foil and wrap tightly.
2. Roast in a preheated 400°F oven for about 45 minutes, until soft.
3. Unwrap and let cool.
4. Peel the cloves and squeeze out the pulp.
5. Wash and rinse the potatoes under cold water. Halve or quarter.
6. In a large pot, cook the potatoes at a slow boil for about 20 minutes.
7. Remove from the heat and drain in a colander.
8. In a large saucepan or bowl, combine the potatoes and the roasted garlic with the remaining ingredients and mash with a potato masher.
9. Serve warm.

APPLEBEE'S
low-fat grilled tilapia with mango salsa

LIGHT AND DELICIOUS, THIS DELICATELY SEASONED GRILLED FISH IS TOPPED WITH FRESH MANGO SALSA AND SERVED ON STEAMED WHITE RICE WITH A TANGY VEGETABLE MEDLEY.

I tilapia fillet (or other white fish fillet)
Vegetable oil
1/8 teaspoon cayenne pepper
Salt and black pepper
White rice
Fresh vegetable medley (choose your favorites)
Lemon pepper

Mango Salsa
I cup diced tomatoes
1/2 cup diced red onion
1/4 cup diced jalapeño
2 tablespoons chopped fresh cilantro
Salt and black pepper, to taste
I teaspoon salad oil
I teaspoon white vinegar
1/2 teaspoon granulated garlic
1/2 cup chopped mango

1. Brush both sides of the tilapia with oil.
2. Shake the seasoning (cayenne, salt, pepper) over both sides of the tilapia.
3. Cook the tilapia on a clean, lightly oiled grill, smooth side down. Cook to an internal temperature of 145°F, turning once during cooking.
4. Cook the rice according to the package directions, and steam the vegetable medley; season with lemon pepper.
5. To make the mango salsa, mix all the ingredients but the mango together in a bowl. Just before serving, add the mango and mix lightly.
6. To serve, top the fish with the salsa.

Serves 1

Tilapia has white or pinkish flesh that's firm, low in fat, sweet, and mild in flavor. The tender skin is edible.

Haddock, red snapper, bass, flounder, and sole all make great substitutes if you don't have any tilapia.

APPLEBEE'S
santa fe chicken

EXPERIENCE THE FLAVOR OF THE SOUTHWEST WITH THIS POPULAR GRILLED
MARINATED CHICKEN DISH. SERVE OVER A BED OF RICE PILAF WITH MIXED
VEGETABLES.

8 boneless, skinless chicken breasts
One 8-ounce block Monterey Jack
 cheese
1 cup Italian bread crumbs
1½ tablespoons grated Parmesan
 cheese
½ teaspoon salt
½ teaspoon ground cumin
½ teaspoon pepper

8 tablespoons (1 stick) butter or
 margarine, melted
1 tablespoon butter or margarine
1 tablespoon all-purpose flour
1 cup milk
1 small red bell pepper, seeded and
 diced
1 small green bell pepper, seeded
 and diced

1. Place one chicken breast between two sheets of waxed paper. Working
   from the center to the edges, pound with a meat mallet until flat and
   rectangular shaped. Repeat with the remaining breasts.
2. Cut half of the cheese block into 8 slices; grate the remaining cheese and
   set aside.
3. Wrap each flattened chicken breast around a slice of cheese; secure with
   wooden picks.
4. Combine the bread crumbs, Parmesan cheese, salt, cumin, and pepper.
5. Roll the secured chicken pieces in the melted butter and then in the
   bread crumb mixture.
6. Place the chicken breasts in a 13 by 9-inch baking dish, being careful not
   to crowd them.
7. Drizzle the remaining melted butter over the breasts.
8. Refrigerate for 1 hour or freeze to bake later (if you decide to freeze,
   increase the baking time by 5 to 10 minutes).
9. Preheat the oven to 400°F.
10. Bake the chicken breasts for 25 to 30 minutes, until cooked through.

11. Melt the 1 tablespoon butter in a saucepan, stir in the flour, whisk in the milk, then bring to a simmer.
12. Stir in the grated Jack cheese, reduce the heat, and simmer until thick, stirring.
13. Place the chicken on individual plates, pour the sauce over, and top with the diced peppers.

Serves 8

Make your own bread crumbs using stale bread.

APPLEBEE'S
spinach pizza

AN APPLEBEE'S SIGNATURE, THIS ULTRATHIN PIZZA TOPPED WITH MUSHROOMS, CREAMY SPINACH, FRESH TOMATOES, AND A RICH BLEND OF ITALIAN CHEESES AND HERBS WILL LEAVE YOU FEELING SATISFIED, NOT STUFFED!

¼ cup rice milk
¼ cup all-purpose flour
⅓ cup nutritional yeast
One 10-ounce package frozen spinach, thawed and squeezed
1 medium onion, chopped
4 cloves garlic, minced
1 tablespoon olive oil
5 medium plum tomatoes, roughly chopped

8 ounces mushrooms, sliced
1 teaspoon dried basil
1 teaspoon parsley flakes
1 teaspoon cayenne pepper
3 pita breads
¼ cup shredded Parmesan cheese
¼ cup shredded Asiago cheese

1. Heat the rice milk in a large saucepan until hot but not boiling.
2. Stir in the flour and continue stirring until the sauce begins to thicken.
3. Reduce the heat and add the nutritional yeast and spinach.
4. Stir constantly until the sauce is thick and gooey, 3 to 4 minutes.
5. In a large skillet, sauté the onion and garlic in the oil until the onion is tender.
6. Stir in the tomatoes, mushrooms, herbs, and cayenne. Cook, stirring, until heated through. Drain off any liquid.
7. Preheat the oven to 425°F.
8. Using a very sharp bread knife, split each pita bread in half to make 2 thin rounds.
9. Place the pita halves, cut side up, on a cookie sheet or pizza pan.
10. Spread the spinach sauce over each.
11. Top with the tomato mixture.
12. Sprinkle with Parmesan and Asiago cheeses.
13. Bake for 5 to 7 minutes. Watch closely so that the edges of the pita don't burn. The pizza is ready when the cheese has melted.

Kids love pizza, and this recipe will get them to eat their greens!

Use drained canned diced tomatoes when fresh tomatoes are not in season.

APPLEBEE'S
tomato-basil soup

RED RIPE TOMATOES, SLOWLY SIMMERED IN A RICH CREAM SAUCE, SEASONED
WITH BASIL AND HERBS.

5 large beefsteak tomatoes, peeled,
seeded, and diced
5 cups V8 juice
16 fresh basil leaves, whole
¼ cup finely minced onion
2 cloves garlic, crushed
½ teaspoon Italian seasoning

1¼ cups heavy cream
8 tablespoons (1 stick) butter,
melted
Salt and pepper
Croutons, for garnish
¼ cup shredded Cheddar cheese,
for garnish

1. Place the tomatoes and the juice in a stockpot over medium heat;
   simmer for 30 minutes.
2. Add the basil leaves, onion, garlic, and Italian seasoning, then puree the
   tomato mixture with a hand blender.
3. Pour into a slow cooker set on low.
4. Slowly add the heavy cream and then the butter. Season with salt and
   pepper.
5. Let simmer on low for 1½ to 2 hours or until the soup has thickened.
   Do not let boil.
6. Garnish with croutons and the Cheddar cheese.

Serves 6

APPLEBEE'S
walnut blondie with maple butter sauce

THIS BLONDIE IS BAKED WITH WALNUTS, TOPPED WITH BOTH ICE CREAM AND
CHOPPED NUTS, AND SERVED WARM COVERED WITH A RICH, HOT MAPLE BUT-
TER SAUCE.

½ teaspoon baking powder
⅛ teaspoon baking soda
⅛ teaspoon salt
1 cup all-purpose flour, sifted
¼ cup chopped walnuts (or more)
1 cup packed light brown sugar
5⅓ tablespoons butter or
   margarine, melted
1 egg, beaten

1 tablespoon vanilla extract
½ cup white chocolate chips

Maple Butter Sauce
¾ cup real maple syrup
8 tablespoons (1 stick) butter
¾ cup packed light brown sugar
¼ cup chopped walnuts (optional)

1. Preheat the oven to 350°F.
2. Add the baking powder, baking soda, and salt to the already sifted flour,
   then sift the dry ingredients again. Add the chopped nuts and mix well.
   Set aside.
3. Add the brown sugar to the melted butter and mix well. Mix in the egg
   and vanilla extract.
4. Stir in the flour mixture, a little at a time, until well incorporated. Stir in
   the white chocolate chips.
5. Spread out the batter in a 9 by 9-inch nonstick pan. Bake for 20 to 25
   minutes. The blondie is cooked when a toothpick comes out clean when
   inserted in the center.
6. To make the maple butter sauce, cook the maple syrup and butter over
   low heat until the butter is melted. Stir in the brown sugar until completely dissolved. If you desire, add the walnuts.
7. Serve the blondie warm with ice cream and the maple butter sauce.

Makes 4 large blondies or 6 smaller ones

Substitute maple-flavored syrup for real maple syrup.

ARBY'S
apple turnovers

WARM, FLAKY PASTRY WRAPPED AROUND A DELICIOUS APPLE FILLING.

4 large apples
½ cup sugar
1 tablespoon cornstarch
¼ teaspoon ground cinnamon

1 teaspoon lemon juice
One 17.3-ounce package frozen
puff pastry sheets, thawed

1. Peel, core, and thinly slice the apples.
2. Over low heat, in a medium saucepan, cook the apples with the sugar, cornstarch, cinnamon, and lemon juice, stirring often. Cook until the apples are tender, then remove from the heat and let cool.
3. Preheat the oven to 400°F.
4. Unfold the pastry on a floured surface. Roll 2 sheets into 12-inch squares, then cut each sheet into four 6-inch squares. You'll use 1½ sheets of pastry.
5. Place ¼ cup of the apple mixture in the center of each square.
6. Brush the edges with water, then fold to form triangles. Be sure to seal the edges firmly with a fork.
7. Place on baking sheets. Bake for 25 minutes or until golden. Let cool on a wire rack.

Serving Suggestion:
In a small bowl, mix together ½ cup confectioners' sugar and 1 tablespoon water. With a spoon, drizzle over the turnovers; allow to set before serving.

Makes 6 turnovers

For best results, use Granny Smith apples.
Substitute pears for the apples for a nice treat, or you can use a combination of apples and pears.

Serve with your favorite ice cream; drizzle with your favorite caramel topping, if desired.

In 1964, the first Arby's restaurant became a reality. When it opened, it wasn't offering the large menu of items customers see today. In fact, the restaurant served only roast beef sandwiches, potato chips, and iced tea. An interesting fact is that the name came from the initials *R. B.,* for "Raffel brothers" who opened the first restaurant.

ARBY'S
barbecue sauce

A TANGY BARBECUE SAUCE FOR GRILLING MEATS AND TOPPING SANDWICHES.

1 cup ketchup	¼ teaspoon onion powder
2 teaspoons water	¼ teaspoon pepper
2 teaspoons dark brown sugar	¼ teaspoon salt
¼ teaspoon Tabasco sauce	½ teaspoon Worcestershire sauce
¼ teaspoon garlic powder	

1. In a small saucepan, combine all the ingredients and cook over medium heat. Stir until the sauce begins to boil, about 7 minutes.
2. Remove the pan from the heat. Let cool, covered.
3. Store covered, in the refrigerator. Keeps for at least 1 month.

Makes about 1 cup

For an even greater kick, add more Tabasco sauce and some diced jalapeño pepper.

ARTHUR TREACHER'S
fried fish

PERFECTLY BATTERED AND LIGHTLY SEASONED GOLDEN FRIED FISH FILLETS.

3 pounds fish fillets
1 egg, beaten
2 cups all-purpose flour
3 cups pancake mix

3 cups club soda
1 tablespoon onion powder
1 tablespoon seasoned salt
Oil, for frying

1. Dip the fish fillets in the egg to moisten, then dip the fish evenly but lightly in the flour. Dust off any excess flour and allow the fillets to air-dry on waxed paper, about 5 minutes.
2. Whip the pancake mix with the club soda to the consistency of buttermilk. It should be pourable, but not too thin and not too thick.
3. Beat in the onion powder and seasoned salt.
4. Add 1 inch of oil to a heavy saucepan and heat to 425°F.
5. Dip the floured fillets into the batter and slide into the oil a few at a time.
6. Brown for about 4 minutes per side.
7. Preheat the oven to 325°F. To keep the fried fillets warm, arrange on a cookie sheet and place in the oven until all the fillets have been fried.

Serves 4

This batter can also be used for chicken pieces.

Use a meat thermometer to test the oil temperature.
Always use caution when placing the fillets into the hot oil.

The chain started in 1969, introducing British fish-and-chips to America. Arthur Treacher's probably became one of the most prolific companies in the expansion of fish and chips in the late 1970s.

The chain is named for Arthur Treacher (1894–1975), an English character actor who was known as "the perfect butler" for his performances as Jeeves and as a butler in several Shirley Temple films. He served as a spokesman for the restaurant chain in its early years, underscoring the British character of its food.

In America, Arthur Treacher is also remembered as the sidekick and announcer of *The Merv Griffin Show* in the late 1960s and early 1970s. Arthur Treacher also played the constable who returned the Banks children home in the motion picture *Mary Poppins*.

BAHAMA BREEZE
jamaican jerk grilled chicken wings

WINGS MARINATED WITH AUTHENTIC SPICY JERK SEASONINGS, SLOW-ROASTED,
AND GRILLED TO A CRISP. SERVE WITH A TANGY DIPPING SAUCE.

Jamaican Marinade
¼ cup olive oil
2 tablespoons Jamaican jerk
  seasoning
¼ cup orange juice
¼ cup rice wine vinegar
1 tablespoon dark Jamaican rum
½ cup chopped red onion
½ teaspoon Cajun blackening spice
1 tablespoon dried oregano
3 green onions, chopped

Juice of 1 lime
1 habanero pepper, seeded and
  minced
4 tablespoons chopped garlic
1 tablespoon chopped fresh thyme
1 teaspoon ground allspice
1 cup water

5 pounds whole chicken wings
Jamaican jerk seasoning

1. Place the Jamaican marinade ingredients in a large bowl and mix to
   evenly combine.
2. Add the chicken wings to the marinade, stir well, cover with plastic
   wrap, and place in the refrigerator.
3. Marinate the chicken wings for 16 to 24 hours before cooking.
4. Preheat the oven to 350°F.
5. Remove the wings from the marinade and place in a clean bowl. Make
   sure the wings are drained well after being removed from the marinade,
   or the jerk seasoning will not fully adhere to the wings. Discard the
   marinade.
6. Rub the wings with the Jamaican jerk seasoning and place on a sheet pan
   with the wing tips facing down.
7. Bake the wings for 20 to 25 minutes until fully cooked. (Precooking the
   wings prevents flare-ups on the grill.)
8. Remove from the oven and allow to cool. Place in the refrigerator to chill
   to 40°F.
9. Preheat the grill to medium heat.

10. Place the chilled wings on the grill and grill for 2½ to 3 minutes on each side. The skin of the wings should develop a crisp texture and a dark color. Make sure the wings are fully heated to 165°F.
11. Serve hot.

Serves 6 to 8

Rice wine vinegar is made from rice, has a gentle but tart flavor, and is milder than other types of vinegar.

The Bahama Breeze™ restaurants specialize in Caribbean-inspired fresh seafood, chicken, and steaks. Founded in Orlando, Florida, in 1996, the chain currently has more than two dozen locations throughout the country.

BASKIN-ROBBINS
cheesecake ice cream

SINCE 1964, THIS CLASSIC CHEESECAKE ICE CREAM HAS BEEN MADE WITH
GRAHAM CRACKER PIECES.

2½ cups heavy cream
1¼ cups sugar
2 eggs, beaten
1½ (8-ounce) packages cream
  cheese, softened

½ teaspoon finely grated lemon
  zest
1 tablespoon lemon juice
1 teaspoon vanilla extract
Graham crackers, broken into bits

1. In a large saucepan, combine 1½ cups of the cream, the sugar, and eggs.
   Cook, stirring, over medium heat just until boiling.
2. In a large bowl, beat the cream cheese with an electric mixer until
   smooth; slowly beat in the hot mixture.
3. Cover and chill thoroughly.
4. Stir in the remaining 1 cup cream, the lemon peel, lemon juice, and
   vanilla.
5. Freeze in an ice cream maker according to the manufacturer's directions.
6. Fold in graham cracker bits to taste.
7. Put into a freezer container with a lid and let sit for 4 hours in the freezer
   before serving.

Serves 8 to 10

Great for birthday parties!

Brothers-in-law Burton "Burt" Baskin and Irvine "Irv" Robbins
started Baskin-Robbins. Founded as separate ventures in 1945, the
stores merged in 1953 and became the Baskin-Robbins we know
today, offering more than a thousand flavors of high-quality ice
cream made the old-fashioned way.

BENIHANA
hibachi steak

SIRLOIN STEAK CUBES HIBACHI-GRILLED WITH MUSHROOMS, ONIONS, AND BEAN SPROUTS.

Four 5-ounce sirloin steaks
4 teaspoons soybean oil
1 large onion, sliced
8 large mushrooms, sliced thick
2 cups bean sprouts

¼ cup soy sauce
4 pinches of salt, or to taste
4 pinches of pepper, or to taste
4 dashes of mustard-based steak
   sauce

1. Preheat the broiler.
2. Broil the steak until rare; cut into 1-inch cubes
3. Heat a nonstick skillet and add the oil to the heated skillet.
4. Add the onion and cook until slightly browned and soft.
5. Place the steak cubes in the skillet with the mushrooms and cook to the desired degree of doneness (rare, medium, well-done).
6. Add the bean sprouts and soy sauce.
7. Add the salt and pepper.
8. Add the steak sauce, and serve.

Serves 4 to 6

This Japanese steak recipe typically has less than 5 grams of carbs.

Benihana started out as a tiny four-table restaurant in New York City's theater district before becoming an international chain. Diners sit around large tables where chefs dramatically chop, slice, stir-fry, and grill.

BENIHANA

japanese fried rice

QUICK, EASY, AND DELICIOUS. A SIGNATURE BENIHANA SIDE DISH.

1 ¼ cups uncooked short-grain Japanese white rice
Soybean oil
2 eggs, beaten
½ cup finely diced green onions

½ cup frozen peas, thawed
1 medium carrot, finely grated
4 teaspoons soy sauce
Salt and pepper

1. Cook the rice according to the package directions. Once done, empty into a mixing bowl.
2. In a large skillet, heat 2 teaspoons of oil. Scramble the eggs into small pieces until cooked. Empty the scrambled eggs into the bowl with the rice and stir together.
3. Using the same pan, add additional oil, the diced green onions, the peas, and the carrot. Let simmer on low heat for 5 minutes.
4. Add several scoops of the cooled rice and egg mixture to the skillet. Keep gradually adding a scoop at a time to the pan and stirring.
5. While mixing, slowly add the soy sauce a teaspoon at a time until the fried rice is a golden brown color.
6. Add salt and pepper to taste.

Serves 4

Use leftover cooked rice.

Frozen peas work well in this recipe. To thaw quickly, place the peas in a colander and run warm water over them.

This side goes great with Benihana Hibachi Steak (page 28).

BENNIGAN'S
broccoli bites

BROCCOLI MIXED WITH BACON BITS, SHREDDED CHEESE, AND DICED ONION; ROLLED IN BREAD CRUMBS; AND LIGHTLY FRIED. IRRESISTIBLE SERVED WITH BENNIGAN'S HONEY MUSTARD DRESSING (PAGE 31).

3 eggs
⅔ cup shredded Monterey Jack cheese
⅔ cup shredded Colby cheese
One 16-ounce box frozen chopped broccoli, thawed and drained well

5 tablespoons bacon bits
1 tablespoon minced yellow onion
2 tablespoons all-purpose flour
Oil, for frying
Italian bread crumbs, as needed

1. Beat the eggs in a small bowl.
2. Place all the remaining ingredients, except for the oil and bread crumbs, in a separate bowl and stir together until thoroughly combined.
3. Refrigerate the mixture for about 1 hour.
4. Heat 4 cups oil in a deep-fryer or large skillet to 350°F.
5. Set up a shallow dish with the bread crumbs.
6. Form the broccoli mixture into walnut-size balls, dip in the egg, and coat each ball evenly with the crumbs.
7. Place the broccoli bites in the hot oil. Make sure they do not stick together. Fry for 1 minute, then remove and place on a dish lined with paper towels to drain.
8. Serve with Honey Mustard Dressing (page 31).

Serves 4

A great way to get the kids to eat their veggies!

Bennigan's got started in 1976 and was one of the earliest theme-based chains of casual-dining restaurants in the United States. These restaurants were famous for their fried mozzarella sticks, Monte Cristo sandwiches, and other tasty but often fatty treats. Bennigan's Irish-themed restaurants had a great ambience, at least in the early days.

BENNIGAN'S
honey mustard dressing

A SMOKY HONEY DIJON DRESSING. SERVE WITH BENNIGAN'S BROCCOLI BITES (PAGE 30).

¾ cup sour cream
⅓ cup mayonnaise
⅓ cup Dijon mustard

⅓ cup honey
1 tablespoon lemon juice

1. In a mixing bowl, combine the sour cream, mayonnaise, and mustard.
2. Mix well using a whisk.
3. Slowly pour in the honey and lemon juice; continue mixing until smooth.

Makes about 1 cup

Use this recipe as a dipping sauce or as a salad dressing!

BENNIGAN'S
hot bacon dressing

THIS WARM DRESSING IMMERSES CRUNCHY BACON BITS IN A SWEET, THICKENED
VINAIGRETTE. SERVE WITH SPINACH OR MIXED GREENS.

6 slices bacon
½ cup finely chopped red onion
2 cups water
½ cup honey
½ cup red wine vinegar

1 tablespoon Tabasco sauce
  (optional)
1½ tablespoons cornstarch
2 tablespoons Dijon mustard

1. Fry the bacon until crisp. Remove with a slotted spoon, drain on paper
   towels, crumble, and set aside. Pour ¼ cup of the bacon drippings into a
   saucepan over medium-high heat. Add the onion and cook, stirring,
   until the onion begins to brown.
2. While the onion is caramelizing, in a mixing bowl, combine the water,
   honey, red wine vinegar, and Tabasco, if using.
3. Using a whisk, mix the ingredients. Add the cornstarch, and whisk well.
4. After the onion has caramelized, add the Dijon mustard to the onion
   and mix together.
5. Add the honey-vinegar mixture to the onion and mix. Continue stirring
   until the mixture thickens and comes to a boil. Remove from the heat
   and garnish with the crumbled bacon. Cool to room temperature and
   store in the refrigerator until needed. To reheat, use a double boiler.

Makes about 3 cups

Make in bulk and save leftovers.

BENNIGAN'S
linguine diablo

AN AMERICAN RESTAURANT'S TAKE ON AN ITALIAN FAVORITE WITH SUCCULENT SCALLOPS, SHRIMP, AND CLAMS.

Marinara Sauce
3 tablespoons vegetable oil
1 cup diced yellow onions
1 tablespoon chopped garlic
One 28-ounce can crushed tomatoes
3½ tablespoons minced fresh parsley
2¼ teaspoons dried oregano
1¼ teaspoons dried basil
1 whole bay leaf
1½ teaspoons salt
Red pepper flakes (optional)

1 pound linguine
1 tablespoon vegetable oil

Garlic-Lemon Butter
8 tablespoons (1 stick) butter, melted
2 teaspoons chopped garlic
1½ teaspoons lemon juice

12 scallops, shucked
12 large shrimp, peeled and deveined
12 clams, in shells
¼ cup grated Parmesan cheese
1 teaspoon chopped fresh parsley

1. To make the marinara sauce, in a large saucepan, heat the oil over medium heat. Add the onions. Cook, stirring, until the onions start to become soft and translucent, about 5 minutes.
2. Add the garlic; cook, stirring, for 2 minutes more.
3. Add the remaining sauce ingredients to the saucepan; stir. Add red pepper flakes if desired. Bring the sauce to a boil.
4. Reduce the heat to low, and simmer, uncovered, for 30 minutes. Once cooked, remove the bay leaf.
5. Cook the linguine until al dente (8 to 10 minutes); drain well. Rinse and mix in the vegetable oil to prevent sticking. Set aside.
6. To make the garlic-lemon butter, mix together the butter, garlic, and lemon juice. Pour the garlic-lemon butter into a large sauté pan over medium-high heat. Be sure not to burn the garlic.

7. When the garlic-lemon butter starts sizzling, add the scallops, shrimp, and clams; cook, stirring, for 5 minutes.
8. Add the marinara sauce and stir the mixture to ensure even heating of all the ingredients.
9. Add the linguine and toss until the noodles are well covered with sauce. Continue to cook for another 2 minutes. Pour the pasta into a large bowl and sprinkle with the Parmesan cheese and garnish with the parsley.

Serves 4

Prepare the garlic-lemon butter and marinara sauce the day before.

BENNIGAN'S

Onion soup

TASTY ONION SOUP TOPPED WITH CRUSTY BREAD AND MELTED CHEESE.

I large onion, quartered and sliced
4 tablespoons (½ stick) butter, melted
2 tablespoons canola oil
3 tablespoons all-purpose flour
4 cups chicken broth

4 cups beef broth
Eight 1-inch slices of crusty baguette
I cup shredded mozzarella cheese or Swiss cheese
¼ cup grated Parmesan cheese

1. In a Dutch oven over medium heat, slowly cook the onion in the butter and oil, stirring occasionally, until the onion is translucent and turning yellow but not browned. When tender, turn the heat to its lowest setting and add the flour, stirring until well blended.
2. Add the chicken and beef broths; heat through.
3. Preheat the broiler. Divide the soup among eight oven-safe bowls.
4. Place a slice of bread on top of each bowl of soup. Sprinkle equal amounts of the cheeses over the bread slices.
5. Place the bowls on an oven rack 4 inches from the heat and broil until the cheese melts. Serve hot.

Serves 8

If you're not serving eight, don't worry. The soup can be kept in the freezer for months and still remain fresh for reheating.

BOSTON MARKET
creamed spinach

A UNIQUE BOSTON MARKET DISH! SPINACH MIXED WITH RICH CHEESES, CREAM, AND GARLIC.

5 tablespoons butter or margarine
¼ cup all-purpose flour
¼ teaspoon salt
1 cup half-and-half
4 ounces cream cheese, cut up
2 tablespoons minced onion

Two 10-ounce boxes frozen
chopped spinach, thawed
¼ cup water
¼ cup grated Pecorino-Romano
cheese

1. In a saucepan over medium-low heat melt 3 tablespoons of the butter. Stir the flour and salt into the pan until creamed together.
2. Slowly stir in the half-and-half, then stir in the cream cheese; raise the heat to medium.
3. Constantly whisk until the mixture becomes thick and smooth; remove from the heat and set aside.
4. In a saucepan over medium-high heat, sauté the onion in the remaining 2 tablespoons butter until translucent.
5. Add the spinach and water to the pan; reduce the heat to low; cover. Cook, stirring occasionally, for 8 minutes.
6. Stir the prepared sauce and the Pecorino-Romano into the pan; stir until completely blended.

Serves 6

Boston Market started out as Boston Chicken. The first store was opened in Newton, Massachusetts, in 1985 by Arthur Cores and his friend Steven (Kip) Kolow. Cores's experience in the gourmet food industry led him to believe that a market existed for fast high-quality, home-style food.

Cores and Kolow borrowed recipes for chicken soup and

oatmeal cookies from their grandmothers, and Cores also concocted some of his own dishes based on traditional side dishes such as mashed potatoes and squash. To their array of vegetable and salad sides, they added sweet corn bread. Their various side dishes would complement the centerpiece of every meal—marinated chicken roasted in brick-fired rotisseries.

BOSTON MARKET
cucumber salad

A CRISP AND COOL SALAD OF CUCUMBERS, TOMATO, AND ONION DRIZZLED
WITH A TASTY VINAIGRETTE.

2 medium cucumbers, with skin,
cut into ½-inch slices
¼ red onion, cut into ½-inch dice
1 large ripe tomato, diced
1 cup oil-and-vinegar dressing

1 teaspoon dried dill weed
½ teaspoon parsley flakes
¼ cup olive oil
Salt and pepper

1. Combine the cucumbers with the rest of the ingredients, except the salt and pepper, in a plastic refrigerator container; cover tightly.
2. Allow the salad to marinate for 24 hours in the fridge before serving. Do not freeze.
3. Add salt and pepper to taste.

Serves 4 to 6

This recipe is low in both fat and calories.

BOSTON MARKET
dill potato wedges

TENDER POTATO WEDGES WITH DILL, GARLIC, AND BUTTER FLAVORING.

2 medium red potatoes, unpeeled
Butter-flavored cooking spray

½ teaspoon garlic salt
½ teaspoon dried dill weed

1. Preheat the oven to 400°F.
2. Cut the potatoes lengthwise into wedges and bake for 45 minutes or until tender.
3. Spray the cut sides of the potatoes with cooking spray.
4. Dust with the garlic salt and dried dill weed and pan-fry until slightly browned.

Serves 2

Be sure to use red potatoes because they keep their consistency and do not get mushy after baking.

BOSTON MARKET
macaroni and cheese

A RICH CHEESE SAUCE—COMPLETE WITH AMERICAN, CHEDDAR, AND BLUE
CHEESES—MIXED WITH SEMOLINA ROTINI PASTA.

1 tablespoon minced onion	¼ cup cubed Cheddar cheese
4 tablespoons (½ stick) butter or	1 teaspoon salt
margarine, melted	Pinch of pepper
¼ cup all-purpose flour	¼ teaspoon dry mustard
2 cups milk	4 ounces semolina rotini pasta,
4 ounces American cheese, cubed	cooked al dente
¼ cup cubed blue cheese	

1. Preheat the oven to 400°F.
2. Sauté the onion in the butter until translucent.
3. Stir in the flour and cook for 2 minutes.
4. Slowly stir in the milk.
5. Stir in the cheeses, salt, pepper, and mustard.
6. Continue to cook over medium heat, stirring constantly, until thickened.
7. Stir in the prepared macaroni.
8. Lightly butter a casserole dish and pour the pasta mixture into the dish.
9. Bake for 20 minutes.

Serves 4

This recipe can be prepared for a fraction of the cost that you would
pay at Boston Market.

When pasta is cooked al dente, there should be a slight resistance in
the center when the pasta is chewed.
    Choose different types of pastas for different looks!

BOSTON MARKET
meat loaf

RICH, MOIST MEAT LOAF MADE WITH SAVORY SEASONINGS AND COVERED WITH
ZESTY HICKORY BARBECUE SAUCE.

½ cup ketchup
1½ tablespoons hickory barbecue
sauce
1 tablespoon sugar
1½ pounds lean ground beef
⅓ cup all-purpose flour

¾ teaspoon salt
½ teaspoon onion powder
¼ teaspoon pepper
2 cloves garlic, minced
¾ cup Italian bread crumbs
1 egg, beaten

1. Preheat the oven to 400°F.
2. In a large bowl, stir together the ketchup, barbecue sauce, and sugar;
   set aside ¼ cup of the mixture.
3. With your hands, mix in the remaining ingredients.
4. Form the mixture into a loaf and place in a greased 9 by 5-inch loaf pan.
5. Bake, covered, for 30 minutes.
6. Uncover and drain the fat from the pan, then slice the meat loaf while
   still in the pan.
7. Drizzle the reserved tomato mixture evenly over the meat loaf.
8. Bake, uncovered, for an additional 30 minutes, or until cooked through.

Serves 5

You can make this recipe with ground turkey instead of beef.

BOSTON MARKET

spicy rice

THIS SIDE DISH WILL GO WITH ANY POULTRY, FISH, PORK, OR BEEF DISH.

¼ cup orzo (rice-shaped pasta)
¾ cup white rice
1 tablespoon finely chopped
  pimiento
½ teaspoon celery leaf flakes
1 teaspoon parsley flakes

¼ teaspoon dry mustard
One 14-ounce can chicken broth
¼ cup olive oil
½ teaspoon salt
Pepper

1. In a 2-quart saucepan, combine all the ingredients except the salt and pepper. Stir often and bring to a boil.
2. Cover and remove from the heat. Let stand for 15 minutes. Fluff the rice mixture with a fork every 5 minutes.
3. Add salt and pepper to taste.

Serves 6

Use leftover rice and cut the preparation time in half.

BOSTON MARKET
Squash casserole

FRESH ZUCCHINI AND YELLOW SQUASH BLENDED WITH CORN BREAD AND A TOUCH OF THYME. TOPPED WITH CHEDDAR CHEESE AND BAKED UNTIL GOLDEN BROWN.

1 box Jiffy corn muffin mix	1/2 teaspoon pepper
4 1/2 cups diced zucchini	1/2 teaspoon thyme
4 1/2 cups diced yellow squash	1 tablespoon chopped fresh
1 1/2 cups chopped yellow onions	parsley
12 tablespoons (1 1/2 sticks) butter,	3 chicken bouillon cubes
melted	1 teaspoon minced garlic
1 teaspoon salt	8 ounces Cheddar cheese, diced

1. Prepare corn bread as directed on the Jiffy box; set aside to cool.
2. Preheat the oven to 350°F.
3. Place the zucchini and yellow squash in a large saucepan and add water to cover.
4. Cook over medium-low heat until tender; remove from the heat.
5. Drain the squash, reserving 1 cup of the water for the casserole.
6. In a large saucepan on medium-low heat, sauté the onions in the butter until the onions turn clear.
7. Add the salt, pepper, thyme, and parsley.
8. Add the chicken bouillon cubes and garlic to the onions; stir and sauté for another minute.
9. Add the drained squash and diced cheese, and stir.
10. Crumble the prepared corn bread into the squash and add the reserved cup of cooking water and mix well.
11. Place the squash mixture in a 13 by 11-inch baking dish that has been sprayed with cooking spray.
12. Cover the casserole. Bake for 50 to 60 minutes or until golden brown. Remove the lid for the last 20 minutes of the baking time.

Serves 8

The corn bread can be prepared ahead of time or even store-bought.

BOSTON MARKET
stuffing

A MOIST VEGETABLE STUFFING PREPARED WITH A FLAVORFUL BROTH AND BAKED
TO PERFECTION.

One 10-ounce can sliced carrots, undrained

One 14-ounce can sliced mushrooms, undrained

One 14-ounce can chicken broth

2 ribs celery, cut into 5 pieces each

1 tablespoon rubbed sage

½ teaspoon poultry seasoning

1 tablespoon chicken bouillon powder

3 tablespoons melted butter

3 English muffins, cut into ½-inch cubes

One 8-ounce bag plain croutons (6 cups)

1 tablespoon parsley flakes

2 tablespoons onion flakes

1. Preheat the oven to 350°F.
2. Empty the sliced carrots and their liquid into a Dutch oven. Add the mushrooms and their liquid; set aside.
3. Pour the chicken broth into a blender. Add the celery pieces, sage, poultry seasoning, bouillon powder, and butter. Blend for a few seconds or until the celery is finely minced.
4. Add the English muffin cubes, croutons, parsley flakes, and onion flakes to the Dutch oven.
5. Add the blender mixture and stir with a rubber spatula until completely moist.
6. Cover and bake for about 45 minutes, until steaming hot.

Serves 8

BROOKLYN CAFE
sun-dried tomato seared scallops

SCALLOPS AND SUN-DRIED TOMATOES IN A CITRUS VINAIGRETTE.

¼ cup chopped dry-packed
sun-dried tomatoes
1 bunch fresh basil
⅔ cup orange juice
1 tablespoon lemon juice
6 tablespoons olive oil

1 tablespoon minced garlic
3 zucchini, cut into thin strips
Salt and pepper
1 tomato, diced
10 sea scallops

1. If the sun-dried tomatoes are moist, dry in a 200°F oven for about 15 minutes, until dry.
2. Grind the sun-dried tomatoes in a blender until they become a smooth powder; remove from the blender and set aside.
3. Add the basil (reserve 2 sprigs for garnish), orange juice, and lemon juice to the blender. Blend on medium speed while drizzling ¼ cup of the olive oil into the mixture.
4. Heat a nonstick skillet over medium heat; add 1 tablespoon olive oil and the garlic. Sauté the garlic for 15 seconds (do not burn), then add the zucchini. Cook, stirring frequently, for 2 minutes, until the zucchini softens. Season with salt and pepper. Add the tomato, then take off the heat.
5. Heat another nonstick skillet over medium-high heat. Season the scallops with salt and pepper and all but 1 teaspoon of the reserved sun-dried tomato powder. Add the remaining 1 tablespoon olive oil to the pan and add the scallops slowly to prevent spattering.
6. Let cook for about 3 minutes, then flip them over. Let cook for another 2 minutes; transfer to a paper towel–lined plate.
7. To serve, mound the zucchini mixture in the middle of two dinner plates. Place 5 scallops around each mound. Drizzle the vinaigrette around the dish. Garnish with a basil sprig and a sprinkling of tomato powder.

Serves 2

Whether you want just a salad and a glass of wine or their signature lobster enchiladas, Brooklyn Cafe does it all. Zagat ranked the café among its Top 40 Most Popular Restaurants in Atlanta. The exposed brick walls and European-inspired light fixtures create an ideal setting for an upscale lunch or a romantic evening out.

BULLFISH GRILL
shrimp and cheese grits

FRESH SHRIMP SAUTÉED WITH GARLIC, MUSHROOMS, BACON, AND GREEN
ONIONS, SERVED OVER CHEESE GRITS.

6 cups water
½ teaspoon salt
2 cups quick-cooking grits
1 cup grated sharp Cheddar
   cheese
Pinch of ground nutmeg
Tabasco sauce
12 slices bacon, coarsely
   chopped

2 pounds large shrimp, peeled and
   deveined
8 ounces button mushrooms,
   sliced
2 cups sliced green onions
2 large cloves garlic, minced
2½ tablespoons fresh lemon juice
Salt and pepper
¼ cup chopped fresh parsley

1. Bring the water and salt to a boil in a large, heavy saucepan.
2. Whisk in the grits. Reduce the heat, cover, and simmer, stirring occasionally, until the mixture is thick and the grits are tender, about 10 minutes.
3. Whisk in the cheese and nutmeg. Season to taste with the Tabasco sauce. Cover and set aside.
4. Cook the bacon in a large skillet over medium heat until browned but not crisp. Using a slotted spoon, transfer the bacon to a small bowl. Pour off half the drippings from the skillet.
5. Add the shrimp to the same skillet and cook just until pink, about 2 minutes per side.
6. Using a slotted spoon, transfer the shrimp to a plate.
7. Add the mushrooms to the same skillet and sauté until tender, about 4 minutes.
8. Add the green onions and garlic and sauté for 3 minutes.
9. Return the shrimp and bacon to the skillet. Mix in the lemon juice. Season with salt, pepper, and the Tabasco sauce.
10. Bring the grits back to a simmer. Add water by tablespoons if the grits are too thick.

11. Spoon the grits onto plates. Spoon the shrimp mixture over. Sprinkle with parsley and serve.

Serves 4

Grits come from corn kernels that are dried, hulled, and ground, then boiled.

Bullfish Grill specializes in hand-cut steaks and fresh seafood. They're known for serving Grand Champion Angus Beef and fresh seafood flown in daily.

CALIFORNIA PIZZA KITCHEN

bbq chicken pizza

THIS IS THE ORIGINAL, AND NOW MOST POPULAR, BARBECUE CHICKEN PIZZA INTRODUCED IN THE FIRST CALIFORNIA PIZZA KITCHEN IN 1985. A DELICIOUS AND UNIQUE DISH THAT INCLUDES BARBECUE CHICKEN, BARBECUE SAUCE, SMOKED GOUDA, AND MOZZARELLA CHEESE.

1 boneless, skinless chicken breast
1 tablespoon olive oil
½ cup Bull's-Eye original barbecue sauce
Store-bought pizza dough or dough mix
Flour, cornmeal, or semolina, for handling the dough

2 tablespoons shredded smoked Gouda cheese
1 cup shredded mozzarella cheese
½ small red onion, sliced into ½-inch pieces
2 tablespoons chopped fresh cilantro

1. Cook the chicken in the oil in a large skillet over medium heat for 5 to 6 minutes. Be careful not to overcook. Set aside in the refrigerator.
2. Once the chicken is chilled, coat with half the barbecue sauce, cut into bite-size pieces, and set aside.
3. Preheat the oven to 425°.
4. Follow the instructions on the store-bought pizza dough or dough mix to prepare enough dough for a 10-inch crust. Form the pizza dough into a ball and roll out on a floured surface until 10 inches wide, round, and flat.
5. Put the pizza crust onto a baking sheet and spread the remaining barbecue sauce evenly over the crust.
6. Sprinkle the Gouda cheese and ½ cup of the mozzarella over the sauce.
7. Add the barbecue chicken and red onion, then cover with the remaining ½ cup mozzarella. Sprinkle the cilantro on top of the mozzarella.
8. Bake for 10 minutes or until the crust is crisp and golden.

Serves 6 to 8

Use leftover chicken when preparing this dish. It's so easy to prepare that the kids can help, too!

CALIFORNIA PIZZA KITCHEN
chicken-tequila fettuccine

SPINACH FETTUCCINE WITH CHICKEN, RED, YELLOW, AND GREEN PEPPERS, RED ONION, AND FRESH CILANTRO IN A TEQUILA, LIME, AND JALAPEÑO CREAM SAUCE.

1 pound dried or fresh spinach fettuccine

⅓ cup plus 2 tablespoons chopped fresh cilantro

2 tablespoons minced fresh garlic

2 tablespoons minced jalapeño pepper (seeds and veins removed)

3 tablespoons butter, melted

½ cup chicken stock

2 tablespoons gold tequila

2 tablespoons lime juice

3 tablespoons soy sauce

1¼ pounds boneless, skinless chicken breasts, diced

¼ medium red onion, sliced thin

½ each medium red, yellow, and green bell pepper, sliced thin

1½ cups heavy cream

1. Boil salted water to cook the pasta; cook until al dente, 8 to 10 minutes for dried pasta, about 3 minutes for fresh. The pasta may be cooked ahead of time, rinsed and oiled, and then reheated in boiling water.
2. Cook the ⅓ cup cilantro, the garlic, and jalapeño in 2 tablespoons of the butter over medium heat for 4 to 5 minutes.
3. Add the stock, tequila, and lime juice. Bring to a boil, then cook until reduced to a pastelike consistency; set aside.
4. Pour the soy sauce over the diced chicken; set aside for 5 minutes.
5. Meanwhile, cook the onion and peppers, stirring occasionally, in the remaining 1 tablespoon butter over medium heat. When the vegetables become limp, add the chicken and soy sauce; toss and add the reserved tequila-lime paste and the cream.
6. Bring the sauce to a boil; boil until the chicken is cooked through and the sauce is thick (about 3 minutes).
7. Toss with the drained fettuccine and the remaining 2 tablespoons cilantro.

Serves 4

If you are out of cilantro, you can substitute parsley in this recipe.

CARRABBA'S ITALIAN GRILL

italian butter

⅛ teaspoon dried oregano
⅛ teaspoon dried basil
⅛ teaspoon dried rosemary
⅛ teaspoon black pepper

Pinch of red pepper flakes
1 large clove garlic, crushed
2 to 3 tablespoons extra virgin
olive oil

1. Mix together the dried herbs, the black pepper, and the red pepper flakes.
2. Add the crushed garlic to the herb mixture.
3. Put the mixture on a plate and drizzle with the olive oil.
4. Use as a dip with your favorite hot bread.

Serves 1 or 2

Carrabba's Italian Grill is not your typical restaurant chain. It was founded by Johnny Carrabba and Damian Mandola in Houston in 1986, both men coming from longtime restaurant families. The main thing that makes Carrabba's stand out from the other chains is the quality and consistency of the food.

CARRABBA'S ITALIAN GRILL
meatballs

THE TRUE MEATBALL OF ITALIAN CHEFS, MADE WITH THREE TYPES OF MEAT.

8 ounces ground pork
8 ounces ground veal
8 ounces ground beef
2 eggs, beaten
¼ cup grated Parmesan cheese
4 cloves garlic, chopped fine and sautéed

⅓ cup plain bread crumbs
¼ cup finely chopped fresh parsley
Salt and pepper, to taste
1 cup olive oil

1. Preheat the oven to 375°F.
2. Combine all the ingredients except the olive oil in a medium bowl.
3. Heat the oil in a large sauté pan over medium-high heat.
4. Roll the mixture into 1½-inch balls and fry until brown on all sides but not cooked through completely.
5. Remove with a slotted spoon to a plate lined with paper towels.
6. Put the meatballs in an ovenproof pan and bake for 20 to 25 minutes, until the meatballs are cooked throughout. You can also continue to cook these in a tomato sauce if desired.

Serves 4

THE CHEESECAKE FACTORY
avocado egg rolls

· ·

CHUNKS OF FRESH AVOCADO, SUN-DRIED TOMATO, RED ONION, AND CILANTRO
DEEP-FRIED IN A CRISP CHINESE WRAPPER. SERVED WITH A TAMARIND-CASHEW
DIPPING SAUCE.

· ·

Dipping Sauce

4 teaspoons white vinegar
1 teaspoon balsamic vinegar
½ cup honey (I use slightly less)
½ teaspoon tamarind concentrate
Pinch of ground turmeric
½ cup chopped cashews
⅔ cup chopped fresh cilantro
2 cloves garlic
2 green onions
1 tablespoon sugar
1 teaspoon pepper
1 teaspoon ground cumin
¼ cup olive oil

Egg Rolls

1 large avocado, pitted, peeled, and
   diced
2 tablespoons chopped dry-packed
   sun-dried tomatoes
1 tablespoon finely chopped red
   onion
½ teaspoon chopped fresh cilantro
Pinch of salt
4 egg roll wrappers
1 egg, beaten
Oil, for frying

1. To make the dipping sauce, combine the vinegars, honey, and tamarind in a microwave-safe bowl. Stir until the tamarind is dissolved.
2. Microwave for 1 minute.
3. Using a food processor, puree the tamarind mixture, turmeric, cashews, cilantro, garlic, green onions, sugar, pepper, and cumin.
4. Pour the mixture into a bowl and stir in the oil.
5. Cover and refrigerate until needed.
6. To make the egg rolls, stir together the avocado, sun-dried tomato, red onion, cilantro, and salt.
7. Place some of the filling in the center of one of the egg roll wrappers.
8. Fold one corner up one quarter of the way over the filling. Brush the

remaining corners and edges with the beaten egg, fold over the left and right sides, then fold the top corner over all and press to seal.

9. Repeat with the remaining wrappers.
10. Deep-fry the egg rolls in 375°F oil for 3 to 4 minutes, until browned. Drain on paper towels.
11. Serve with the chilled dipping sauce.

Serves 2 to 4

You can bake these instead of deep-frying for a healthy alternative.

This restaurant was started by Evelyn Overton in 1949 as a small-scale bakery operated out of her family's basement in Detroit. Today, the restaurants are a major chain and have much more on their menu than just cheesecake.

THE CHEESECAKE FACTORY

banana cream cheesecake

BANANA CREAM CHEESECAKE TOPPED WITH BAVARIAN CREAM AND FRESH SLICED BANANAS.

Crust
20 vanilla sandwich cookies
4 tablespoons (½ stick) margarine, melted

Filling
Three 8-ounce packages cream cheese, softened
⅔ cup sugar
2 tablespoons cornstarch
3 eggs
¾ cup mashed bananas (about 2)
½ cup heavy cream
2 teaspoons vanilla extract
1 cup store-bought Bavarian cream
2 ripe bananas, sliced

1. To make the crust, place the cookies in a blender; pulse until finely crushed. Add the margarine; process with pulses until combined. Press the mixture onto the bottom of a 10-inch springform pan; refrigerate.
2. Preheat the oven to 350°F.
3. To make the filling, beat the cream cheese in a large bowl with an electric mixer at medium speed until creamy. Add the sugar and cornstarch; beat until blended. Add the eggs, one at a time, and continue beating. Mix in the bananas, heavy cream, and vanilla until incorporated.
4. Pour the cream cheese mixture into the chilled crust.
5. Place the pan on a cookie sheet and bake for 15 minutes. Reduce the oven temperature to 200°F and continue baking for 1 hour and 15 minutes or until the center is almost set.
6. Loosen the edges of the cheesecake; let cool completely on a wire rack before removing the rim of the pan. Refrigerate, uncovered, for 6 hours. Allow the cheesecake to stand at room temperature for 15 minutes before serving.
7. Top with dollops of Bavarian cream and the sliced bananas.

Serves 6 to 8

Use overripe bananas in this recipe.

THE CHEESECAKE FACTORY

cajun jambalaya pasta

A CAJUN-SPICED CHICKEN-AND-SHRIMP SAUCE WITH PEPPERS AND ONIONS
SERVED OVER FRESH LINGUINE.

8 tablespoons (1 stick) butter
2 teaspoons Cajun blackening
  spice
1 pound boneless, skinless chicken
  breasts, cut into small pieces
1 pound fresh linguine
½ cup clam juice
½ green bell pepper, cut into thin
  strips

½ red bell pepper, cut into thin
  strips
½ yellow bell pepper, cut into thin
  strips
1 small red onion, cut into thin
  strips
8 ounces medium shrimp, peeled
  and deveined
½ cup diced tomato

1. Place the butter in a skillet over medium heat. Allow the butter to melt slightly. Add the Cajun spice to the pan and stir together with the melted butter. Add the chicken to the pan and continue to cook until the chicken is about half done.
2. While the chicken is cooking, carefully place the pasta in boiling salted water and cook until al dente.
3. Pour the clam juice into the pan. Add the peppers and onions. Cook for another minute, making sure the vegetables are heated through and the chicken is almost done.
4. Add the shrimp to the pan. Toss the ingredients together and continue to cook until the shrimp are almost done.
5. Add the tomato to the pan. Continue to cook the mixture until both the shrimp and the chicken are cooked through.
6. Serve the pasta on plates or bowls and add the jambalaya mixture.

Serves 4

THE CHEESECAKE FACTORY
chicken fettuccine

FETTUCCINE WITH CHICKEN, FRESH TOMATO, AND A GARLIC-PARMESAN SAUCE.

8 ounces fettuccine
2 tablespoons olive oil
1 tablespoon chopped garlic
¼ red onion, minced
6 medium mushrooms, sliced thin
¼ cup white wine
¼ cup chicken broth
1 tomato, peeled, seeded, and diced

6 fresh basil leaves, chopped
2 grilled boneless chicken breasts, cut into thin strips
2 tablespoons butter
Salt and pepper
Parmesan cheese for garnish
Minced green onions for garnish

1. Add the pasta to boiling salted water. As the pasta cooks, heat the olive oil in a 12-inch sauté pan.
2. Add the garlic to the pan and sauté for about 30 seconds.
3. Add the red onion and mushrooms and sauté for 2 minutes.
4. Add the white wine and reduce by half, then add the chicken broth and reduce by half.
5. Add the tomato, basil, and grilled chicken.
6. Sauté for 1 minute, then add the butter to the sauce.
7. Mix with the cooked, drained pasta. Add salt and pepper to taste.
8. Top with grated Parmesan cheese and garnish with green onions and serve.

Serves 2 to 4

Precooked, sliced, and frozen chicken breasts will save time.

You can substitute linguine or any other pasta in this recipe.

THE CHEESECAKE FACTORY

crab cakes

MADE WITH FRESH CRABMEAT, AND DELICIOUS WITH TARTAR OR REMOULADE SAUCE.

8 ounces lump crabmeat

3 tablespoons plain bread crumbs (such as Progresso)

2 tablespoons mayonnaise

2 tablespoons minced green onion (green part only)

2 tablespoons minced red bell pepper

½ beaten egg

1 teaspoon minced fresh parsley

1 teaspoon Old Bay seasoning

½ teaspoon yellow mustard

¼ cup panko (Japanese bread crumbs; available at Asian markets)

Vegetable oil, for frying

Store-bought tartar or remoulade sauce, for serving

1. Measure all the ingredients for the crab cakes, except the panko and vegetable oil, into a large bowl. Use a spatula to carefully fold the ingredients together. Avoid over-stirring.
2. Use your hands or a spoon to fill six cups of a clean muffin tin with equal amounts of the crab mixture. Press down a bit on each crab cake so that the top is flat, but don't press too hard.
3. Cover the muffin tin with plastic wrap and refrigerate the cakes for a couple of hours to help them stay together when they're browned in the oil.
4. After the crab cakes have chilled completely, heat about ¼ inch of vegetable oil in a large skillet over medium-low heat.
5. Fill a shallow bowl with the panko bread crumbs.
6. Carefully turn the crab cakes out onto a plate.
7. Gently roll each crab cake around in the panko bread crumbs. Each crab cake should be covered in a light coating of panko.

8. Test the oil by dropping a pinch of the panko crumbs into the oil. If it sizzles, the oil is ready.
9. Sauté the crab cakes in the hot oil for 1½ to 3 minutes on each side, until the cakes are golden brown.
10. Drain the crab cakes on paper towels or a rack, then serve them hot with your favorite sauce.

Makes 6 crab cakes

THE CHEESECAKE FACTORY
oreo cheesecake

. . . .

THE CREAMY RICHNESS OF CHEESECAKE WITH CRUSHED OREO COOKIES OVER AN OREO CRUST.

. . . .

Crust
2 tablespoons butter, melted
1½ cups Oreo cookie crumbs
(about 25 Oreo cookies, finely chopped)

Filling
Three 8-ounce packages cream cheese, softened
1 cup sugar
5 eggs
¼ teaspoon salt
2 teaspoons vanilla extract
¼ teaspoon salt
¼ cup all-purpose flour
8 ounces sour cream
5 Oreo cookies, coarsely chopped, for filling
10 Oreo cookies, coarsely chopped, for topping

1. Have all the ingredients at room temperature before beginning.
2. Preheat the oven to 325°F.
3. To make the crust, mix the melted butter with the Oreo cookie crumbs and press onto the bottom and 1½ inches up the sides of a 9-inch springform pan; set aside.
4. To make the filling, beat the cream cheese with an electric mixer on low until fluffy.
5. Slowly add the sugar and continue beating the cream cheese until mixed well.
6. Add the eggs one at a time and continue to beat until blended.
7. Measure the vanilla, salt, and flour; pour into the cream cheese mixture, and beat until smooth. Add the sour cream and beat.
8. Stir in the 5 coarsely chopped Oreo cookies with a spoon.
9. Pour the cream cheese mixture into the springform pan and sprinkle the 10 coarsely chopped Oreo cookies over the filling.
10. Place the pan in the middle of oven and bake for 1 hour and 15 minutes.

11. After that time, keep the oven door open and let the cheesecake stay in the oven for 1 hour. Remove from the oven and let cool enough to place in the refrigerator for 24 hours. To serve, run a knife or metal spatula around the sides of the pan to loosen the cake, and remove the pan.

Serves 4 to 6

Refrigerate this for 24 hours before serving for the best flavor.

THE CHEESECAKE FACTORY
pumpkin cheesecake

RICH AND CREAMY PUMPKIN CHEESECAKE WITH A CINNAMON GRAHAM CRACKER CRUST.

Crust
2 cups graham cracker crumbs
1 tablespoon sugar
1 teaspoon ground cinnamon
5 tablespoons butter, melted

Filling
Two 8-ounce packages cream
    cheese, softened
1 cup sour cream

1 ¼ cups granulated sugar
3 tablespoons packed light brown
    sugar
1 teaspoon vanilla extract
One 15-ounce can pumpkin puree
2 teaspoons pumpkin-pie spice
½ teaspoon ground cinnamon
4 eggs, beaten
Whipped cream and nuts, to
    garnish (optional)

1. Preheat the oven to 350°F.
2. To make the crust, mix the ingredients until crumbly, not pasty. Pat into a 9-inch springform pan, forming the crust along the bottom and up the sides. Set aside.
3. To make the filling, in a mixer, beat the cream cheese, sour cream, granulated and brown sugars, and vanilla until smooth. Add the pumpkin puree and the spices and blend. Add the eggs one at a time and blend again until mixed. Pour into the pan over the crust.
4. Bake for 40 to 45 minutes, until the center is almost set.
5. Turn the oven off and leave the cheesecake in the oven for an additional 30 minutes.
6. Remove from the oven and allow to cool. Refrigerate for several hours, until the cheesecake cools completely and firms.
7. To serve, run a knife or metal spatula around the sides of the pan to loosen the cake, and remove the pan. Garnish with whipped cream and nuts, if desired.

Serves 10 to 12

Make your own pumpkin-pie spice by combining 1 tablespoon allspice, 2 tablespoons ground cinnamon, 1 tablespoon ground cloves, 2 teaspoons ground nutmeg, and 2 teaspoons ground ginger.

CHI-CHI'S
baked chicken chimichangas

A SPICY TORTILLA-WRAPPED CHICKEN-AND-REFRIED-BEAN FILLING, BAKED UNTIL
GOLDEN AND CRISP, SERVED WITH SALSA, SOUR CREAM, AND GUACAMOLE.

½ cup chopped onion
2 cloves garlic, minced
2 tablespoons olive oil
⅓ cup chili powder
One 16-ounce jar Chi-Chi's salsa
¼ cup water
½ teaspoon ground cumin
½ teaspoon ground cinnamon

1 pound cooked boneless, skinless
    chicken breasts, shredded
Salt
Six 10-inch flour tortillas, warmed
1 cup Chi-Chi's refried beans
Olive oil
Sour cream
Guacamole

1. Preheat the oven to 425°F. Grease a rimmed 15 by 10-inch baking pan.
2. In large saucepan, sauté the onion and garlic in the oil until tender. Stir
   in the chili powder, ⅔ jar salsa, water, cumin, and cinnamon. Pour the
   mixture into a blender or a food processor fitted with the metal blade.
   Process until smooth. Pour back into the saucepan; stir in the chicken.
   Add salt to taste.
3. Working with one tortilla at a time, spoon a heaping tablespoon of the
   refried beans down the center of each tortilla. Top with about ½ cup of
   the chicken mixture.
4. Place the chimichangas in the greased baking pan, seam-side down.
   Brush all the sides with oil.
5. Bake for 15 minutes or until golden brown and crisp, turning every
   5 minutes.
6. Serve with the remaining salsa, sour cream, and guacamole.

Serves 6

Another great way to make use of leftover chicken.

This recipe can also be made into a casserole by layering the
ingredients in an oiled casserole dish. Bake until heated
through.

CHI-CHI'S
pork tenderloin with bourbon sauce

ZESTY MARINATED PORK SERVED WITH A TOMATO-AND-BOURBON-BASED SAUCE.

Marinade
One 10-ounce can Chi-Chi's diced tomatoes and green chiles, drained
1/3 cup bourbon
1/3 cup soy sauce

1/3 cup Worcestershire sauce
1/2 cup chopped onion
2 tablespoons honey
2 tablespoons Dijon mustard
1/4 teaspoon pepper

2 pounds pork tenderloin

1. Combine all the marinade ingredients in a resealable plastic bag. Mix well. Add the pork tenderloin. Seal the bag and turn several times to coat the meat. Place in the refrigerator for at least 8 hours or overnight, turning the bag occasionally.
2. Preheat the broiler. Remove the meat from the marinade; reserve the marinade.
3. Place the meat on a broiler pan, and broil 7 to 8 inches from the heat source for 7 to 9 minutes on each side, until cooked thoroughly throughout.
4. In a small saucepan, bring the remainder of the marinade to a boil; boil for 1 minute. Serve with the meat.

Serves 4 to 6

CHI-CHI'S
salsa verde chicken kabobs

SWEET AND SPICY MARINATED CHICKEN KABOBS, SERVED ON A BED OF CAB-
BAGE, JICAMA, AND CARROTS WITH GRILLED BANANA.

One 16-ounce jar Chi-Chi's salsa verde
1/4 cup olive oil
2 tablespoons lime juice
3 cloves garlic
1 boneless, skinless chicken breast, cut into 1 1/2-inch strips
2 cups finely shredded cabbage

1 1/2 cups finely julienned jicama
1 cup shredded carrots
1/3 cup coarsely chopped fresh cilantro
Pinch of salt
Pinch of pepper
2 large ripe bananas or plantains

1. In a blender or food processor, combine the salsa verde, oil, lime juice, and garlic. Process until smooth.
2. Remove 2/3 cup of the mixture and set aside in the refrigerator.
3. Place the chicken in a resealable plastic bag; pour the remaining salsa verde mixture over the chicken. Seal the bag and turn over several times to coat the pieces thoroughly. Refrigerate, turning the bag occasionally, for at least 4 hours or overnight.
4. In a large bowl, combine the cabbage, jicama, carrots, and cilantro. Stir in the reserved 2/3 cup salsa verde mixture. Add the salt and pepper; set aside.
5. Preheat the grill to medium heat. Thread the chicken pieces onto 8 long bamboo skewers (be sure to presoak the skewers in water for 30 minutes before using).
6. Grill the kabobs over medium hot coals for 5 minutes on each side or until no longer pink in the center.
7. Slice the bananas lengthwise, and grill for 2 minutes on each side.
8. Serve the chicken and bananas on top of the cabbage mixture.

Serves 2

If Chi-Chi's salsa verde is not available in your area, look for a salsa made from tomatillos, cilantro, and onions. Spicy and sweet!

CHI-CHI'S
steak and mushroom quesadillas

MARINATED AND GRILLED STEAK WITH A MEDLEY OF SAUTÉED PEPPERS AND
ONIONS, SERVED IN A ZESTY TORTILLA TOPPED WITH CHEESE AND PICO DE GALLO.

Marinade
2 tablespoons soy sauce
2 tablespoons pineapple juice
2 cloves garlic, crushed
Salt and pepper to taste

4 ounces flank or skirt steak
¼ cup sliced red bell pepper
¼ cup sliced green bell pepper
¼ cup sliced yellow onion
⅓ cup sliced mushrooms
1 tablespoon garlic butter
(combine 1 tablespoon softened
butter with ⅛ teaspoon finely
minced garlic)

One 12-inch jalapeño-Cheddar or
plain flour tortilla
½ cup shredded Cheddar-Jack
cheese
½ cup pico de gallo
Shredded iceberg lettuce
Sour cream
Guacamole
Chi-Chi's salsa con queso or other
dipping sauce

1. Combine all the marinade ingredients, and marinate the steak for at least
   2 hours prior to grilling.
2. Preheat the grill to 350°F.
3. Grill the steak to the preferred doneness. Remove the steak from the grill
   and slice thinly.
4. Sauté the red pepper, green pepper, onion, and mushrooms in the garlic
   butter until the vegetables are semisoft and have a light golden color to
   them.
5. Lay the tortilla over medium-high heat on the grill or in a large sauté
   pan on the stove top. Top the tortilla with the cheese, pico de gallo,
   sautéed vegetables, and the grilled steak.
6. Allow to heat until the cheese has melted. Once the cheese has melted,
   fold the tortilla in half. Remove the tortilla from the heat and cut into
   four wedges.

7. Place the cut tortilla on a large serving plate and garnish with the shredded lettuce, sour cream, and guacamole. Serve the salsa con queso in individual bowls for dipping.

Serves 4

Prepare this dish with boneless, skinless chicken breasts.

CHILI'S
baby back ribs

FULL RACK OF RIBS "DOUBLE-BASTED" WITH BARBECUE SAUCE. TYPICALLY
SERVED WITH CINNAMON APPLES AND HOME-STYLE FRIES.

6 pounds pork baby back ribs

2 cups water

Sauce

1 cup white vinegar

½ cup tomato paste

1 tablespoon dry mustard

¼ cup packed dark brown sugar

1 teaspoon liquid smoke

3 tablespoons Worcestershire sauce

1¼ teaspoons salt

½ teaspoon onion powder

2 cloves garlic, minced

¼ teaspoon paprika

2 teaspoons lemon juice

1. Preheat the oven to 350°F.
2. Cut the rib slabs in half, leaving 6 to 8 ribs per section. In a large roasting pan, arrange the ribs evenly, then add the water. Cover the pan tightly with a lid or foil to prevent steam from escaping. Bake for 3 hours.
3. About 2 hours into the baking time, make the sauce. In a large saucepan, combine all the sauce ingredients. Simmer over low heat for 1 hour, stirring occasionally.
4. Prepare the coals in a barbecue. Remove the ribs from the roasting pan. Discard the water.
5. Cover the ribs with the sauce, saving about 1½ cups of the sauce for later use at the table. Grill the ribs on the barbecue for about 5 minutes per side, or until slightly charred.
6. Serve with the remaining sauce and lots of paper towels or moist towelettes.

Serves 6 to 8

Place the ribs in a slow cooker, pouring the sauce over. Let cook on low for 6 to 8 hours or on high for 3 to 4 hours until the meat is very tender.

When the first Chili's restaurant opened in Dallas in 1975, the menu consisted of little more than burgers, chili, and tacos—yet there was a never-ending line out the door. Today, their permanent and limited-time menu items are more exciting and innovative than ever.

CHILI'S
beef fajitas

JUICY STEAK SLOW-COOKED TO PERFECTION! SERVED WITH SIZZLING ONIONS
AND BELL PEPPERS.

1½ pounds sirloin steak
One 4-ounce can diced green
  chiles
1 envelope onion soup mix
2 cups water
1 large red onion

1 large green bell pepper
Olive oil
Eight 8-inch flour tortillas
Shredded Cheddar cheese
Salsa

1. Cut the sirloin steak into bite-size pieces.
2. Place in a slow cooker with the chiles, soup mix, and water. Cook on low for 6 to 8 hours.
3. Cut the onion and green pepper into small strips; sauté in oil until tender.
4. Warm the tortillas in the microwave.
5. Drain the beef mixture. Spread in the center of each tortilla, then top with the cheese, salsa, and the onion and pepper mixture. Roll up the tortillas to enclose the filling.

Serves 4

Goes great with Mexican rice and refried beans.

CHILI'S
chicken enchilada soup

A SPICY SOUP WITH TOMATOES, CHEESE, AND CHICKEN, SERVED WITH CHEDDAR CHEESE, TORTILLA CHIPS, AND PICO DE GALLO.

½ cup vegetable oil
¼ cup chicken bouillon powder
3 cups diced yellow onions
2 teaspoons ground cumin
2 teaspoons chili powder
2 teaspoons granulated garlic
½ teaspoon cayenne pepper
2 cups masa harina
4 quarts water

2 cups canned crushed tomatoes
8 ounces Velveeta, cubed
3 pounds cooked chicken breast, shredded

Garnish
I cup shredded Cheddar cheese
4 cups crushed tortilla chips
I cup pico de gallo

1. To a large pot, add the oil, bouillon powder, onions, cumin, chili powder, granulated garlic, and cayenne pepper. Sauté until the onions are soft and clear, about 5 minutes.
2. In a large bowl, combine the masa harina with 1 quart of the water. Stir until all the lumps have dissolved. Add to the sautéed onions and bring the mixture to a boil. Cook, stirring constantly, for an additional 2 to 3 minutes.
3. Add the remaining 3 quarts water to the pot. Add the tomatoes and return to a boil, stirring occasionally. Add the cheese and stir until it melts. Add the chicken; heat and serve.
4. Garnish with shredded Cheddar cheese, crumbled tortilla chips, and pico de gallo.

Serves 16 to 20

This soup can be transferred to various-sized containers and frozen for future meals.

Masa harina is the traditional flour used to make tortillas, tamales, and other Mexican dishes.

CHILI'S
chocolate chip paradise pie

A WARM, CHEWY "CANDY BAR," LAYERED WITH CHOCOLATE CHIPS, WALNUTS, AND COCONUT. SERVE TOPPED WITH A SCOOP OF VANILLA ICE CREAM AND DRIZZLED WITH HOT FUDGE AND CARAMEL.

Crust
3 tablespoons butter
1/3 cup graham cracker crumbs
3 tablespoons sugar
1/3 cup chocolate chips

Filling
1/2 cup all-purpose flour
1/4 cup sugar
3/4 teaspoon baking powder
1/3 cup milk

1 tablespoon vegetable oil
1 teaspoon vanilla extract
1/3 cup semisweet or milk chocolate chips
1/4 cup shredded coconut
1/4 cup crushed walnuts or almonds

To Serve
Vanilla ice cream
Hot fudge sauce
Caramel syrup

1. Preheat the oven to 350°F.
2. To make the crust, melt the butter and combine with the graham cracker crumbs and sugar.
3. Press into the bottom of a 1-quart baking dish. Top evenly with the chocolate chips.
4. Bake for 5 minutes or until the chocolate is melted. Spread the melted chips out evenly over the crust.
5. To make the filling, combine the dry ingredients in a large mixing bowl.
6. Add the milk, oil, and vanilla and stir until smooth. Stir in the chocolate chips, coconut, and nuts. Pour into the crust.
7. Bake, uncovered, for 35 to 40 minutes, until a toothpick comes out clean.
8. Serve warm with vanilla ice cream, hot fudge, and caramel syrup.

Serves 4

Use a prepared piecrust for this recipe.

CHILI'S
margarita grilled chicken

TENDER, JUICY CHICKEN BREAST, MARINATED WITH MARGARITA FLAVORING
AND GRILLED TO PERFECTION. SERVE WITH BLACK BEANS, MEXICAN RICE, AND
HOMEMADE OR STORE-BOUGHT PICO DE GALLO.

I cup liquid margarita mix
¼ cup tequila
I tablespoon minced garlic

4 boneless, skinless chicken breasts
Salt and pepper

1. Combine the margarita mix, tequila, and garlic in a dish with the chicken breasts and let marinate for 2 hours in the refrigerator. When ready to prepare, drain and season with salt and pepper.
2. Preheat the grill to medium-high heat.
3. Spray the grill with olive oil cooking spray and cook the chicken breasts until done, 6 to 8 minutes on each side.

Serves 4

Make your own margarita mix using 4 parts lemon juice, 1 part lime juice, and 1 part Key lime juice.

CHILI'S
salsa

MAKE CHILI'S FAMOUS SALSA AT HOME. GREAT WITH YOUR FAVORITE CHIPS.

4 teaspoons fresh or canned (not pickled) diced jalapeño pepper
¼ cup diced onion
One 14½-ounce can tomatoes and green chiles

One 14½-ounce can whole peeled tomatoes, with juice
¾ teaspoon garlic salt, or to taste
½ teaspoon cumin, or more to taste
¼ teaspoon sugar, or to taste

1. Place the jalapeño and onion in a food processor; pulse for just a few seconds.
2. Add both cans of tomatoes and the garlic salt, cumin, and sugar.
3. Process all the ingredients until well blended, but do not puree. You want the salsa to be chunky.
4. Serve immediately or refrigerate.

Serves 4

CHILI'S
southwestern chicken chili

HEARTY CHICKEN CHILI MADE WITH FLAVORFUL SEASONINGS, WHITE BEANS,
AND CHOPPED GREEN CHILE.

¼ cup vegetable oil
½ cup diced onion
1⅓ cups diced green bell peppers
2 tablespoons diced jalapeño pepper
3 tablespoons minced garlic
4½ cups water
2 tablespoons plus 2 teaspoons chicken bouillon powder
2 teaspoons lime juice
2 tablespoons sugar
3 tablespoons cornstarch
3 tablespoons ground cumin
2½ tablespoons chili powder
4 teaspoons paprika
4 teaspoons dried basil
2 teaspoons minced fresh cilantro

1½ teaspoons cayenne pepper
½ teaspoon ground oregano
½ cup canned crushed tomatillos
One 4-ounce can diced green chiles, drained
Two 15-ounce cans navy or small white beans, rinsed and drained
One 15-ounce can dark red kidney beans, rinsed and drained
3 pounds cooked chicken breast, diced

Garnish
Shredded Cheddar or Jack cheese
Sour cream
Tortilla chips

1. In a 5-quart (or larger) pot, heat the oil over medium heat. Add the onion and sauté along with the green pepper, jalapeño, and garlic. Cook until the vegetables are tender.
2. In a large bowl, combine the water, chicken bouillon powder, lime juice, sugar, cornstarch, cumin, chili powder, paprika, basil, cilantro, cayenne pepper, and oregano. Add to the vegetable mixture.
3. Add the tomatillos and diced green chiles to the pot; bring to a boil. Add the navy beans and kidney beans, and chicken; simmer for 10 minutes.
4. Serve topped with shredded cheese and sour cream, with the tortilla chips on the side.

Serves 4

CHILI'S
southwestern egg rolls

CRISPY FLOUR TORTILLAS WRAPPED AROUND SAUTÉED CHICKEN, CORN, BLACK
BEANS, SPINACH, JALAPEÑO AND RED BELL PEPPER, AND MELTED JACK CHEESE.
SERVE WITH A CREAMY STORE-BOUGHT AVOCADO-RANCH DIPPING SAUCE.

2 tablespoons vegetable oil
1 boneless, skinless chicken breast
2 tablespoons minced green onion
2 tablespoons minced red bell pepper
1/3 cup frozen corn kernels
1/4 cup canned black beans, rinsed and drained
2 tablespoons frozen chopped spinach, thawed and squeezed
2 tablespoons diced jalapeño pepper
Pinch of cayenne pepper

1 1/2 teaspoons minced fresh parsley
1/2 teaspoon ground cumin
1/2 teaspoon chili powder
1/3 teaspoon salt
3/4 cup shredded Monterey Jack cheese

Five 6-inch flour tortillas
4 cups oil, for deep-frying

Store-bought avocado-ranch salad dressing, for dipping
Chopped tomato
Chopped onion

1. Rub 1 tablespoon of the vegetable oil over the chicken breast. In a medium saucepan over medium heat, cook the chicken for about 5 minutes per side, until the meat is no longer pink and the juices run clear. Remove from the heat and set aside.
2. Heat the remaining 1 tablespoon vegetable oil in the saucepan over medium heat. Stir in the green onion and red bell pepper. Cook, stirring for 5 minutes or until tender.
3. Dice the chicken and mix it into the pan with the onion and green bell pepper. Mix in the corn, black beans, spinach, jalapeño, parsley, cumin, chili powder, salt, and cayenne pepper. Cook, stirring for 5 minutes or until well blended and the vegetables are tender. Remove from the heat and stir in the Monterey Jack cheese so that it melts.
4. Wrap the tortillas with a clean, lightly moistened cloth. Microwave on

high for 1 minute, or bake, wrapped in foil, in a preheated 350°F oven for 5 minutes.

5. Spoon even amounts of the mixture into each tortilla. Fold the ends of the tortilla, then roll tightly around the mixture. Secure with toothpicks. Arrange in a medium dish, cover with plastic wrap, and place in the freezer. Freeze for at least 4 hours before frying.

6. In a large, deep skillet, heat the oil to 375°F. Deep-fry each frozen stuffed tortilla for 10 minutes or until dark golden brown. Drain on paper towels before serving.

7. Slice each egg roll diagonally lengthwise and arrange on a plate around a small bowl of the dipping sauce. Garnish the dipping sauce with the chopped tomato and onion.

Serves 5 or 6

Prepare this recipe the night before any party, then deep-fry just before serving.

CHILI'S
southwestern vegetable soup

IF YOU LIKE A SOUP THAT IS PACKED WITH VEGGIES, IS LOW IN FAT, AND HAS SOME OF THAT SOUTHWESTERN ZING TO IT, THIS IS THE ONE FOR YOU!

6 cups chicken broth
One 14.5-ounce can diced tomatoes, with juice
1 cup water
1 cup canned dark red kidney beans, with liquid
1 cup frozen corn kernels
1 cup frozen cut green beans
1 small green bell pepper, diced

½ cup diced Spanish onion
½ cup tomato sauce
6 corn tortillas, minced
1½ teaspoons chili powder
Pinch of garlic powder

Garnish
1 cup shredded Cheddar cheese
1 cup crumbled tortilla chips

1. Mix the soup ingredients in a pot over high heat.
2. Bring the soup to a boil, reduce the heat, and let simmer for 45 minutes.
3. Serve in soup bowls and garnish with the cheese; sprinkle the crumbled tortilla chips on top of the cheese.

Serves 6

CHURCH'S
fried chicken

BIG, JUICY, FULL-FLAVORED SOUTHERN FRIED CHICKEN. SERVE WITH MASHED
POTATOES AND GRAVY AND COLESLAW.

1 tablespoon sugar
1 ½ cups self-rising flour
½ cup cornstarch
1 tablespoon seasoned salt
2 teaspoons paprika
½ teaspoon baking soda
½ cup biscuit mix

1 envelope Italian dressing mix
1 envelope onion soup mix
One 2- to 3-pound chicken, cut
   into 8 pieces
2 eggs, beaten with ¼ cup cold
   water
1 cup corn oil, for frying

1. Preheat the oven to 350°F.
2. Combine all the dry ingredients in a large bowl. Mix to blend the
   ingredients thoroughly.
3. Dip the chicken pieces into the egg mixture and then into the dry
   coating mix; repeat so each piece is double-coated.
4. Preheat the oil in a heavy skillet over medium-high heat. Brown the
   pieces skin side down for 5 minutes.
5. Turn and brown the undersides of the pieces for a few minutes. Transfer
   to an oiled pan. Cover with foil, sealing it on only three sides of the pan.
6. Bake for 45 to 50 minutes. Remove the foil, then bake for another
   5 minutes or until the coating is crisp.

Serves 4 to 6

Combine all the dry ingredients and store them in a sealed container
for future use.

George W. Church, Sr., of San Antonio, Texas, founded Church's in 1952, at a time when only hot dogs and ice cream were being marketed as fast food. Church, a retired chicken incubator salesman in his sixties, drew on his more than twenty years in the poultry industry in conceiving the idea of marketing low-cost, freshly fried chicken as a convenience food.

The first Church's Fried Chicken to Go, in downtown San Antonio, across the street from the Alamo, sold only fried chicken. French fries and jalapeño peppers were added to the menu in 1955. Today, there are more than 1,500 restaurants throughout the United States.

CRACKER BARREL
baby limas

BABY LIMAS COOKED IN A CHICKEN-BASED BROTH AND FLAVORED WITH BACON
AND A HINT OF GARLIC.

1 cup water	1 clove garlic, lightly smashed
1 chicken bouillon cube	One 16-ounce bag frozen baby
1 slice bacon	lima beans
2 pinches red pepper flakes	Salt and pepper

1. Bring the water and bouillon to a boil.
2. Add the bacon, red pepper flakes, garlic, and beans. Cover the pan, reduce the heat, and let the beans simmer. Cook for at least 25 minutes.
3. Drain and discard the bacon and garlic clove. Serve the beans seasoned with salt and pepper to taste.

Serves 4

If additional liquid is needed, use boiling water.

Cracker Barrel opened in 1969 and serves good ol' country cookin'. Their corn bread comes from cornmeal, not a mix; mashed potatoes are made from real potatoes; and scratch biscuits come with real butter.

CRACKER BARREL
banana pudding

ENJOY THE OLD-FASHIONED GOODNESS OF A RICH PUDDING WITH BANANAS OVER A VANILLA COOKIE BASE.

1½ cups sugar
½ cup plus 2 tablespoons all-purpose flour
½ teaspoon salt
4 cups milk
5 egg yolks, beaten

4 tablespoons (½ stick) butter
2 teaspoons vanilla extract
One 12-ounce box vanilla wafers
7 bananas, sliced about ⅓ inch thick
One 16-ounce container whipped topping

1. In a large saucepan over medium-low heat, combine the sugar, flour, salt, and milk. Stir until completely blended.
2. When the mixture begins to boil, cook for 2 minutes, stirring constantly as it begins to thicken.
3. Remove from the heat and add ½ cup of the hot mixture to the beaten egg yolks and stir until blended.
4. Place the pudding mixture back on the stove over medium heat and add the egg yolk mixture; continue to cook, stirring, for 3 minutes.
5. After 3 minutes, turn the heat off, add the butter and vanilla, and beat with a whisk until blended.
6. Remove from the stovetop and let cool for about ten minutes.
7. Spray a 13 by 9-inch baking pan with cooking spray and arrange the vanilla wafers to cover the bottom and sides of the pan.
8. Slice the bananas and cover the wafers with the banana slices. Pour the pudding into the pan, covering the bananas and wafers.
9. Allow the banana pudding to cool in the refrigerator. When the pudding has set, cover with the whipped topping.

Serves 6

For a quicker version of this recipe, you can buy two boxes of banana-flavored pudding and follow the package directions. Then start following the recipe directions from step 6.

CRACKER BARREL
cherry-chocolate cobbler

CHOCOLATE DECADENCE WITH A CHERRY FILLING AND NUT TOPPING.

1 ½ cups all-purpose flour
½ cup sugar
2 teaspoons baking powder
½ teaspoon salt
4 tablespoons (½ stick) butter,
cut into small pieces
One 6-ounce package semisweet
chocolate chips

¼ cup milk
1 egg
One 21-ounce can cherry
pie filling
½ cup finely chopped nuts

1. Preheat the oven to 350°F.
2. In a large bowl, combine the flour, sugar, baking powder, salt, and butter; cut with a pastry blender until the crumbs are the size of large peas.
3. Using a double boiler, melt the semisweet chocolate chips.
4. Remove from the heat and let cool slightly at room temperature (about 5 minutes).
5. Add the milk and egg to the melted chocolate and mix well.
6. Blend the chocolate into the flour mixture.
7. Spread the cherry pie filling in the bottom of a 2-quart casserole. Drop the chocolate batter randomly over the cherries. Sprinkle with the nuts.
8. Bake for 40 to 45 minutes, until the top is golden. Serve hot.

Serves 6

CRACKER BARREL
fried apples

TENDER AND JUICY APPLE SLICES FRIED JUST RIGHT AND TOPPED WITH CIN-
NAMON AND NUTMEG.

¼ cup solid bacon drippings
6 tart apples, peeled, cored, and
  cut into eighths
1 teaspoon lemon juice

¼ cup packed light brown sugar
⅛ teaspoon salt
1 teaspoon ground cinnamon
Pinch of ground nutmeg

1. In a large skillet, melt the bacon drippings.
2. Pour the apple slices over the bottom of the skillet.
3. Pour the lemon juice over them, then the brown sugar, then the salt.
4. Cover and cook over low heat for 15 minutes or until the apples are tender and juicy.
5. Sprinkle with the cinnamon and nutmeg.

Serves 6

After cooking bacon, let the drippings cool and strain through a cheesecloth. Store refrigerated in a glass container until ready to use.

DAIRY QUEEN
heath blizzard

CREAMY-SMOOTH DQ SOFT SERVE BLENDED WITH BITS OF HEATH BAR.

2 Heath candy bars, frozen	I quart vanilla ice cream
½ cup milk	2 teaspoons fudge topping

1. Bash the candy bars into small pieces before removing them from the wrappers.
2. Add all the ingredients to a blender and blend until the mixture is nice and creamy.
3. To increase the thickness, place in the freezer for 20 to 30 minutes until the desired consistency.

Serves 2 or 3

You can also make this delicious dessert with Butterfinger candy bars, Oreo cookies, or Reese's peanut butter cups. For a reduced-fat treat, use vanilla frozen yogurt and low-fat milk.

Dairy Queen got its start in the late thirties, when J. F. McCullough, who lived in a small Illinois town, noticed that his daughter, before eating her ice cream, would mash it and allow it to melt a bit in order to get it soft enough to eat. With a friend, Sherb Noble, his tinkering with that idea led to the first sale of a new soft ice cream product in 1938, which sold for the extravagant price of ten cents a portion, but even then it was an instant hit.

DAIRY QUEEN
ice cream

A SMOOTH AND CREAMY FROZEN DELICACY!

1 envelope unflavored gelatin	1 teaspoon vanilla extract
¼ cup cold water	¼ teaspoon salt
1 cup milk	1½ cups heavy cream
1 cup sugar	

1. Sprinkle the gelatin over the water and let stand for 5 minutes.
2. Meanwhile, heat the milk to almost a simmer over medium-low heat.
3. Remove from the heat.
4. Stir in the sugar, vanilla, and salt with a wire whisk until the sugar is completely dissolved, at least 2 minutes.
5. Stir into the gelatin mixture and let cool.
6. Stir in the cream. Cover and refrigerate for 6 hours.
7. Transfer to an ice cream maker and process according to the manufacturer's directions for about 20 minutes or until creamy.

Serves 2

You can get creative with this recipe by adding your favorite topping: gummy bears, M&M's, chocolate syrup, or fresh strawberries.

DAIRY QUEEN
onion rings

CRISPY GOLDEN FRIED RINGS OF BUTTERMILK-SOAKED ONIONS.

2 Vidalia onions
2 cups buttermilk
I cup water
2 cups white cornmeal
2 cups fine cracker crumbs

2 cups all-purpose flour
4 cups oil, for deep-frying

1. Slice the onions ½ inch thick and use only the larger rings.
2. In a large bowl, combine the buttermilk and water.
3. In a separate bowl, combine the cornmeal and cracker crumbs.
4. Put the flour in another separate bowl.
5. Take each ring and coat it with the flour, then with the buttermilk, and then with the cornmeal mixture.
6. Heat the oil to 425°F. Carefully drop each ring into the hot oil and fry until golden.
7. Drain on paper towels.

Serves 2

DENNY'S
country fried steak

GOLDEN-FRIED CHOPPED-BEEF STEAKS SMOTHERED IN RICH COUNTRY GRAVY.

Four 5-ounce top round steaks

Corn oil

Seasoned salt

2 to 3 tablespoons red wine

2 cups biscuit mix

Salt and pepper

8 tablespoons (1 stick) butter

⅓ cup corn oil

Country Gravy (page 85)

1. The night before, put the steaks in a single layer on a dish. Brush them on both sides with an even coating of corn oil. Dust them on both sides with a generous amount of seasoned salt. Drizzle each steak with the wine. Seal the dish in foil or plastic wrap and refrigerate the steaks for about 24 hours prior to preparing the final dish.
2. Remove the steaks from the fridge and coat both sides well in the biscuit mix. Season with salt and pepper, to taste.
3. Preheat the oven to 375°F.
4. Combine the butter with the ⅓ cup oil in a large skillet and heat until melted.
5. Place the steaks in the skillet. Brown both sides of each steak until crispy.
6. Transfer the steaks to a baking dish and cover and seal with foil. Bake for about 30 minutes, or until golden brown on each side.
7. Serve with country gravy.

Serves 4

Prepare this recipe using chicken cutlets instead of beef.

DENNY'S
country gravy

COUNTRY FRIED STEAK WOULDN'T BE THE SAME WITHOUT IT!

1 medium clove garlic, minced	2 cups water
¼ cup bacon drippings	1 teaspoon kosher salt
1 cup all-purpose flour	1 tablespoon pepper
3 cups heavy cream	

Brown the garlic in the bacon drippings in a large heavy saucepan. Stir in the flour until smooth. Cook over low heat for a few minutes, stirring frequently. Add the cream and water, stirring constantly. Simmer until the gravy thickens and is hot. Season with the salt and pepper.

The restaurant chain that we know as Denny's began in Lakewood, California, in 1953 with a dream and a doughnut stand called Danny's Donuts. The owner, Harold Butler, started his business with a solid commitment: "We're going to serve the best cup of coffee, make the best doughnuts, give the best service, keep everything spotless, offer the best value, and stay open twenty-four hours a day."

While customers were happy, they wanted sandwiches and other entrées that were as good as the coffee and doughnuts, and the menu grew. In 1954, Danny's Donuts became Danny's Coffee Shops.

In 1959, Danny's was renamed Denny's to avoid confusion with another small chain in southern California called Coffee Dan's. Doughnuts were phased out and the menu grew to include sandwiches and other entrées.

DOLLYWOOD
dipped chocolate chip cookies

THE OLD-FASHIONED GOODNESS OF CHOCOLATE CHIP COOKIES DIPPED IN
CHOCOLATE FOR ADDED TASTE.

2¼ cups all-purpose flour
1 teaspoon baking soda
1 teaspoon salt
16 tablespoons (2 sticks) butter, softened
¾ cup granulated sugar
¾ cup packed dark brown sugar
1 teaspoon vanilla extract
2 eggs

One 12-ounce package semisweet chocolate chips

Chocolate Dip
One 6-ounce package semisweet chocolate chips
One 6-ounce package white chocolate chips
Vegetable oil

1. Preheat the oven to 375°F.
2. In a small bowl, combine the flour, baking soda, and salt; set aside.
3. In a large bowl, combine the butter, granulated and brown sugars, and vanilla; mix until creamy.
4. Beat in the eggs. Gradually add the flour mixture. Stir in the 12 ounces semisweet chips.
5. Drop by level teaspoonfuls onto an ungreased baking sheet. Bake for 9 to 11 minutes. The cookies should still be soft when removed from the oven. Place on a rack to cool.
6. To make the chocolate dip, in separate small saucepans, melt the semisweet and white chocolate chips.
7. Add a small amount of vegetable oil to each saucepan.
8. Dip each cookie halfway in the dark chocolate and return to the rack to cool.
9. Once the chocolate has cooled (and solidified), dip the other half of each cookie in the white chocolate. Allow to cool.

Makes about 2 dozen cookies

Dollywood, opened in 1985, is Dolly Parton's theme park, complete with shows, festivals, and good old-fashioned southern cooking!

EL POLLO LOCO
beans

PINTO BEANS COOKED WITH TENDER SERRANO PEPPERS.

¼ cup corn oil

5 serrano peppers

2 teaspoons ground serrano
pepper

One 28-ounce can pinto beans,
drained

¾ cup water

1. Heat the oil in a large saucepan.
2. Add the whole peppers. Sauté until tender.
3. Add the ground pepper, the beans, and the water. Stir well.
4. Bring to a boil, then reduce the heat. Simmer for 17 minutes, stirring often, until thick.

Serves 4

A perfect side for tacos, fajitas, quesadillas, and your other favorite Mexican dishes.

El Pollo Loco, pronounced "El Po-yo Lo-co," is Spanish for "The Crazy Chicken." This chain started out in 1975 as a roadside chicken stand in Mexico. Its success spread rapidly throughout Mexico and into the United States. It is billed as "a wholesome, delicious alternative to traditional fast-food fare."

EL POLLO LOCO
pollo asada

GRILLED CHICKEN, GUACAMOLE, PICO DE GALLO, AND FRESH CILANTRO IN A GRILLED FLOUR TORTILLA.

Marinade
1 cup white vinegar
1 cup olive oil
½ cup white wine
Pinch of dried oregano
Pinch of dried thyme
Pinch of salt
2 cloves garlic, minced
1½ teaspoons Tabasco sauce

1 whole chicken, cut into 8 pieces
2 cups cooked Mexican rice
One 15.5-ounce can red beans in
　sauce, warmed
Eight 8-inch flour tortillas
　(optional)
1 cup guacamole
1½ cups pico de gallo
½ cup chopped fresh cilantro

1. Mix together all the marinade ingredients in a large bowl.
2. Add the chicken to the bowl; cover.
3. Marinate for several hours in the refrigerator (overnight works best).
4. Preheat the grill to low heat.
5. Grill the chicken slowly until done.
6. Serve with Mexican rice and beans or in a soft tortilla that's been warmed on the grill.
7. Top with guacamole, pico de gallo, and cilantro.

Serves 4

HARD ROCK CAFE
baked potato soup

TASTEFULLY SEASONED SOUP MADE WITH BAKED POTATOES, BACON, ONIONS, AND CHEDDAR CHEESE.

8 slices bacon
1 cup diced yellow onions
2/3 cup all-purpose flour
6 cups hot chicken broth
4 cups diced peeled baked potatoes
2 cups heavy cream
1/4 cup chopped fresh parsley
1 1/2 teaspoons granulated garlic
1 1/2 teaspoons dried basil
1 1/2 teaspoons salt

1 1/2 teaspoons Tabasco sauce
1 1/2 teaspoons coarsely ground pepper
1 cup grated Cheddar cheese
1/4 cup diced green onions (white part)

Garnish
Crumbled bacon
Chopped fresh parsley
Grated Cheddar cheese

1. Fry the bacon until crisp. Drain on paper towels and crumble; save the drippings.
2. Cook the yellow onions in the bacon drippings over medium-high heat until soft, about 3 minutes.
3. Add the flour, whisking to prevent lumps. Cook for 4 minutes.
4. Add the chicken broth slowly, whisking to prevent lumps, and cook until the liquid thickens.
5. Reduce the heat to a simmer and add the potatoes, cream, crumbled bacon, parsley, garlic, basil, salt, Tabasco sauce, and pepper. Simmer for 10 minutes; do not boil.
6. Add the grated cheese and green onions. Heat until the cheese melts.
7. Serve, garnished as desired with crumbled bacon, parsley, and grated cheese.

Serves 6

Leftover baked potatoes work well in this recipe.

Hard Rock Cafe was started in 1971 in London as a "specialty theme" restaurant catering to rock 'n' roll lovers worldwide. It has become the world's leading collector and exhibitor of rock 'n' roll memorabilia, which can be seen on display in the restaurants. All this and great food as well.

HARD ROCK CAFE
bbq beans

TANGY BARBECUE-SEASONED PINTO BEANS TOPPED WITH CRISP BACON.

Two 15-ounce cans pinto beans, with liquid
2 teaspoons cornstarch
2 tablespoons water
1/2 cup ketchup
1/3 cup white vinegar
1/4 cup packed dark brown sugar
2 tablespoons diced onion

1 teaspoon yellow mustard
1/2 teaspoon chili powder
1/4 teaspoon salt
1/4 teaspoon coarsely ground pepper
1/2 cup crumbled cooked bacon, for serving

1. Preheat the oven to 350°F.
2. Pour the entire contents of the cans of pinto beans into a 2-quart casserole.
3. Dissolve the cornstarch in a small bowl with the 2 tablespoons water. Add this solution to the beans and stir.
4. Add the remaining ingredients except the bacon to the casserole, stir well, and cover.
5. Bake for 90 minutes or until the sauce thickens. Stir every 30 minutes. After removing the beans from the oven, let the beans cool for 5 to 10 minutes before serving, topped with crumbled bacon.

Serves 6

HARD ROCK CAFE
bbq ribs

A FULL RACK OF TENNESSEE-STYLE RIBS WITH HARD ROCK'S AUTHENTIC HICKORY
BARBECUE SAUCE.

2 cups water
2 cups liquid smoke
One 3½-pound slab St. Louis–style
   ribs

Barbecue Sauce
¼ cup chicken broth
2 cups ketchup
1 teaspoon real maple syrup
½ teaspoon garlic powder
¼ teaspoon pepper

2½ tablespoons vegetable oil
1¾ teaspoons liquid smoke
1 teaspoon yellow mustard
1¼ tablespoons packed dark brown
   sugar
1½ tablespoons Worcestershire sauce
1 bay leaf
3 tablespoons white vinegar
3 tablespoons orange juice

1. Preheat the oven to 375°F.
2. In a large bowl, mix together the water and liquid smoke.
3. Marinate the ribs in the mixture for 15 minutes.
4. Place the ribs in a roasting pan and cover with foil; discard the marinade.
   Bake for 3 hours or until fully cooked and just tender. Remove from the
   oven and let cool at room temperature for no more than 30 minutes.
5. To make the barbecue sauce, place the chicken broth, ketchup, maple
   syrup, garlic powder, pepper, vegetable oil, liquid smoke, yellow mustard, brown sugar, Worcestershire sauce, and bay leaf in a stockpot and
   bring to a boil.
6. Add the white vinegar and orange juice, reduce the heat, and simmer for
   5 minutes. Don't overboil, because the orange juice and vinegar will make
   the sauce bitter. Remove and discard the bay leaf after the cooking process.
7. Preheat the grill to 225°F.
8. Place the cooked ribs on the grill, bone side down, brush with the sauce,
   then turn them over to grill the meat. Brush, bone side up, with the
   barbecue sauce. Grill 8 to 10 minutes per side, or until the surface of the
   ribs starts to char. Brush with additional sauce before serving.

Serves 6

HARD ROCK CAFE
homemade chicken noodle soup

THIS TRADITIONAL CHICKEN NOODLE SOUP IS A CLASSIC AMERICAN DISH.

Vegetable oil
2 pounds skinless, boneless chicken
  breasts
2 tablespoons olive oil
1 cup chopped onions
½ cup diced celery
5 cups chicken broth
1 cup water

1 cup sliced carrots
1 teaspoon salt
½ teaspoon pepper
½ teaspoon minced fresh parsley,
  plus extra for garnish
2 cups egg noodles
2 cups oyster crackers

1. Preheat the oven to 350°F.
2. Grease a rimmed baking sheet with vegetable oil. Add the chicken and
   bake for 30 minutes. Remove from the oven and set aside.
3. In a large saucepan, heat the olive oil over medium heat. Add the onions
   and celery and cook, stirring, for 4 minutes or until onions are caramelized.
4. Dice the chicken and add it to the pan along with the remaining
   ingredients, except the noodles and crackers.
5. Bring the soup to a boil, reduce the heat, and simmer for 30 minutes.
6. Add the noodles and simmer for an additional 15 minutes, or until the
   noodles are tender. Serve in individual bowls with a pinch of minced
   fresh parsley sprinkled on top and with the soup crackers.

Serves 6

This can be easily portioned and placed in freezer containers for
future use.

HARD ROCK CAFE
pulled pork

THIS SLOW-ROASTED PORK IS HAND-PULLED, SO IT'S TENDER AND JUICY.

4 cups apple cider vinegar
½ cup Tabasco sauce
½ cup sugar

4 cups hot water
3 pounds pork shoulder

1. In a large bowl, combine the apple cider vinegar, Tabasco sauce, sugar, and hot water. Stir until the sugar is dissolved. Pour the marinade over the pork, cover, and refrigerate overnight.
2. Preheat the oven to 450°F.
3. Remove the pork from the marinade and place in a baking pan. Save the marinade. Roast the pork until browned, about 1 hour.
4. Reduce the oven temperature to 300°F, pour some of the reserved marinade over the pork, cover, and slow-roast for an additional 2 hours or until the meat pulls away from the bone easily. Pull the pork apart into long shreds using two forks.

Serves 6

You can also prepare this in a slow cooker. Cook on low for 6 to 8 hours or on high for 3 to 4.

HARD ROCK CAFE
shrimp fajitas

GARLIC- AND CILANTRO-FLAVORED SHRIMP WITH SAUTÉED PEPPERS AND ONION,
TOPPED WITH SOUR CREAM, AND WRAPPED IN WARM FLOUR TORTILLAS.

1 pound medium shrimp, peeled
and deveined
1 cup chopped fresh cilantro
2 cloves garlic, minced
⅓ cup lime juice
Four 9-inch flour tortillas

1 tablespoon olive oil
2 large bell peppers (1 red,
1 green), thinly sliced
1 large onion, thinly sliced
½ cup sour cream

1. Preheat the oven to 350°F.
2. Stir together the shrimp, cilantro, garlic, and lime juice. Let stand at room temperature for 20 minutes.
3. Meanwhile, wrap the tortillas in foil and place in the oven until hot, about 15 minutes.
4. Heat the oil in a wide nonstick skillet over medium-high heat. Add the peppers and onion. Cook, stirring occasionally, until the vegetables are limp, about 10 minutes. Remove the vegetables from the pan and keep warm.
5. Add the shrimp mixture to the pan, increase the heat to high, and cook, stirring often, until the shrimp are opaque in the center (cut to test), about 3 minutes. Return the vegetables to the pan, stirring to mix with the shrimp.
6. Spoon the shrimp mixture onto the warm tortillas, top with the sour cream, and roll up.

Serves 4

HARDEE'S
cinnamon "flake" biscuits

A HOT FRESHLY BAKED CINNAMON BISCUIT TOPPED WITH SWEET CREAMY ICING.

"Flake" Mixture
One 13-ounce box bran flakes
1 tablespoon ground cinnamon
2 tablespoons packed light brown sugar
2 tablespoons butter, melted

Biscuit Dough
2½ cups biscuit mix, plus extra as needed
2 tablespoons granulated sugar

½ cup dark raisins
⅓ cup buttermilk
½ cup tonic water
½ teaspoon vanilla extract

Icing
2 tablespoons butter, melted
1 teaspoon vanilla extract
2 tablespoons sour cream
Pinch of salt
1½ cups confectioners' sugar

1. Preheat the oven to 400°F. Grease two 8-inch round cake pans.
2. To make the "flake" mixture, empty the box of cereal into a blender. Add the cinnamon and brown sugar and pulse on high speed for about 3 seconds, until the mixture is crumbled but not powdered.
3. Empty into a small bowl. Stir in the melted butter with a fork. Set aside.
4. To make the biscuit dough, using a 2-quart mixing bowl, stir the biscuit mix together with the granulated sugar and raisins.
5. Pour the buttermilk, tonic water, and vanilla into the biscuit mixture. Use a fork to mix until all of the liquid is absorbed, then knead in the bowl with your hands, adding enough biscuit mix to make the dough smooth and prevent it from sticking to the sides of the bowl.
6. Break the dough into 5 portions in the bowl. Sprinkle the "flake" mixture over the dough and then work it in until most of it is evenly distributed throughout the dough.
7. Divide the dough into 12 equal parts and shape each portion into a ½-inch-thick patty. Arrange the patties close together in the prepared cake pans. Bake for 25 minutes or until golden.
8. While the biscuits are baking, make the icing: in a small bowl with an

electric mixer on high speed, beat the melted butter, vanilla, sour cream, salt, and confectioners' sugar until smooth.

9. When the biscuits are done, remove the pans to a wire rack and coat the tops of the biscuits with the icing.

Serves 4 to 6

Make your own buttermilk: For this recipe, combine ⅓ cup milk with 1 teaspoon lemon juice or white vinegar.

The first Hardee's hamburger stand opened in 1960. The concept was simple: charcoal-broiled hamburgers and milk shakes sold at the time for fifteen cents each.

HOOTERS
buffalo shrimp

LOOKING FOR AN APPETIZER WITH SOME KICK? TRY THIS ALTERNATIVE TO HOT WINGS. SERVE WITH BLUE CHEESE.

Buffalo Sauce
¼ cup Crystal hot sauce
4 tablespoons (½ stick) butter
⅛ teaspoon paprika
Pinch of black pepper
Pinch of garlic powder
⅛ teaspoon cayenne pepper

Shrimp
1 egg, beaten
½ cup milk
1 cup all-purpose flour
12 large shrimp, peeled and
    deveined, tails left on
Vegetable oil, for deep-frying

1. To make the Buffalo sauce, combine the ingredients in a small saucepan over medium heat; heat until the butter is melted. Cover and keep warm.
2. For the shrimp, beat the egg and milk in a small bowl.
3. Place the flour in a bowl or a large resealable plastic bag.
4. Coat 6 of the shrimp with the egg mixture, then toss them in the flour.
5. Repeat the process with the remaining 6 shrimp. Make sure they are all well coated with flour. Refrigerate for about 5 minutes to help set the coating.
6. Pour 4 cups oil into a deep-fryer and heat to 375°F.
7. Deep-fry the shrimp for 8 to 10 minutes, until cooked and golden. Remove, drain on paper towels, and toss with the Buffalo sauce.

Serves 2 to 4

Remove the tails before breading to make popcorn shrimp.

The first Hooters opened October 4, 1983, in Clearwater, Florida. During its history, the Hooters concept has undergone very little change. The current logo, uniform, menu, and ambience are all very similar to what existed in the original restaurant. This lack of change is understandable given the tremendous success the Hooters concept has enjoyed.

Hooters has continued to rank high among the industry's growth leaders. The casual beach-themed establishments feature "oldies" jukebox music, sports on television, and a menu that includes seafood, sandwiches, salads, and spicy chicken wings.

HOOTERS
buffalo wings

WORLD-FAMOUS CHICKEN WINGS!

4 tablespoons (½ stick) butter	¼ teaspoon salt
¼ cup Crystal hot sauce	10 chicken wings, cut into thirds
Pinch of black pepper	(wing tips discarded)
2 cloves garlic, minced	Vegetable oil, for deep-frying
½ cup all-purpose flour	Celery sticks
¼ teaspoon paprika	Blue cheese dressing
¼ teaspoon cayenne pepper	

1. In a small saucepan, melt the butter over low heat. Add the hot sauce, black pepper, and garlic and stir until well mixed.
2. In a gallon-sized resealable plastic bag, mix the flour, paprika, cayenne pepper, and salt.
3. Rinse the chicken wings under cold water and drain. Drop the wings into the bag a few at a time, resealing the bag and shaking to coat after each addition. When all the wings have been coated, remove from the bag and place on a waxed paper–lined plate or tray. Refrigerate for at least 1 hour to help set the coating.
4. Pour 2 inches of oil into a deep-fryer and heat to 375°F.
5. Carefully lower a few wings at a time into the oil. Deep-fry for 15 to 20 minutes, until light brown. Drain the wings on paper towels and repeat with the remaining wings.
6. Preheat the oven to 400°F.
7. Place the cooked wings in a large ovenproof bowl or baking pan; pour the sauce over the wings and stir to coat thoroughly.
8. Place in the oven for about 5 minutes or until the wings are hot.
9. Serve the wings with celery sticks and blue cheese dressing on the side.

Serves 2 or 3

To create "Atomic Wings," add more cayenne pepper and hot sauce.

HOUSTON'S
buttermilk-garlic dressing

A CREAMY GARLIC-FLAVORED DRESSING FOR SALAD.

⅔ cup sour cream
1 cup mayonnaise
¼ teaspoon crushed garlic
½ teaspoon salt
1 teaspoon paprika

½ teaspoon pepper
1 teaspoon dry mustard
2 tablespoons sugar
½ cup buttermilk

1. Blend all the ingredients in a blender until smooth.
2. Let the dressing sit, refrigerated, for a couple of hours for the flavors to meld. Shake well before serving.

Serves 4

Reduce calories and fat by using low-fat or fat-free sour cream, mayonnaise, and buttermilk.

Houston's has offered a family-style dining experience since it opened in 1975. Their menu is designed to satisfy the smallest of appetites as well as the most robust cravings for charbroiled steaks and seafood.

HOUSTON'S
spinach and artichoke dip

PECORINO ROMANO CHEESE GIVES THIS DISH A DISTINCTIVE, UNIQUE FLAVOR.
SERVE WITH MULTICOLORED TORTILLA CHIPS.

Two 10-ounce boxes frozen
spinach, thawed
1 tablespoon minced garlic
2 tablespoons minced onion
4 tablespoons (½ stick) butter
¼ cup all-purpose flour
2 cups heavy cream
¼ cup chicken broth
2 teaspoons lemon juice

½ teaspoon Tabasco sauce
½ teaspoon salt
⅔ cup grated Pecorino Romano
cheese
¼ cup sour cream
One 12-ounce jar artichoke hearts,
drained and coarsely chopped
½ cup shredded white Cheddar
cheese

1. Drain the spinach and squeeze through a cheesecloth to remove as much liquid as possible; mince and set aside.
2. In a heavy saucepan over medium heat, cook the garlic and onion in the butter, stirring, for 3 to 5 minutes, until golden.
3. Stir in the flour and cook, stirring, for 1 minute.
4. Slowly stir in the cream and broth and cook until boiling.
5. Once boiling, stir in the lemon juice, Tabasco sauce, salt, and Pecorino Romano cheese; stir until the cheese has melted.
6. Remove from the heat and let cool for 5 minutes.
7. Stir in the sour cream, then fold in the spinach and artichoke hearts.
8. Sprinkle the Cheddar evenly over the top.
9. Microwave to melt the Cheddar cheese, and serve.

Serves 12

IHOP
banana-nut pancakes

BANANA-FLAVORED PANCAKES WITH FRESH BANANA, CHOPPED PECANS, AND
WHIPPED CREAM.

Banana Syrup
½ cup light corn syrup
½ cup sugar
½ cup water
¼ teaspoon banana extract
¼ teaspoon vanilla extract

Pancakes
¼ cup vegetable oil
1¼ cups all-purpose flour
1½ cups buttermilk

1 egg
2 tablespoons sugar
1½ teaspoons baking powder
1 teaspoon baking soda
½ teaspoon banana extract
¼ teaspoon salt

½ cup chopped pecans
1 banana
Whipped cream, for serving

1. To make the banana syrup, stir the corn syrup, sugar, and water together in a small saucepan over high heat. Remove from the heat once the mixture boils. Mix in the banana and vanilla extracts.
2. Using an electric mixer, mix together all the ingredients for the pancakes. The batter should be smooth.
3. Preheat a griddle to medium heat; coat with cooking spray.
4. To make the pancakes, using a ladle, pour ¼ cup of the batter onto the griddle and allow the batter to spread out. Immediately sprinkle about ¾ tablespoon of the pecans into the center of the pancake, so that the pecans are set in place.
5. Cook the pancakes for 1 to 2 minutes on each side. The edges will lift slightly and the surfaces should be slightly browned.
6. Slice the banana, and place a few slices on top of a stack of 3 pancakes. Serve with the syrup, whipped cream, and the remaining chopped pecans on top.

Serves 4

IHOP restaurants are operated by International House of Pancakes, Inc. IHOP features moderately priced high-quality food and beverage items. It is best known for its award-winning pancakes, omelets, and other breakfast specialties and also offers a broad array of lunch, dinner, and snack items.

IHOP
colorado omelet

A MEAT-LOVER'S DELIGHT: BACON, SAUSAGE, ROAST BEEF, HAM, ONION, GREEN
PEPPER, AND CHEDDAR CHEESE. SERVE WITH SALSA.

I tablespoon butter
¼ cup diced yellow onion
¼ cup diced green bell pepper
¼ cup diced cooked lean ham
3 or 4 eggs, beaten
2 tablespoons water
¼ teaspoon salt
I teaspoon vegetable oil

¼ cup diced tomato (optional)
⅓ cup sliced cooked small breakfast sausage links
¼ cup crumbled lean fried bacon
⅓ cup shredded or diced deli
roast beef
¾ cup finely shredded Cheddar
cheese

1. In a saucepan over medium-low heat, melt the butter and add the onion
   and green pepper.
2. Stir until the onion and pepper are soft but not browned.
3. Add the diced ham and stir until the ham is heated through.
4. Immediately remove from the heat and set the mixture aside.
5. In a mixing bowl, combine the eggs, water, and salt; beat or stir well. Set
   aside.
6. Heat a 12-inch nonstick skillet over medium-low heat; add the oil or
   spray with nonstick cooking spray.
7. Pour the egg mixture into the pan and sprinkle with the vegetable and
   ham mixture, tomato if desired, sausage, bacon, half the roast beef, and
   ½ cup of the cheese.
8. Cover the pan until the omelet starts to set, 2 to 3 minutes.
9. Immediately remove the lid and fold the omelet from the sides to the
   middle or in half. Sprinkle with the rest of the roast beef and the
   remaining ¼ cup cheese.

Serves 2

For a healthier dish, you can replace the eggs with egg whites or your
favorite egg substitute and use turkey meat.

IHOP

cream of wheat pancakes

THE CREAM OF WHEAT GIVES THESE PANCAKES THE BEST FLAVOR AND TEXTURE.
IF YOU WISH, SERVE WITH BACON STRIPS OR SAUSAGE LINKS, AND GARNISH
WITH FRESH FRUIT.

3½ cups plain nonfat yogurt
¼ cup honey
One 28-ounce box pancake mix
One 18-ounce box Cream of
Wheat cereal

2 teaspoons baking powder
5½ cups nonfat milk
8 eggs, beaten
1 cup vegetable oil

1. Mix the yogurt and honey until smooth; cover and set aside in the refrigerator.
2. In a large bowl, combine the pancake mix, Cream of Wheat, and baking powder; set aside.
3. In a separate large bowl, combine the milk, eggs, and vegetable oil; stir into the dry ingredients and mix until the batter is smooth.
4. For each serving, ladle 3 scant ¼-cup portions of batter onto a medium-hot lightly greased griddle. Cook until the pancake tops begin to bubble; flip the pancakes over. Cook until golden.
5. Serve each plate with ¼ cup of the yogurt and honey mixture.

Serves 12

IHOP
pancakes

MADE WITH BUTTERMILK FOR AN AUTHENTIC COUNTRY FLAVOR.

1¼ cups sifted all-purpose flour	1¼ cups buttermilk
1 teaspoon baking powder	2 tablespoons butter, melted
1 teaspoon baking soda	¼ cup sugar
Pinch of salt	
1 egg, beaten	

1. Sift together the flour, baking powder, baking soda, and salt.
2. In a separate bowl, combine the egg and buttermilk. Add to the flour mixture, stirring only until smooth.
3. Blend in the melted butter and sugar.
4. Cook on a medium-hot lightly greased griddle, using about ¼ cup of batter for each pancake. Drop the batter onto the griddle in 5-inch-wide circles.
5. Cook until the pancakes are brown on one side and around the edges, then flip and brown the other side.

Serves 4

You can add fruit topping such as apple, strawberry, or peach to finish off this breakfast treat. You can also add fresh fruit such as blueberries or chopped apples to the batter. For whole wheat pancakes, replace all-purpose flour with whole wheat flour.

IHOP
swedish pancakes

SWEDISH PANCAKES CAN BE SERVED FOR BREAKFAST OR DESSERT, BUT SWEDES
PREPARE THEM FOR SUPPER.

3 eggs
1 ½ cups sifted all-purpose flour
1 tablespoon granulated sugar
½ teaspoon salt
1 cup milk, plus extra as needed

½ cup cream or milk
2 tablespoons butter, melted
2 cups lingonberry sauce
Confectioners' sugar, for garnish

1. Beat the eggs very well.
2. Sift together the flour, sugar, and salt.
3. Add ½ cup of the milk to the eggs and fold in the flour mixture.
4. Then add the remaining ½ cup milk, the cream, and butter. Add more milk if the consistency is too thick.
5. Ladle the batter onto the surface of a hot griddle or crepe pan, creating 5-inch-diameter circles. These pancakes should be thin and will need only 1 or 2 minutes on each side to brown.
6. Place 2 tablespoons of lingonberry (Swedish cranberry) sauce in the center of each pancake and roll the pancake up like a jelly roll.
7. Serve sprinkled with confectioners' sugar.

Serves 4

You can substitute any fruit jam for the lingonberry sauce.

JOE'S CRAB SHACK
crab cakes

A MUST-HAVE RECIPE FOR SEAFOOD LOVERS. SERVE AS AN APPETIZER WITH TARTAR SAUCE OR DIJONAISE SAUCE FOR DIPPING.

1 egg yolk	¼ teaspoon Old Bay seasoning
⅓ cup mayonnaise	¼ teaspoon salt
2½ teaspoons Worcestershire sauce	1¼ cups fresh bread crumbs
1 teaspoon lemon juice	3 tablespoons chopped fresh parsley
1 teaspoon dry mustard	1 pound lump crabmeat
1 teaspoon black pepper	All-purpose flour, for coating
¼ teaspoon red pepper flakes	Oil, for deep-frying

1. Beat together the first nine ingredients.
2. Fold in the bread crumbs and parsley.
3. Fold in the crabmeat.
4. Form into 4 to 6 patties.
5. Lightly coat the patties in flour on both sides. Refrigerate for at least 30 minutes before frying.
6. Deep-fry the crab cakes in 350°F oil (use just enough oil to cover the crab cakes) until browned.

Serves 4 to 6

What started off as a little beachside shack offering seafood in Houston, Texas, is now a renowned restaurant chain. Specializing in crab preparations and other delightful seafood, Joe's Crab Shack is a fun place to be. The look of a shanty by the seaside gives a casual feel to the place, which is always full of people and brimming with energy.

JOE'S CRAB SHACK
étouffée

A CHOICE OF CRAWFISH, CHICKEN, OR SHRIMP SMOTHERED IN A RICH CREAM
SAUCE, SERVED OVER RICE PILAF.

I teaspoon chopped garlic	½ cup condensed cream of celery
¾ cup diced onion	soup
¼ cup diced celery	I cup water
½ cup diced green bell pepper	8 ounces crawfish meat or
2 tablespoons butter	8 ounces cubed chicken or
½ teaspoon salt	8 ounces peeled and deveined
½ teaspoon cayenne pepper	shrimp
½ teaspoon paprika	3 tablespoons sliced green onions
¼ teaspoon dry mustard	I tablespoon chopped fresh
½ teaspoon Worcestershire sauce	parsley
One 10.75-ounce can condensed	3 cups Rice Pilaf (page 111)
cream of mushroom soup	

1. Sauté the garlic, onion, celery, and green pepper in the butter until soft.
2. Stir in the spices, soups, water, and meat of your choice.
3. Bring to a simmer and continue cooking until the meat is cooked through.
4. Stir in the green onions and parsley.
5. Scoop ½ cup of the rice pilaf into the center of six bowls or soup plates.
6. Pour the étouffée over the rice.

Serves 6

The literal translation of the French word *étouffée* (pronounced AY-too-FAY) is "smothered"—as in smothered in lots of rich sauce.

JOE'S CRAB SHACK
rice pilaf

TENDER RICE AND SAUTÉED VEGETABLES WITH A HINT OF GARLIC AND BUTTER.

1⅔ cups water	1⅓ cups white rice
1 tablespoon plus 1 teaspoon butter	¼ cup chopped celery
	¼ cup chopped onion
1 bay leaf	¼ cup chopped red bell pepper
¼ teaspoon white pepper	½ teaspoon minced garlic

1. Bring the water, the 1 tablespoon butter, the bay leaf, and the white pepper to a boil in a saucepan.
2. Add the rice, cover, reduce the heat, and cook until the rice is tender and the water is absorbed, about 20 minutes.
3. Sauté the celery, onion, red pepper, and garlic in the 1 teaspoon butter until tender.
4. Stir the sautéed vegetables into the rice.

Serves 6

JOE'S CRAB SHACK
seafood-stuffed mushrooms

TENDER MUSHROOMS LOADED WITH SEAFOOD STUFFING AND TOPPED WITH
MONTEREY JACK CHEESE. SERVE WITH GARLIC TOAST, FOR DIPPING.

16 large mushroom caps
1¼ cups Seafood Stuffing
(page 113)

1 cup store-bought Alfredo sauce
¼ cup grated Monterey Jack
cheese

1. Place the mushroom caps, stem side up, in a baking dish.
2. Spoon 1 tablespoon of the hot seafood stuffing into each cap.
3. Pour the Alfredo sauce over the stuffed mushrooms.
4. Sprinkle the Monterey Jack cheese over the top.
5. Broil for 8 to 10 minutes, until the top is browned.

Serves 8

JOE'S CRAB SHACK
seafood stuffing

A WONDERFUL COMBINATION OF FISH, SHRIMP, AND CRAB COMBINED WITH
CROUTONS TO MAKE A FLAVORFUL STUFFING.

½ bunch celery, trimmed and
diced
3 large onions, diced
1½ tablespoons minced garlic
4 tablespoons (½ stick) margarine,
melted
8 ounces pollack fillets
8 ounces small shrimp, peeled
and chopped

1 ounce shrimp soup base
¼ teaspoon cayenne pepper
¼ teaspoon white pepper
2 cups plain croutons
¼ cup Italian bread crumbs
8 ounces crab claw meat

1. Sauté the celery, onions, and garlic in the margarine until translucent.
2. Add the pollack and cook for 5 to 7 minutes. The fish is done when it
   separates into flakes and appears opaque throughout.
3. Add the shrimp and cook for 2 minutes.
4. Drain most, but not all, of the liquid from the pan.
5. Stir in the shrimp soup base and the cayenne and white peppers.
6. Fold in the croutons and bread crumbs.
7. Fold in the crabmeat.

Serves 6 to 8

Use this recipe to prepare Joe's Crab Shack Seafood-Stuffed Mushrooms (page 112) or Joe's Crab Shack Stuffed Shrimp en Brochette
(page 114).

JOE'S CRAB SHACK
stuffed shrimp en brochette

PLUMP SHRIMP WITH JOE'S FAMOUS CRABMEAT STUFFING.

20 jumbo shrimp, peeled and deveined
½ cup Seafood Stuffing (page 113)
10 slices jalapeño pepper, halved
2 slices Monterey Jack cheese, cut into 20 equal-sized pieces
1 pound thin-sliced bacon
Oil, for deep-frying

1. Slice the shrimp down the middle of the side opposite the vein, but don't cut all the way through.
2. Lay the shrimp cut side up and press 1 teaspoon of the stuffing into each shrimp.
3. Place a jalapeño half over the stuffing on each shrimp. Then place a piece of cheese over the jalapeños.
4. Wrap each stuffed shrimp in a slice of bacon.
5. Thread 5 of the shrimp on a bamboo skewer; repeat with the remaining shrimp.
6. Deep-fry the shrimp in 400°F oil (use just enough oil to cover the shrimp) until the bacon is browned; or grill the shrimp over a high flame, turning once, until the bacon is browned; or broil the shrimp, turning once, until the bacon is browned.

Serves 4

If you like scallops, you can replace the shrimp with scallops and omit the seafood stuffing. The bacon gives this recipe such a wonderful flavor.

JOHNNY CARINO'S
five-cheese chicken fettuccine

PASTA WITH SLICED CHICKEN IN A FIVE-CHEESE CREAM SAUCE.

1 cup store-bought Alfredo sauce
Pinch of black pepper
Pinch of cayenne pepper
Pinch of salt
Pinch of garlic salt
3 ounces cooked chicken,
  sliced
2 tablespoons grated Parmesan
  cheese
2 tablespoons grated Pecorino
  Romano cheese
2 tablespoons grated mozzarella
  cheese
2 tablespoons grated provolone
  cheese
2 tablespoons grated Asiago
  cheese
10 ounces cooked fettuccine

1. In a warm skillet, combine the Alfredo sauce, black pepper, cayenne pepper, salt, garlic salt, and chicken. Cook over low heat, stirring, until the sauce begins to boil and the chicken is heated through.
2. As the sauce continues to boil, begin to mix in the cheeses until a dense smooth sauce is formed.
3. Remove from the heat, add the pasta, toss, and serve.

Serves 2

Asiago is an Italian cheese whose flavor is reminiscent of sharp Cheddar and Parmesan.

Carino's is a full-service restaurant offering pizza and freshly prepared pasta, beef, chicken, and pork dishes inspired by the cuisine of southern Italy. Their headquarters are in Austin, Texas.

JUNIOR'S
famous no. 1 cheesecake

COMMONLY KNOWN AS NEW YORK'S BEST CHEESECAKE, THIS IS REALLY THAT
GOOD. NOW YOU CAN EXPERIENCE BROOKLYN'S FAMOUS DESSERT.

Sponge Cake Layer
½ cup cake flour, sifted
1 teaspoon baking powder
Pinch of salt
3 extra-large eggs, separated
⅓ cup plus 2 tablespoons sugar
1 teaspoon vanilla extract
3 drops lemon extract
3 tablespoons butter, melted
¼ teaspoon cream of tartar

Cream Cheese Filling
Four 8-ounce packages cream
   cheese, softened
1⅔ cups sugar
¼ cup cornstarch
1 tablespoon vanilla extract
2 extra-large eggs
¾ cup heavy cream

1. Preheat the oven to 350°F. Generously butter a 9-inch springform pan.
2. To make the sponge cake layer, combine the cake flour, baking powder, and salt in a bowl and set aside.
3. In a large bowl, with an electric mixer on high speed, beat the egg yolks for 3 minutes. Then, with the mixer still running, gradually add the ⅓ cup sugar and continue beating until thick light-yellow ribbons form in the bowl, about 5 minutes more. Beat in the vanilla and lemon extracts.
4. Sift the flour mixture over the yolk mixture and stir it in by hand until no more white flecks appear. Blend in the butter.
5. In a separate bowl, using clean, dry beaters, beat the egg whites and cream of tartar together on high speed until frothy.
6. Gradually add the 2 tablespoons sugar and continue beating until stiff peaks form (the whites should stand up in stiff peaks but not be dry). Stir about ⅓ cup of the whites into the batter; then gently fold in the remaining whites (don't worry if a few white flecks remain).
7. Gently spoon the batter into the prepared pan. Bake the cake just until the center of the cake springs back when lightly touched, about

10 minutes (watch carefully). Let the cake cool in the pan on a wire rack while you make the cream cheese filling. Do not remove the cake from the pan.

8. To make the cream cheese filling, place one package of the cream cheese, ⅓ cup of the sugar, and the cornstarch in a large bowl. Beat with an electric mixer on low speed until the mixture is creamy, about 3 minutes. Then beat in the remaining 3 packages of cream cheese.

9. Increase the mixer speed to high and beat in the remaining 1⅓ cups sugar, then beat in the vanilla. Blend in the eggs, one at a time, beating the batter well after each addition. Blend in the cream. At this point, mix the filling only until completely blended (just as they do at Junior's). Be careful not to overmix the batter.

10. Gently spoon the cream cheese filling on top of the baked sponge cake layer. Wrap the bottom of the pan with foil. Set the springform pan in a large shallow pan and place in the oven. Add enough hot water to the shallow pan to come about 1 inch up the sides of the springform pan. Bake the cheesecake until the center barely jiggles when you shake the pan, about 1 hour.

11. Let the cake cool on a wire rack for 1 hour. Then cover the cake with plastic wrap and refrigerate in the pan until it's completely cold, at least 4 hours or overnight. Remove the sides of the springform pan. Slide the cake off the bottom of the pan onto a serving plate. Or, if you wish, simply leave the cake on the removable bottom of the pan and place it on the serving plate. If any cake is left over, cover it with plastic wrap and store in the refrigerator.

Serves 12 to 16

Substitute mascarpone cheese for the cream cheese.

Founded by Harry Rosen in 1950, Junior's has become a landmark restaurant in New York City. It is nationally known for having arguably the best cheesecake in the country!

KFC
buttermilk biscuits

THESE FRESHLY BAKED, WARM, BUTTERY, FLAKY BUTTERMILK BISCUITS HAVE
BECOME ONE OF THE MOST POPULAR ITEMS ON THE KFC MENU. ONE TASTE AND
YOU WILL KNOW WHY.

1½ cups all-purpose flour
1 teaspoon salt
1 tablespoon sugar

1 tablespoon baking powder
⅓ cup vegetable shortening
⅔ cup buttermilk

1. Preheat the oven to 425°F.
2. Sift together the dry ingredients into a large bowl.
3. Cut in the shortening.
4. Make a nest in the flour mixture and add the buttermilk. Gently knead the mixture with your hands until thoroughly combined and a soft dough forms.
5. On a floured cutting board, pat the dough to a ½-inch thickness and cut with a biscuit cutter or the rim of a glass.
6. Place the biscuits on a cookie sheet and bake for 12 minutes, or until golden brown.

Makes about 9 biscuits

If you don't have a pastry cutter, you can use two knives or a wide-tined fork to cut in the shortening.

KFC—also known as Kentucky Fried Chicken—was begun in 1930 by Harland Sanders in Sanders's Court & Café in Corbin, Kentucky. In 1939 he began using a pressure fryer, which allowed him to serve his customers more quickly. Colonel Sanders created his famous Original Recipe chicken in 1940. KFC is now in more than eighty countries around the world.

KFC

honey barbecue wings

SWEET YET TANGY WINGS GLAZED IN HONEY BARBECUE SAUCE.

1 cup all-purpose flour
1 teaspoon salt
½ teaspoon pepper
20 chicken drummettes (small
fleshy parts of chicken wings)

2 cups Bull's-Eye barbecue sauce
¾ cup honey
Vegetable oil, for deep-frying

1. Combine the flour, salt, and pepper in a dish and coat the chicken in the flour mixture.
2. Heat the barbecue sauce and honey in a saucepan. Once warm, reduce the heat to a simmer.
3. Add the oil to a deep-fryer and heat to 375°F.
4. Deep-fry the chicken, 6 to 8 pieces at a time, for 15 minutes or until cooked thoroughly.
5. Drain the chicken on paper towels and smother with the barbecue sauce mixture.

Serves 5

KFC
original recipe fried chicken

WHAT'S THE SECRET BEHIND COLONEL SANDERS'S FAMOUS ELEVEN HERBS AND SPICES? TO THIS DAY, HIS SECRET RECIPE HAS NEVER BEEN REVEALED, LEAVING CURIOUS MINDS TO SPECULATE. I'VE TRIED MANY DIFFERENT COMBINATIONS, BUT THERE IS ONLY ONE THAT COMES OUT TASTING JUST LIKE THE ORIGINAL. TO MAKE THIS, YOU'LL NEED A PRESSURE FRYER.

1 egg, beaten
1 cup buttermilk
One 3-pound chicken, cut into
  6 pieces
1 cup all-purpose flour
1 teaspoon ground oregano
1 teaspoon chili powder
1 teaspoon dried sage
1 teaspoon dried basil
1 teaspoon dried marjoram

1 teaspoon pepper
2 teaspoons salt
2 tablespoons paprika
1 tablespoon onion salt
1 teaspoon garlic powder
2 tablespoons Accent
1 can lard (or one 3-pound can
  Crisco), enough to cover chicken
  in fryer (see Secret Recipe Tips)

1. Combine the egg and buttermilk in a large bowl. Soak the chicken pieces in the mixture.
2. Add the flour to a separate bowl and fold in all the herbs and spices.
3. Roll the chicken in the seasoned flour until completely covered.
4. Add the lard to a pressure fryer and heat to 365°F. Be sure to follow the manufacturer's directions for your pressure fryer.
5. Use a utensil to lower 4 pieces of the chicken into the hot oil, and lock the lid in place. Be careful not to burn yourself with the hot oil.
6. Allow to fry for 8 to 10 minutes, until the chicken is golden brown and thoroughly cooked.
7. Once the pieces are cooked, release the pressure according to the manufacturer's directions and remove the chicken to paper towels or a metal rack to drain.
8. Repeat with the remaining 2 pieces of chicken.

Makes 6 pieces

The real secret to making this is the Accent in the recipe and using a pressure fryer!

Make sure the oil is at 365°F before frying the chicken. To avoid making a mess, use a utensil when adding the chicken. Quickly lock the lid on the pressure fryer once all the pieces of chicken have been added.

For crispier chicken, use Crisco instead of lard and double-coat the chicken with the flour mixture.

LUBY'S CAFETERIA
spaghetti salad

A ZESTY COLD SALAD OF SPAGHETTI, CUCUMBER, RED ONION, AND TOMATOES
WITH AN ITALIAN VINAIGRETTE DRESSING.

I pound spaghetti, noodles broken in half
One 16-ounce bottle Italian vinaigrette dressing
I tablespoon grated Parmesan cheese
I tablespoon sesame seeds
I tablespoon poppy seeds
2 teaspoons seasoned salt

I teaspoon paprika
½ teaspoon garlic powder
½ teaspoon black pepper
½ teaspoon cayenne pepper
I medium cucumber, peeled and diced
I medium red onion, diced
2 medium tomatoes, diced
Fresh parsley sprigs, for garnish

1. Cook the spaghetti according to the package directions. Drain, rinse with cold water, and drain again well. Transfer to a large bowl.
2. In a separate bowl, whisk together the Italian dressing, cheese, sesame and poppy seeds, seasoned salt, paprika, garlic powder, and black and cayenne peppers until well blended.
3. Stir in the cucumber and onion.
4. Pour the mixture over the spaghetti and toss lightly to coat evenly.
5. Cover and refrigerate for at least 2 hours or up to 24 hours.
6. Top with the tomatoes and garnish with parsley sprigs.

Serves 12

In 1947, Bob Luby and his cousin Charles R. Johnston opened the first Luby's Cafeteria in San Antonio, Texas. Their 180-seat cafeteria was packed for both lunch and dinner. Their success has been attributed to consistently serving quality food at reasonable prices.

MACARONI GRILL
chocolate cake with fudge sauce

CHOCOLATE CAKE SMOTHERED WITH WARM HOMEMADE CHOCOLATE GANACHE
AND SPRINKLED WITH PECANS.

Cake
3 ½ cups all-purpose flour
1 tablespoon baking soda
1 cup cocoa powder
1 ½ cups sugar
1 ¾ cups mayonnaise
1 ¾ cups brewed coffee, at room
temperature
1 ½ teaspoons vanilla extract

Fudge Sauce
1 cup heavy cream
8 ounces semisweet chocolate,
coarsely chopped

Vanilla ice cream, for serving
½ cup chopped pecans, for garnish

1. Preheat the oven to 350°F. Grease a 13 by 9-inch pan.
2. To make the cake, sift together the flour, baking soda, cocoa powder, and sugar into a large bowl.
3. Beat in the mayonnaise, coffee, and vanilla, but do not overmix. The batter should be thick.
4. Pour the batter into the prepared pan.
5. Bake for 25 minutes or until a toothpick inserted in the center comes out clean. Let the cake cool in the pan 10 minutes, then remove from the pan and allow to cool completely on a wire rack.
6. To make the fudge sauce, bring the cream to a simmer in a saucepan over medium heat. Be careful not to burn.
7. Remove from the heat and add the chocolate.
8. Let sit for 5 minutes.
9. Whisk the glaze until smooth.
10. To serve, place a large square of cake on each plate. Pour the warm fudge sauce over the cake. Top with a scoop of vanilla ice cream and sprinkle with the pecans.

Serves 6 to 8

Romano's Macaroni Grill bills itself as a chain of casual Italian-dining restaurants located around the world. The first Romano's Macaroni Grill was opened in San Antonio, Texas, in 1988 by Phil Romano. The chain is known for its great Italian dishes. Have fun with the paper tablecloths and crayons!

MACARONI GRILL
focaccia

A THICK ITALIAN FLATBREAD FLAVORED WITH AN OLIVE OIL, SALT, AND ROSE-MARY TOPPING.

½ cup olive oil
3 cups all-purpose flour
¾ cup semolina flour
½ teaspoon salt

1½ tablespoons quick-rising dry yeast
1½ cups hot milk (120° to 130°F)
1 tablespoon fresh rosemary leaves

1. Pour 1½ teaspoons of the olive oil into a 9-inch square cake pan; spread to cover the bottom and sides.
2. Place the all-purpose flour, semolina flour, 2 tablespoons of the olive oil, ¼ teaspoon of the salt, and all of the yeast in the bowl of a mixer fitted with the dough hook (or you can mix by hand).
3. Mix on medium speed until all the ingredient are blended. Reduce the speed to low and slowly add the hot milk. Increase the speed to medium and continue mixing for 5 minutes, then knead for about 10 minutes by hand.
4. Dust the bottom of the cake pan with a little flour. Remove the dough from the bowl and spread out evenly in the pan. Cover with a towel and let the dough rest for 30 minutes.
5. Preheat the oven to 400°F.
6. Remove the towel and brush the dough with 1 to 2 tablespoons of the olive oil. Dust the top with the remaining ¼ teaspoon salt and the rosemary. Bake for 20 minutes.
7. Remove from the oven and drizzle with the remaining oil.

Serves 6 to 8

Store in a plastic bag at room temperature, and use within a few days.

MACARONI GRILL
insalata florentine

FULLY LOADED SALAD WITH SPINACH, ORZO PASTA, GRILLED CHICKEN, SUN-DRIED TOMATOES, CAPERS, PINE NUTS, BLACK OLIVES, GARLIC-LEMON VINAIGRETTE, AND PARMESAN.

4 ounces shredded spinach
4 ounces chilled grilled chicken, sliced
1 diced ripe plum tomato
2 tablespoons pine nuts, lightly toasted
¼ cup sun-dried tomatoes packed in oil, julienned
2 tablespoons drained capers
¼ cup sliced black olives

¼ cup julienned radicchio
5 ounces cooked orzo pasta, chilled
⅓ cup Roasted Garlic–Lemon Vinaigrette (page 131)
2 tablespoons shaved Grana Padano cheese
Shaved Parmesan cheese, for garnish
Cracked pepper, for garnish

1. In the order listed, place all the ingredients, except the Parmesan cheese and cracked pepper, in a chilled mixing bowl.
2. Toss and serve in individual bowls. Garnish with shaved Parmesan cheese and cracked pepper.

Serves 4

Orzo is the Italian term for rice-shaped pasta, slightly smaller than a pine nut. It is frequently used in soups and salads.

To toast pine nuts on the stove top, place in a dry skillet and cook over medium heat, shaking the pan, until toasted.

MACARONI GRILL
pasta gamberetti e pinoli

SHRIMP, MUSHROOMS, PINE NUTS, SPINACH, AND LEMON BUTTER WITH ANGEL HAIR PASTA. RETAIL PRICE: $12.99 PER PLATE.

2 tablespoons butter
2 teaspoons minced garlic
1/2 cup fresh shiitake mushrooms, thinly sliced
12 medium shrimp, peeled and deveined
1/4 cup dry white wine
1/2 cup heavy cream
1/3 cup lemon juice
4 tablespoons (1/2 stick) cold butter

Salt and white pepper
2 tablespoons plain bread crumbs
5 1/2 cups spinach, washed and dried
6 ounces cooked angel hair pasta
1 tablespoon pine nuts, toasted

1. In a large skillet, melt the 2 tablespoons butter over medium-high heat. Add the garlic and sauté for about 30 seconds, just enough to make the garlic sizzle. Add the mushrooms and sauté briefly.
2. Add the shrimp and sauté for about 30 seconds, until the shrimp is just half cooked.
3. Add the wine and, using a wooden spoon, stir to loosen any brown bits on the bottom of the pan. Let cook for 2 minutes, stirring, to finish cooking the shrimp and reduce the liquid. Remove the shrimp to a warm plate and cover with foil.
4. Add the heavy cream to the pan and let cook for 3 minutes to reduce. Stir in the lemon juice. Remove the pan from the heat and add the 4 tablespoons cold butter, 1 tablespoon at a time, stirring in the next piece after the one before it has just melted.
5. Season with salt and white pepper and stir in the bread crumbs. Return the pan to the heat, add the spinach, and cook, stirring, for 1 1/2 minutes or just until the spinach has wilted.
6. Return the shrimp to the pan and stir to coat and heat through.
7. To serve, divide the angel hair pasta between two warmed serving dishes

or bowls. Arrange the shrimp on top, spoon the remaining contents of the pan equally over the shrimp, and sprinkle with the toasted pine nuts.

Serves 2

Angel hair pasta is a long delicate noodle and is served with light sauces.

To toast pine nuts in the oven, spread the nuts in a single layer on a baking pan and bake in a preheated 350°F oven for 6 to 8 minutes, until slightly browned. Shake the pan once or twice to toast the nuts evenly.

MACARONI GRILL
reese's peanut butter cake

RICH AND DELICIOUS CAKE TOPPED WITH CREAMY PEANUT BUTTER AND A
WARM CHOCOLATE GLAZE.

Cake
12 tablespoons (1½ sticks) butter,
softened
¾ cup creamy peanut butter
2 cups packed light brown sugar
3 eggs
2 cups all-purpose flour
1 tablespoon baking powder
½ teaspoon salt
1 cup milk
1 teaspoon vanilla extract

Peanut Butter Filling
One 8-ounce package cream
cheese, softened
½ cup creamy peanut butter

Chocolate Glaze
½ cup water
4 tablespoons (½ stick) butter
½ cup cocoa powder
1 cup confectioners' sugar
1 teaspoon vanilla extract

1. Preheat the oven to 350°F. Grease and flour two 9-inch round cake pans.
2. In a large bowl, cream the butter and peanut butter until the mixture
   becomes fluffy. Mix in the brown sugar. Add the eggs, one at a time,
   mixing well after each addition.
3. In a small bowl, combine the flour, baking powder, and salt. Add the
   flour mixture to the butter mixture along with the milk and blend. Add
   the vanilla.
4. Pour the batter into the prepared pans. Bake for about 45 minutes, until
   a toothpick inserted in the center of each cake comes out clean. After the
   cake has cooled for 5 minutes, place a covered cake board or cooling rack
   over the cake and turn over. Gently remove the pan from the cake. Allow
   to cool completely before frosting.
5. To make the peanut butter filling, cream the cream cheese and peanut
   butter together until fluffy.
6. Spread ¾ cup of the peanut butter filling over the top of each cake. Let
   chill in the refrigerator.
7. To make the chocolate glaze, combine the water and butter in a small

saucepan. Bring to a boil. Add the cocoa, confectioners' sugar, and vanilla to the butter-water mixture. Mix until smooth.

8. Using a metal spatula dipped in hot water, spread half of the warm chocolate glaze over the peanut butter topping on each cake. The glaze will thicken as it cools.

Makes two 9-inch cakes

MACARONI GRILL
roasted garlic–lemon vinaigrette

A HONEY-SWEETENED, ROASTED GARLIC VINAIGRETTE DRESSING WITH A HINT OF CITRUS. SERVE OVER YOUR FAVORITE SALAD GREENS.

¼ cup red wine vinegar
3 tablespoons honey
½ teaspoon salt

1 tablespoon roasted garlic
¾ cup virgin olive oil
Juice of ½ lemon

1. Combine the vinegar, honey, salt, and roasted garlic in a blender or food processor. Puree until the ingredients form a paste.
2. With the food processor still running, add the olive oil and lemon juice.
3. Transfer to an airtight container and refrigerate until ready to serve.

Serves 2 to 4

To roast garlic, place an unpeeled bulb of garlic on a sheet of aluminum foil and wrap tightly. Roast in a preheated 400°F oven for about 45 minutes, until soft. Unwrap and allow to cool. Peel the cloves and squeeze out the pulp.

MACARONI GRILL

sesame shrimp

SAUTÉED SHRIMP AND VEGETABLES FLAVORED WITH TOASTED SESAME SEEDS, SOY SAUCE, AND WHITE WINE. SERVE OVER IMPORTED CAPELLINI PASTA.

¼ cup diced carrot
¼ cup diced onion
¼ cup diced celery
½ cup diced mushrooms
I tablespoon olive oil

6 large shrimp, peeled and
  deveined
I teaspoon sesame seeds, toasted
I tablespoon soy sauce
I tablespoon white wine

1. Sauté the carrot, onion, celery, and mushrooms in the oil over medium heat until soft.
2. Add the shrimp and cook for 2 to 3 minutes, until pink and opaque.
3. Add the sesame seeds, soy sauce, and white wine.
4. Stir to combine, then serve.

Serves 1 or 2

To toast sesame seeds, place in a dry skillet and cook over medium heat, shaking the pan, until toasted.

MACARONI GRILL
shrimp portofino

SUCCULENT SAUTÉED SHRIMP WITH SAVORY MUSHROOMS AND ARTICHOKE HEARTS IN A LEMON-BUTTER SAUCE. SERVE OVER CAPELLINI PASTA OR RICE.

16 medium mushrooms
2 teaspoons chopped garlic
8 tablespoons (1 stick) butter, melted
16 large shrimp, peeled and deveined
½ teaspoon pepper

3 cloves garlic, minced
¼ cup lemon juice
One 6-ounce jar marinated artichoke hearts
4 slices lemon
2 tablespoons chopped fresh parsley

1. Sauté the mushrooms and garlic in the butter over medium heat until almost tender, about 5 minutes.
2. Add the shrimp and sauté until the shrimp are cooked, about 3 minutes. Be careful not to overcook the shrimp.
3. Add the pepper, garlic, lemon juice, and artichoke hearts and heat through.
4. Serve, garnished with the lemon slices and parsley.

Serves 4

OLIVE GARDEN
angel hair and three-onion soup

MADE WITH A BLEND OF THREE TYPES OF ONIONS, THIS AUTHENTIC OLIVE
GARDEN SOUP RECIPE IS BEST MADE WITH HOMEMADE CHICKEN BROTH.

8 ounces pearl onions
1 medium red onion, sliced thin
1 medium Vidalia onion, sliced
   thin
¼ cup olive oil
6 cups chicken broth
Salt

¼ teaspoon red pepper flakes
8 ounces angel hair pasta, broken
   into 2-inch pieces
¼ cup chopped fresh Italian
   parsley
1 tablespoon plus 1 teaspoon
   grated Romano cheese

1. Place the onions and oil in a large saucepan over low heat and cook,
   stirring occasionally, for about 20 minutes, until the onions are soft.
2. Increase the heat, add the broth, and salt to taste. Sprinkle with the red
   pepper flakes, bring to a boil, then reduce the heat and simmer for
   1 hour.
3. Add the pasta and parsley and cook until the pasta is al dente. Sprinkle
   with the grated Romano cheese.

Serves 6

Olive Garden was opened in 1982 and specializes in Tuscan dishes.
Hundreds of Olive Garden team members have traveled to Tuscany
to learn how authentic Italian food is prepared and to experience
Italy firsthand. Those recipes are served to their devoted customers
daily.

OLIVE GARDEN
beef fillets in balsamic sauce

GRILLED BEEF TENDERLOIN WITH A BALSAMIC VINEGAR–WINE SAUCE.

¼ cup extra virgin olive oil, plus
   extra for the fillets
4 tablespoons (½ stick) butter
1 medium yellow onion, sliced thin
Salt and pepper
½ cup dry white wine
½ cup dry Marsala wine

½ cup beef broth
2 tablespoons balsamic vinegar
Six 6-ounce beef tenderloin fillets
Pinch of finely chopped fresh
   parsley
6 fresh rosemary sprigs

1. Heat the oil and butter in a large sauté pan over medium heat. Add the sliced onion and a pinch each of salt and pepper; cook for 10 minutes or until the onion is softened and browned.
2. Add both wines, the broth, and vinegar and bring to a boil. Reduce the heat and simmer for 10 to 15 minutes, until the sauce is reduced by half.
3. Rub the fillets with oil; season with salt and pepper.
4. Preheat the grill to 350°F.
5. Grill the fillets to the desired doneness.
6. Strain the onion from the sauce and arrange on a platter. Top with the sauce and the steaks. Garnish with the parsley and sprigs of rosemary.

Serves 6

Balsamic vinegar is a full-flavored vinegar used in many dishes.

OLIVE GARDEN
bread sticks

SERVE WARM WITH AN ALFREDO OR MARINARA DIPPING SAUCE.

I loaf frozen bread dough	Garlic powder, for dusting
Cooking spray	Dried oregano, for sprinkling

1. Allow the dough to thaw at room temperature in a large greased mixing bowl.
2. When the dough is soft enough to knead, break off pieces and shape into cigar-sized sticks.
3. Place these 3 inches apart on sprayed cookie sheets. Let rise in a warm place until doubled in size, about 1 hour and 15 minutes.
4. Preheat the oven to 375°F.
5. Holding the can of cooking spray about 8 inches from the sticks, lightly spray the top of each stick, dust with garlic powder, and sprinkle with oregano.
6. Bake for 20 to 25 minutes, until golden brown.
7. Let cool on the cookie sheets on racks for a few minutes before serving.

Serves 4 to 6

OLIVE GARDEN
bruschetta al pomodoro

A TRADITIONAL TOPPING OF ROMA TOMATOES, FRESH BASIL, AND EXTRA VIRGIN
OLIVE OIL. SERVE WITH TOASTED CIABATTA BREAD.

4 ripe Roma tomatoes, coarsely
chopped
6 to 8 fresh basil leaves, chopped
¼ cup plus 2 tablespoons extra
virgin olive oil

Salt and pepper
8 slices crusty bread
3 cloves garlic

1. In a medium bowl, combine the tomatoes, basil, and oil, and season
   with salt and pepper to taste.
2. Toast the bread lightly on both sides, then rub the garlic across the
   bread's surface and top with the tomato mixture.

Serves 4

OLIVE GARDEN
chicken crostina

A FLAVORFUL CHICKEN ENTRÉE FEATURING A GOLDEN POTATO-PARMESAN CRUST AND PAIRED WITH LINGUINE PASTA AND A CREAMY GARLIC SAUCE.

Potato Crust
1½ cups Italian bread crumbs
¼ cup grated Parmesan cheese
4 tablespoons (½ stick) butter, melted
½ teaspoon garlic powder
¼ cup chopped fresh parsley
1 small potato, peeled and grated
Salt and pepper to taste

1½ cups plus 1 tablespoon all-purpose flour
1 tablespoon salt

1 tablespoon pepper
1 tablespoon Italian seasoning
6 boneless, skinless chicken breasts
Olive oil as needed
1 pound linguine
1 tablespoon roasted garlic
1 cup white wine
1½ cups heavy cream
1 cup grated Parmesan cheese
2 tablespoons chopped fresh parsley
1 cup diced ripe Roma tomatoes

1. Mix all the ingredients for the potato crust in a bowl and set aside.
2. Mix the 1½ cups flour, the salt, pepper, and Italian seasoning in a shallow dish. Dredge the chicken in the mixture, shaking off any excess.
3. Heat 3 tablespoons olive oil in a large skillet. Cook the chicken breasts two at a time over medium-high heat until golden brown and crisp, or until the internal temperature reaches 165°F. Add more oil for each batch as necessary.
4. Preheat the broiler.
5. Place the cooked chicken breasts on a baking sheet or large ovenproof dish and top with the potato crust mixture. Transfer the baking sheet to the oven and broil until the crust is golden brown, 1 to 2 minutes.
6. Cook the linguine according to the package directions. Drain and set aside.
7. Heat 2 tablespoons olive oil in a saucepan. Add the roasted garlic and cook for 1 minute. Stir in the 1 tablespoon flour and the wine and bring to a boil. Add the cream, 1 cup Parmesan cheese, 1 tablespoon of the

parsley, and the tomatoes. The sauce is done when it is bubbling throughout and begins to thicken.

8. Coat the pasta with some of the sauce, then serve topped with the chicken and the remaining sauce. Garnish with the remaining 1 tablespoon chopped parsley.

Serves 6

Fettuccine can also be used in this recipe.

OLIVE GARDEN
chicken san marco

FETTUCCINE TOSSED WITH A CHICKEN AND SAUTÉED VEGETABLE SAUCE SEASONED WITH ITALIAN HERBS.

San Marco Sauce
3 tablespoons olive oil
2 pounds boneless, skinless chicken thigh meat, cut into 1-inch cubes
2 large yellow onions, cut into ⅛-inch dice
1 cup julienned carrots
1 tablespoon finely chopped garlic
1 cup chicken broth
One 28-ounce can Italian plum tomatoes, with juice
2 teaspoons Wondra flour

Vegetables
3 tablespoons olive oil
1 cup julienned green bell pepper
1 cup julienned red bell pepper
1 cup zucchini, sliced ¼ inch thick, then halved
1 cup yellow squash, sliced ¼ inch thick, then halved
¾ cups coarsely chopped broccoli florets
¾ teaspoon salt
½ teaspoon pepper
1 teaspoon dried oregano
1 teaspoon dried rosemary

Pasta
6 cups cooked fresh fettuccine
1 tablespoon olive oil

Grated Parmesan cheese, for serving

1. To make the sauce, preheat a heavy nonaluminum 6-quart pot over medium-high heat and add the 3 tablespoons olive oil.
2. Once the oil is hot, add the chicken cubes and sauté for 5 minutes or until slightly browned on all sides.
3. Add the onions and carrots and sauté for about 2 minutes.
4. Add the garlic and sauté for about 30 seconds. Do not burn the garlic.
5. Then add the chicken broth to the pot. Stir to loosen the browned bits from the pot.
6. Add the tomatoes with their juice and the flour; lower the heat to a simmer. Cover and let simmer, stirring occasionally, until the chicken cubes are tender, 5 to 10 minutes.

7. While the sauce is cooking, prepare the vegetables. Add the 3 tablespoons olive oil to a skillet and sauté the green and red peppers, zucchini, squash, and broccoli over medium heat until just tender and crisp.
8. Add the vegetables to the sauce when the chicken is cooked through; mix together.
9. Add the salt, pepper, and herbs.
10. Toss the cooked pasta with the 1 tablespoon olive oil to prevent sticking, then add to the sauce. Mix the chicken, vegetables, and sauce and serve along with Parmesan cheese.

Serves 6

Wondra flour is a quick-mixing flour. It dissolves instantly even in cold liquids. Perfect for lump-free sauces and gravies.

Regular crushed or whole tomatoes can be used in place of Italian plum tomatoes.

OLIVE GARDEN
chocolate lasagna

LAYERS OF RICH CHOCOLATE CAKE AND SWEET BUTTERCREAM ICING.

Cake
6 cups cake flour, sifted
5¼ cups granulated sugar
2¼ cups Hershey's cocoa
  powder
2 tablespoons baking soda
¾ pound butter (3 sticks),
  softened
4½ cups milk
12 eggs
1 tablespoon vanilla extract

Buttercream
⅔ cup water
¼ cup meringue powder
12 cups sifted confectioners' sugar
  (about 3 pounds)
1¼ cups shortening
¾ teaspoon salt
1 teaspoon almond extract
1 teaspoon vanilla extract
1 teaspoon butter flavoring
One 12-ounce package semisweet
  chocolate chips

1. Preheat the oven to 350°F. Grease three 10-inch springform pans.
2. To make the cake, in a mixing bowl, combine the sifted flour, sugar, cocoa, and baking soda.
3. Add the butter and mix well.
4. Add the milk, eggs, and vanilla and mix.
5. Pour about 5 cups of the cake batter into each prepared pan.
6. Bake for 45 minutes or until a toothpick inserted in the center of each cake comes out clean.
7. Let cool for 10 minutes before you remove the cakes from the pans. Transfer to wire racks to cool.
8. To make the buttercream, combine the water and the meringue powder; whip at high speed until peaks form. Add 4 cups of the sugar, one cup at a time, beating at low speed after each addition.
9. Add the shortening and the remaining 8 cups sugar. Add the salt, extracts, and butter flavoring; beat at low speed until smooth. Thin out one half of the frosting with a little water. The thinned frosting will be used as the filling between the layers.
10. Place one 10-inch cake on a large round cake platter. Spread one half of

the thinned frosting on top. Sprinkle with semisweet chocolate chips. Place the second cake on top of the first. Frost the top with the remaining thinned frosting. Sprinkle with semisweet chocolate chips. Place the third layer on top of the second. Frost the top with all of the buttercream that was not thinned. Sprinkle with semisweet chocolate chips.

Makes one 10-inch 3-layer cake

Cake flour is a finely milled flour made from soft wheat. It has a very low gluten content.

OLIVE GARDEN
fettuccine alfredo

PARMESAN CREAM SAUCE WITH A HINT OF GARLIC, SERVED OVER FETTUCCINE.

1 pound fettuccine
1½ cups milk
1½ cups heavy cream
½ cup grated Parmesan cheese
½ cup grated Romano cheese

6 jumbo egg yolks
Salt and cracked pepper
1 teaspoon garlic powder
½ teaspoon parsley flakes

1. Cook the fettuccine according to the package directions.
2. Heat the milk and cream in a large, heavy saucepan until the mixture comes to a simmer.
3. Slowly whisk in the cheeses and then remove from the heat.
4. Place the egg yolks in a bowl and slowly whisk in a portion of the hot milk and cream mixture.
5. Slowly pour the egg yolk mixture back into the milk and cream mixture in the pan.
6. Season to taste with salt and pepper.
7. Add the cooked fettuccine to the saucepan. Sprinkle in the garlic powder and stir until the sauce thickens to the desired consistency.
8. Sprinkle with the parsley. Serve immediately.

Serves 4 to 6

For a healthier alternative, use fat-free cheeses, low-fat milk, and whole wheat pasta.

OLIVE GARDEN
fettuccine assortito

FETTUCCINE COMBINED WITH SAUTÉED VEGETABLES AND HAM, TOSSED WITH A
FONTINA CHEESE SAUCE.

Fontina Cheese Sauce
6 tablespoons (¾ stick) butter
¼ cup plus 2 tablespoons
  all-purpose flour
3 cups milk
6 ounces Fontina cheese, shredded
Salt and pepper

3 tablespoons butter or margarine
3 tablespoons olive oil
1 cup julienned green bell pepper

1 cup julienned red bell pepper
1¾ cups coarsely chopped
  broccoli florets
1 cup zucchini, sliced ¼ inch thick
1 cup yellow squash, sliced ¼ inch
  thick
1 cup julienned carrots
1¾ cups julienned ham
1 pound cooked fettuccine
  (al dente)

1. To make the sauce, melt the butter in a heavy nonaluminum pot. Add the flour and cook, stirring with a wire whisk, on medium heat for 2 minutes.
2. Add the milk and bring just to a boil. Turn off the heat and add the Fontina cheese, whisking it into the hot milk. Add salt and pepper to taste.
3. For the pasta, add the butter and olive oil to a large skillet over medium heat and sauté the vegetables and ham together until the vegetables are slightly tender. Stir frequently.
4. Toss the fettuccine with the vegetable and ham mixture; add the sauce and toss again to coat all the ingredients.

Serves 4 to 6

OLIVE GARDEN
five-cheese lasagna

LAYERS OF PASTA WITH FIVE TYPES OF CHEESE, TOPPED WITH MARINARA SAUCE.

Cream Sauce
4 tablespoons (½ stick) butter
¼ cup all-purpose flour
2 cups milk

Cheese Filling
¼ cup minced oil-packed sun-dried
   tomatoes, drained
1 tablespoon minced garlic
3½ cups ricotta cheese
3 eggs
1 cup grated Parmesan cheese

¼ cup grated Fontina cheese
½ cup grated Romano cheese
½ teaspoon salt
1 teaspoon pepper

One 10-ounce box lasagna noodles
   (spinach or egg)
4 cups shredded mozzarella
   cheese
1 cup grated Fontina cheese
2 cups hot marinara sauce
1 cup grated Parmesan cheese

1. To make the cream sauce, melt the butter over medium heat in a heavy 1-quart saucepan.
2. Add the flour and stir until blended, 1 to 2 minutes.
3. Add the milk, stirring with a wire whisk as it comes to a simmer. Cook, stirring, until thickened, 3 to 4 minutes. Set aside and let cool.
4. To make the cheese filling, combine the filling ingredients in a 3-quart bowl and mix well.
5. Add 1½ cups of the cooled cream sauce to the filling and mix well. Refrigerate, setting aside ½ cup of the cream sauce for later use.
6. Cook the lasagna noodles according to the package directions. Drain and run under cold water.
7. Preheat the oven to 350°F.
8. Place 3 lasagna noodles in a lightly oiled 13 by 9-inch baking dish, overlapping them slightly. Spread 1½ cups cheese filling over the noodles; sprinkle with 1 cup of the mozzarella and ¼ cup of the Fontina cheese. Repeat the pasta and cheese layering three more times; top with

the remaining 3 lasagna noodles. Spread the ½ cup reserved cream sauce over the top and cover the lasagna with foil.

9. Bake, covered, for 1 hour.

10. Remove the lasagna from the oven and let it sit for 15 minutes before serving. Serve topped with hot marinara sauce and the Parmesan cheese.

Serves 4

Fontina cheese, made from cow's milk, is a firm, creamy, delicate Italian cheese with a slightly nutty taste. You may have to go to an Italian market to get fine Fontina cheese.

OLIVE GARDEN
fried mozzarella

MOZZARELLA FINGERS, LIGHTLY BREADED WITH A HINT OF ITALIAN HERBS, DEEP FRIED, AND SERVED WITH MARINARA SAUCE.

One 1-pound package mozzarella cheese
2 eggs, beaten
¼ cup water
1½ cups Italian bread crumbs
½ teaspoon garlic salt

1 teaspoon Italian seasoning
⅔ cup all-purpose flour
⅓ cup cornstarch
Vegetable oil, for deep-frying
2 cups homemade or store-bought marinara sauce, warmed

1. Cut the mozzarella into either sticks or triangles.
2. Beat the eggs with the water and set aside.
3. Mix the bread crumbs, garlic salt, and Italian seasoning and set aside.
4. Blend the flour with the cornstarch and set aside.
5. Heat 2 inches of vegetable oil in a deep-fryer to 360°F.
6. Dip each cheese stick in the flour mixture, then in the egg wash, and then coat with the prepared bread crumbs.
7. In batches of 4, place carefully in the hot oil and fry until golden; this takes just a few seconds, so watch carefully.
8. When golden, remove the sticks from the hot oil and drain on paper towels.
9. Serve with marinara sauce, for dipping.

Serves 4

OLIVE GARDEN
lemon cream cake

A MOIST, LIGHT CAKE WITH A HINT OF LEMON, LAYERED WITH LEMON FILLING.

Cake
1¾ cups cake flour
1 tablespoon baking powder
1 teaspoon salt
1¼ cups sugar
½ cup vegetable oil
6 eggs, separated
¾ cup water

1 tablespoon grated lemon zest
½ teaspoon cream of tartar

Lemon Filling
1 cup heavy cream
2½ cups lemon pie filling

8 slices lemon

1. Preheat the oven to 350°F.
2. To make the cake, in a large bowl, combine the flour, baking powder, salt, and ½ cup of the sugar. Add the oil, egg yolks, water, and lemon zest. Beat with an electric mixer until smooth.
3. Using clean beaters in a small bowl, beat the egg whites and cream of tartar until peaks form. Slowly add the remaining ¾ cup sugar, and beat until stiff peaks form.
4. Fold one third of the whites into the batter, then quickly fold in the remaining whites until no streaks remain.
5. Turn the batter into an ungreased 10-inch tube pan. Bake for 1 hour or until a toothpick inserted in the center of the cake comes out clean.
6. Invert the tube pan on a rack and let the cake cool completely in the pan. When cool, loosen the edges of the cake to remove it from the pan.
7. To make the filling, beat the cream to stiff peaks. Fold in the lemon pie filling. Refrigerate until firm.
8. To assemble, slice the cake horizontally into 3 equal layers. Cover the bottom layers with ⅓ cup of the filling. Spread the remaining filling on the top layer. Decorate with the lemon slices.

Makes one 10-inch 3-layer tube cake

You can bake this cake ahead of time: Let cool completely and wrap tightly, unsliced, then place in the freezer until needed. Remove from the freezer and let thaw on the counter for a couple of hours. Prepare the lemon filling and slice and fill the cake.

OLIVE GARDEN
oven-roasted potatoes

BAKED CHUNKS OF POTATOES AND BELL PEPPERS SEASONED WITH ROSEMARY
AND SPRINKLED WITH ROMANO CHEESE.

2 medium baking potatoes	½ teaspoon salt
1 medium green bell pepper	½ teaspoon pepper
1 medium red bell pepper	1 teaspoon minced garlic
¼ cup olive oil	1 tablespoon plus 1 teaspoon
2 teaspoons chopped fresh	chopped fresh parsley
rosemary	½ cup grated Romano cheese

1. Preheat the oven to 350°F.
2. Peel the potatoes and cut into ½-inch cubes. Core and seed the green and red peppers and cut into ½-inch cubes. Set aside.
3. Mix the olive oil, rosemary, salt, pepper, and garlic in a small bowl.
4. In a small baking pan, toss the potatoes and peppers with the oil and rosemary mixture. Bake for 10 minutes or until the potatoes are fork-tender.
5. Sprinkle the potatoes with the parsley and Romano cheese.

Serves 2

Use leftover baked or steamed potatoes and frozen peppers.

OLIVE GARDEN
pasta e fagioli

WHITE AND RED BEANS, GROUND BEEF, TOMATOES, AND SHELL PASTA IN A
SAVORY BROTH.

2 pounds ground beef
1 tablespoon olive oil
1½ cups onions, chopped
2 cups carrots, sliced thin
2 cups celery, diced
One 28-ounce can diced tomatoes
2 cups canned red kidney beans
2 cups canned white kidney beans
Two 48-ounce cans beef broth

1 tablespoon dried oregano
2 teaspoons pepper
1½ teaspoons Tabasco sauce
Three 16-ounce jars spaghetti
   sauce
8 ounces shell pasta
1 tablespoon plus 2 teaspoons
   chopped fresh parsley

1. Sauté the beef in the oil in a 10-quart pot until the beef starts to brown.
   Add the onions, carrots, celery, and tomatoes and simmer for about 10
   minutes.
2. Drain and rinse the beans and add to the pot. Also add the beef broth,
   oregano, pepper, Tabasco sauce, spaghetti sauce, and pasta.
3. Add the chopped parsley. Simmer until the celery and carrots are tender,
   about 45 minutes. Ladle the soup into bowls.

Serves 10

OLIVE GARDEN
pizza bianco

SEASONED PIZZA CRUST WITH A MEDLEY OF ITALIAN CHEESES FOR A FILLING,
TOPPED WITH ONIONS, OLIVES, TOMATO, MOZZARELLA, AND A BLEND OF ITAL-
IAN SPICES.

Cheese Filling
½ cup ricotta cheese
¼ cup grated Parmesan cheese
¼ cup shredded mozzarella cheese
¼ cup shredded Fontina cheese
1 tablespoon minced yellow onion
1½ tablespoons milk
¼ teaspoon salt

2 thick 6-inch-diameter ready-to-
serve seasoned pizza crusts

Toppings
¼ cup sliced green onions
⅓ cup diced black olives
⅓ cup chopped tomato
½ cup grated mozzarella cheese
½ cup grated Parmesan cheese
Pinch of dried oregano, or to taste
Pinch of dried basil, or to taste

1. Preheat the oven to 375°F.
2. Combine all the ingredients for the cheese filling and mix thoroughly.
3. Divide the filling in half and spread on each crust.
4. Divide each of the toppings in half. Sprinkle the green onions, olives,
   and tomato over each crust.
5. Top with the mozzarella and Parmesan, oregano, and basil.
6. Bake the pizzas for 8 to 10 minutes, until the filling is hot and the cheese
   has melted.
7. Cut each pizza into 6 wedges.

Makes two 6-inch pizzas

OLIVE GARDEN

pork filettino

GRILLED PORK TENDERLOIN MARINATED IN EXTRA VIRGIN OLIVE OIL, GARLIC,
PARSLEY, AND ROSEMARY.

4 pork tenderloins
½ teaspoon salt
½ teaspoon pepper
½ cup extra virgin olive oil
¼ cup chopped fresh rosemary,
plus extra for garnish

¼ cup minced garlic
¼ cup chopped fresh parsley
One 1-ounce package veal
demi-glace

1. Season the tenderloins with the salt and pepper on all sides.
2. Brush with the olive oil and sprinkle with the rosemary, garlic, and
   parsley. Refrigerate, covered, for about 2 hours.
3. Preheat the grill to high heat.
4. Grill the tenderloins to an internal temperature of 165°F.
5. Heat the demi-glace and pour over the pork. Garnish with fresh
   rosemary.

Serves 4

Tenderloin is one of the most tender cuts of pork.

OLIVE GARDEN
salad dressing

CLASSIC ITALIAN SALAD DRESSING BUT THICKER AND MORE FLAVORFUL.

½ cup white vinegar
1 teaspoon lemon juice
2 tablespoons beaten egg
⅓ cup water
⅓ cup vegetable oil
¼ cup light corn syrup
3 tablespoons grated Romano cheese

2 tablespoons dry unflavored pectin (optional)
1¼ teaspoons salt
½ teaspoon minced garlic
¼ teaspoon parsley flakes
Pinch of dried oregano
Pinch of red pepper flakes

1. Mix all the ingredients in a blender on low for about 30 seconds.
2. Chill in the refrigerator for 90 minutes.
3. Serve over your favorite salad.

Makes 1½ cups

OLIVE GARDEN
sangria

SANGRIA'S APPEAL IS ALL ABOUT TAKING YOUR FAVORITE RED WINE AND YOUR
FAVORITE FRUITS AND EXPERIMENTING WITH THEM.

One 1.5-liter bottle dry red wine
1¼ cups grenadine
2 cups cranberry juice cocktail
1½ cups sweet vermouth
1¼ cups sugar water (50% sugar
solution)

1 medium orange, unpeeled and
sliced
12 sliced strawberries
4 cups crushed ice

1. Mix all the ingredients except for the ice in a nice-sized pitcher. Pour the sangria into a glass and then add the ice.
2. Serve each glass with fruit from the pitcher.

Makes about 3 quarts

Sangria is a refreshing party drink that was created in Spain. Every restaurant has its own twist on this fruit-filled drink.

You could also use orange juice and brandy instead of grenadine and sweet vermouth.

OLIVE GARDEN

tiramisù

THE CLASSIC ITALIAN DESSERT. A LAYER OF CREAMY SWEETNESS SET ATOP ESPRESSO-SOAKED SPONGE CAKE.

1 store-bought 10- to 12-inch sponge cake (about 3 inches high)
1½ tablespoons brewed strong black coffee (or instant espresso)
1½ tablespoons brandy or rum
1½ pounds cream cheese or mascarpone cheese, softened
1 to 1½ cups superfine or confectioners' sugar
Unsweetened cocoa powder, sifted

1. Cut across the middle of the sponge cake, forming two layers, each about 1½ inches high.
2. Blend the coffee and brandy. Sprinkle enough of the mixture over the bottom half of the cake to flavor it strongly. Don't moisten the cake too much, or it may collapse on serving.
3. Beat the cheese and 1 cup of the sugar until the sugar is completely dissolved and the cheese is light and spreadable. Test for sweetness during beating, adding more sugar if needed.
4. Spread the cut surface of the bottom layer with half of the cheese mixture.
5. Replace the second layer and top with the remaining cheese mixture.
6. Sprinkle the top liberally with sifted cocoa.
7. Refrigerate the cake for at least 2 hours before cutting and serving.

Makes one 10- to 12-inch 2-layer cake

OLIVE GARDEN
tuscan tea

FRESH-BREWED, SWEETENED LEMON-FLAVORED TEA SERVED IN A TALL GLASS OF ICE.

Lemon-Flavored Syrup
1 cup water
1 cup sugar
Lemon juice

Tuscan Tea
½ cup lemon-flavored syrup
2 cups cold freshly brewed tea
2 lemon wedges, for garnish

1. To make the lemon-flavored syrup, heat the water and sugar in a saucepan until the sugar is dissolved. Remove from the heat, and add lemon juice to taste. Store in a covered jar in the refrigerator.
2. To make the Tuscan tea, mix the ½ cup lemon-flavored syrup with the cold tea. Serve in two tall glasses, over ice. Garnish with the lemon wedges.

Serves 2

Substitute other fruit juices to make all kinds of syrups.

Mix this syrup with water to make lemonade or with your favorite alcohol for a great adult beverage.

OLIVE GARDEN

zuppa toscana

SPICY SAUSAGE, RUSSET POTATOES, AND KALE IN A CREAMY BROTH.

1 pound Italian sausage
8 ounces smoked bacon, chopped
4 cups water
Two 14.5-ounce cans chicken broth
2 large russet potatoes, scrubbed and cubed
2 cloves garlic, crushed
1 medium onion, chopped
2 cups chopped kale or Swiss chard
1 cup heavy cream
Salt and pepper

1. In a skillet over medium heat, brown the sausage, breaking it into small pieces; drain and set aside.
2. In a separate skillet, fry the bacon until brown, drain and set aside.
3. Combine the water, broth, potatoes, garlic, and onion in a pot; simmer over medium heat until the potatoes are tender, 10 to 15 minutes.
4. Add the sausage and bacon; simmer for 10 minutes.
5. Add the kale and cream. Season with salt and pepper to taste and simmer until the soup is heated through. Do not allow to boil.

Serves 4

You can use half-and-half instead of heavy cream, if desired. Remove the sausage casings before frying.

OUTBACK STEAKHOUSE
cyclone pasta

HEAPED PORTIONS OF PENNE PASTA IN ALFREDO SAUCE TOSSED WITH CHICKEN,
HAM, SUN-DRIED TOMATOES, SHIITAKE MUSHROOMS, AND GARLIC.

I cup chopped sun-dried tomatoes	I pound cooked penne pasta
I cup sliced shiitake mushrooms	I tablespoon dried oregano
I medium onion, chopped	I tablespoon dried thyme
One 16-ounce jar Alfredo sauce	¼ cup minced garlic
I cup chopped cooked chicken breast	I cup shredded Parmesan cheese
I cup shredded ham	Crusty Italian bread, for serving

1. Preheat the oven to 375°F.
2. Combine all the ingredients except the Parmesan cheese and Italian bread in a lightly greased 13 by 9-inch baking dish. Top with the Parmesan.
3. Bake for 20 to 30 minutes, until the top begins to brown.
4. Serve with Italian bread.

Serves 4

The company was founded in Florida in 1988. At the time, the sequel to the 1986 hit movie *Crocodile Dundee* was soon to be released. Despite the fact that none of the restaurant's founders had ever been to Australia, the quartet decided to give their venture an Australian theme. The outback is kind of the Wild, Wild West of Australia, so you go there for the western theme. But instead of U.S. western, it's Australian western.

OUTBACK STEAKHOUSE
honey-wheat bushman bread

A DARK HONEY-WHEAT BREAD SERVED WARM WITH WHIPPED BUTTER.

1 ½ cups warm water
2 tablespoons butter, softened
½ cup honey
2 cups bread flour, plus extra
2 cups whole wheat flour
1 tablespoon cocoa powder
1 tablespoon sugar
2 teaspoons instant coffee powder

1 teaspoon salt
2 ¼ teaspoons (1 envelope) active
  dry yeast
1 teaspoon caramel food coloring
  (optional)
3 tablespoons cornmeal, for
  dusting
Whipped butter, for serving

1. Place all of the ingredients except the cornmeal and whipped butter in a bread machine and follow the manufacturer's directions. The dough will be a little on the wet side and sticky, but if it seems too wet, add more bread flour. When the dough is done, let it rise for 1 hour in the machine.
2. Remove from the machine, punch down, and divide into 8 portions. Form the portions into tubular-shaped loaves 6 to 8 inches long and 2 inches wide.
3. Sprinkle the entire surface of the loaves with the cornmeal and place the loaves on two cookie sheets. Cover with plastic wrap and let rise for 1 hour.
4. Preheat the oven to 350°F.
5. Bake for 20 to 25 minutes. The internal temperature of a loaf of yeast bread when baked to perfection is 210°F. Use an instant-read thermometer to check. Serve warm with whipped butter.

Makes 8 loaves

OUTBACK STEAKHOUSE
key lime pie

A RICH KEY LIME–FLAVORED FILLING IN A GRAHAM CRACKER CRUST.

3 egg yolks
½ cup Key lime juice
One 14-ounce can sweetened
condensed milk

¼ teaspoon vanilla extract
Pinch of salt
One 9-inch graham cracker crust

1. Preheat the oven to 325°F.
2. In a medium bowl, whisk the egg yolks until blended; whisk in the Key lime juice.
3. Add the sweetened condensed milk, vanilla, and salt, whisking until blended.
4. Pour into the crust and bake for about 15 minutes, until the filling has set.
5. Remove from the oven and let cool completely on a wire rack. Refrigerate until ready to serve.

Makes one 9-inch pie

OUTBACK STEAKHOUSE
marinated steak

THE CLASSIC OUTBACK SIRLOIN SEASONED WITH A SPECIAL BLEND OF SIGNATURE SPICES AND SEARED ON A RED-HOT GRILL.

4 beef sirloin steaks
1 cup beer
1 tablespoon packed dark brown sugar

1 teaspoon seasoned salt
½ teaspoon pepper
½ teaspoon onion powder
½ teaspoon garlic powder

1. Place the steaks in a shallow pan, pour the beer over, and marinate for 1 hour in the refrigerator.
2. Remove the steaks from the beer.
3. Combine the dry ingredients and rub over the steaks.
4. Let rest for 30 minutes in the refrigerator.
5. Preheat the grill to medium-high heat.
6. Grill the steaks to the desired degree of doneness.

Serves 4

For the best results, let the steak marinate in the dry ingredients overnight, in the refrigerator.

OUTBACK STEAKHOUSE
walkabout soup

A CREAM- AND CHEESE-BASED SOUP WITH ONIONS. SERVED WITH A SPRINKLING OF CHOPPED GREEN ONION AND MOZZARELLA CHEESE.

½ stick (4 tablespoons) butter
2½ cups chopped yellow onions
3 tablespoons all-purpose flour
½ teaspoon paprika
1½ teaspoons salt
¼ teaspoon pepper

3 cups milk
2 cups vegetable broth
1 cup shredded Cheddar cheese
⅓ cup cream
1 green onion, chopped
¼ cup shredded mozzarella cheese

1. Melt the butter in a large saucepan over medium heat.
2. Add the onions and cook, stirring, for 10 minutes or until tender.
3. Remove from the heat and stir in the flour, paprika, salt, and pepper.
4. Slowly add the milk, stirring until smooth.
5. Add the vegetable broth a third at a time, stirring after each addition until well blended.
6. Place over low heat, stirring until creamy, thickened, and hot.
7. Add the Cheddar cheese and cream and stir to melt the cheese.
8. Pour into bowls and sprinkle the green onion and mozzarella on top.

Serves 4

Make your own chicken, beef, or vegetable broth at home and freeze it for future use.

PANDA EXPRESS
orange-flavored chicken

TENDER, JUICY CUBED CHICKEN, LIGHTLY BATTERED AND DEEP-FRIED, SERVED
WITH A SWEET AND TANGY ORANGE SAUCE WITH GREEN ONIONS. DELICIOUS
WITH STEAMED RICE.

1 pound boneless, skinless chicken breasts
1 egg white
1 teaspoon salt
1 teaspoon sugar

Orange Sauce
1 cup water
½ cup ketchup
½ cup sugar
2 tablespoons apple cider vinegar
1 tablespoon soy sauce

1 tablespoon plus 1 teaspoon cornstarch
2 teaspoons sesame oil
2 tablespoons vegetable oil
1 tablespoon grated orange zest
2 tablespoons chopped green onions

4 cups vegetable oil, for deep-frying
1 cup cornstarch

1. Cut the chicken breast into ½-inch cubes; set aside.
2. Combine the egg white, salt, and sugar in a bowl and stir vigorously until the ingredients are thoroughly mixed. Add the chicken cubes to the egg white mixture and stir to coat well.
3. To make the orange sauce, combine the water, ketchup, sugar, vinegar, soy sauce, 1 tablespoon plus 1 teaspoon cornstarch, and sesame oil; stir and set aside. Place a pot over high heat. When the pot is hot, add the 2 tablespoons vegetable oil and heat. Add the orange zest and green onions and cook, stirring, for about 20 seconds, taking care not to burn the orange zest.
4. Pour the combined sauce ingredients into the pot and cook over medium heat, stirring frequently, until the sauce has thickened, 12 to 15 minutes.
5. Preheat the 4 cups oil to 350°F in a deep-fryer.
6. Meanwhile, put the coated chicken in a resealable plastic bag containing the 1 cup cornstarch. Shake the chicken well for about 20 seconds, until the chicken is covered with the cornstarch. Shake off all the excess

cornstarch and deep-fry the chicken in the hot oil until golden brown, about 2½ minutes. Remove the chicken from the oil with a slotted spoon, drain well on paper towels, and set aside. Add the fried chicken to the pot with the hot orange sauce, stir for about 30 seconds, then serve immediately.

Serves 4

Panda Express is a powerhouse in the Chinese restaurant business. It opened in 1973 and now has more than 820 fast-food Chinese restaurants across the United States.

PANERA BREAD
asian sesame-chicken salad

ALL-NATURAL CHICKEN, ROMAINE LETTUCE, FRESH CILANTRO, SLICED ALMONDS,
SESAME SEEDS, CRISPY WONTON STRIPS, AND AN ASIAN SESAME VINAIGRETTE.

2 wonton wrappers
Canola oil, for frying
2 tablespoons sliced almonds

Asian Sesame Dressing
¼ cup rice wine vinegar
¼ cup toasted sesame oil
2 tablespoons soy sauce
1 teaspoon sesame seeds, toasted

1 teaspoon red pepper flakes
¾ cup canola or vegetable oil
4 cups loosely packed bite-size
pieces romaine lettuce
1 tablespoon chopped fresh cilantro
3 ounces boneless, skinless chicken
breasts, grilled and sliced thin
1 tablespoon sesame seeds

1. Preheat the oven to 350°F.
2. Cut the wonton wrappers into ¼-inch strips.
3. Heat about 2 inches of canola oil to 365°F in a heavy skillet.
4. Fry the wonton strips in the oil until they are crisp, about 30 seconds.
   Remove with a slotted spoon and drain on paper towels.
5. Spread the almonds out on a baking sheet. Toast them in the oven for
   5 minutes, toss them around, and then toast for 5 minutes more.
   Remove from the oven and let cool.
6. To make the dressing, in a bowl, mix together all of the ingredients
   except the canola oil. Use a wire whisk to blend well and then slowly
   drizzle in the oil to create an emulsion.
7. To assemble the salad, in a large bowl, toss the romaine lettuce, cilantro,
   fried wonton strips, chicken, and dressing.
8. Transfer to plates and top with the sesame seeds and almonds.

Serves 4

Panera started as Au Bon Pain Company in 1981, with the single
goal of making great bread broadly available to consumers across
America. Panera Bread understands that great bread makes great
meals, from made-to-order sandwiches to tossed-to-order salads, and
soup served in bread bowls.

PANERA BREAD
broccoli-cheese soup

CHOPPED BROCCOLI, SHREDDED CARROTS, AND SELECT SEASONINGS SIMMERED
IN A VELVETY SMOOTH CHEESE SAUCE.

½ medium onion, chopped
5 tablespoons butter, melted
¼ cup all-purpose flour
2 cups half-and-half
2 cups chicken broth
8 ounces broccoli, coarsely
  chopped

1 cup shredded carrots
Salt and pepper
2 cups grated sharp Cheddar
  cheese
¼ teaspoon ground nutmeg

1. Sauté the onion in 1 tablespoon of the melted butter. Set aside.
2. Using a wire whisk, combine the remaining 4 tablespoons melted butter and the flour in a large pot over medium heat. Cook, stirring frequently, for about 4 minutes.
3. Slowly add the half-and-half; continue stirring. Add the chicken broth, whisking all the time. Simmer for 20 minutes.
4. Add the broccoli, carrots, and sautéed onion. Cook over low heat until the veggies are tender, about 20 minutes.
5. Add salt and pepper to taste.
6. By now the soup should be thickened. Pour in batches into a blender and puree.
7. Return the puree to the pot and place over low heat. Add the grated cheese and stir until well blended. Stir in the nutmeg.

Serves 4

PAT'S KING OF STEAKS
philly cheesesteak

CHEESE-SMOTHERED STEAK SLICES, TOPPED WITH SAUTÉED ONION, SERVED ON A CRUSTY ITALIAN ROLL AND GARNISHED WITH SAUTÉED BELL PEPPERS AND MUSHROOMS.

9 tablespoons soybean oil
1 large Spanish onion, sliced thin
1 medium green bell pepper, sliced
1 medium red bell pepper, sliced
½ cup sliced mushrooms

1½ pounds rib eye steaks or roll steaks, sliced thin
One 15-ounce jar Cheez Whiz
4 crusty Italian rolls
Ketchup, for serving

1. Heat an iron skillet or a nonstick pan over medium heat.
2. Add 3 tablespoons of the oil to the pan and sauté the onion to the desired doneness; remove the onion and set aside. In the same pan, heat 3 more tablespoons of the oil and sauté the peppers and mushrooms. Remove from the pan and set aside.
3. Add the remaining 3 tablespoons oil and sauté the slices of meat quickly on both sides. While it's cooking, break the meat into smaller pieces with two spatulas. Melt the Cheez Whiz in a double boiler or microwave.
4. Divide the meat among the rolls. Add the onion, and pour the Cheez Whiz over the top.
5. Serve with the sautéed green and red peppers and mushrooms for garnish, along with ketchup.

Serves 4

Soybean oil is also known as soya oil.

In 1930, Pat Olivieri started Pat's King of Steaks. Originally, Pat had a hot dog stand in south Philadelphia. One day, he got an idea to cook something different for his own lunch. So he put some cooked hamburger steak and onions on an Italian roll. A cabdriver who was a regular hot dog customer saw this and asked Pat to make him the same thing. After one bite, the cabdriver told Pat that he should sell these sandwiches and forget about making hot dogs. So Pat did. The steak sandwich became a big hit! Over the years, the hamburger steak evolved into sliced steak, and cheese was added. And it became known as the Philly cheesesteak sandwich.

PERKINS RESTAURANT AND BAKERY
pancakes

LIGHT AND FLUFFY PANCAKES TO SERVE WITH YOUR FAVORITE TOPPINGS
AND SYRUP.

4 cups baking mix
3 extra-large eggs, beaten
2½ cups club soda, at room
  temperature

¼ cup vegetable shortening,
  melted
Vegetable oil, for frying

1. Place the baking mix in a large bowl.
2. Add the eggs, club soda, and melted shortening. Using a wire whisk, mix
   until there are no lumps, but do not overmix.
3. Preheat a griddle over medium-high heat.
4. Fry the pancakes, using about 1 tablespoon vegetable oil on the griddle
   for each pancake; use ½ cup batter for each pancake.
5. Flip the pancakes over when you see open bubbles appear on the surface
   and the edges of the pancakes look dry.

Makes 10 pancakes

Founded in 1958, and with nearly five hundred locations in thirty-four states and five Canadian provinces, Perkins tantalizes with in-house bakeshops, while featuring breakfast, lunch, and dinner menus from traditional to innovative. Fresh muffins, pies, and cookies can top off a meal or be taken out for later.

P.F. CHANG'S
chicken-lettuce wrap

QUICKLY COOKED SPICED CHICKEN WRAPPED WITH COOL LETTUCE LEAVES. IT
MAKES A GREAT APPETIZER.

8 dried shiitake mushrooms

Cooking Sauce

4 teaspoons hoisin sauce
1 teaspoon soy sauce
1 teaspoon dry sherry
2 teaspoons oyster sauce
2 teaspoons water
1 teaspoon sesame oil
1 teaspoon sugar
2 teaspoons cornstarch

1 teaspoon cornstarch
2 teaspoons dry sherry
2 teaspoons water
1 teaspoon soy sauce
Salt and pepper to taste

1½ pounds boneless, skinless chicken breasts, cut into thin strips
5 tablespoons plus 1 teaspoon peanut or vegetable oil
1 teaspoon minced fresh ginger
2 cloves garlic, minced
2 small dried chiles (optional)
2 green onions, minced
1 cup minced bamboo shoots
1 cup minced water chestnuts
1½ cups cooked cellophane noodles
1 head icebag or Bibb lettuce separated into leaves, for wrapping

1. Cover the mushrooms with boiling water; let stand for 30 minutes, then drain.
2. Remove and discard the woody stems. Mince the mushrooms. Set aside.
3. Mix all the ingredients for the cooking sauce in a bowl, and set aside.
4. In a medium bowl, combine the 1 teaspoon cornstarch, sherry, water, soy sauce, salt and pepper, and chicken. Stir to coat the chicken thoroughly.
5. Stir in 1 teaspoon of the peanut oil and let sit for 15 minutes to marinate.
6. Heat a wok or large skillet over medium-high heat.
7. Add 3 tablespoons of the oil, then add the chicken and stir-fry for 3 to 4 minutes. Remove from the pan and set aside.

8. Add 2 tablespoons of the oil to the pan.
9. Add the ginger, garlic, chiles, if desired, and green onions; stir-fry for about a minute or so.
10. Add the minced mushrooms, bamboo shoots, and water chestnuts; stir-fry for an additional 2 minutes. Return the chicken to the pan.
11. Add the cooking sauce to the pan. Cook until thickened and hot.
12. Break the cooked cellophane noodles into small pieces, and cover the bottom of a serving dish with them. Pour the chicken mixture on top of the noodles. Serve with lettuce leaves for wrapping.

Serves 4 to 6

P.F. Chang's is unique. It blends classic Chinese design with a modern bistro look. Each location features an original hand-painted mural depicting scenes of life in twelfth-century China. The goal of a P.F. Chang's meal is to attain harmony of taste, texture, color, and aroma by balancing the Chinese principles of *fan* and *t'sai*. *Fan* foods include rice, noodles, grains, and dumplings, while vegetables, meat, poultry, and seafood are *t'sai* foods.

P.F. CHANG'S
chicken with black bean sauce

SLICES OF CHICKEN, STIR-FRIED IN BLACK BEAN SAUCE. SERVE WITH WHITE OR BROWN RICE.

Peking Stir-fry Sauce
½ cup water
2 teaspoons Shao Hsing rice wine or dry sherry
2 teaspoons mushroom soy sauce
2 teaspoons oyster sauce
1 teaspoon sugar
1 teaspoon cornstarch

4 boneless, skinless chicken breasts
1 egg, beaten
¼ cup canola oil

1 tablespoon cornstarch, plus extra for thickening
1 teaspoon minced fresh ginger
2 teaspoons fermented black beans
1 tablespoon minced green onions (white part)
½ teaspoon minced garlic
1½ cups chicken broth
½ teaspoon sugar
Pinch of white pepper

1. To make the Peking stir-fry sauce, mix all the sauce ingredients together until the cornstarch is incorporated. Stir well before using.
2. Cut the whole chicken breasts in half so you have 8 breast fillets. Cut all the breast fillets diagonally into strips.
3. Combine the egg, 2 tablespoons of the canola oil, and the 1 tablespoon cornstarch in a medium bowl. Add the chicken strips in batches and coat on all sides with the egg mixture.
4. Heat a wok. Add the remaining 2 tablespoons oil, then the chicken, and cook until the chicken is opaque all over.
5. Remove the chicken and any excess oil from the wok.
6. Add the ginger, black beans, and green onions and stir-fry. Add the chicken strips and garlic. Then add the Peking stir-fry sauce and the chicken broth. Add the sugar and the white pepper. *Stir-fry briefly after each addition.*
7. Thicken with a thin paste of cornstarch and water to your liking.

Serves 4

Fermented black beans (aka Chinese black beans) are small black soybeans that have been preserved in salt.

P.F. CHANG'S
sichuan chicken chow fun

WOK-SEARED GROUND CHICKEN WITH CHILI PASTE, GREEN ONIONS, AND SICH-
UAN PRESERVED VEGETABLES, TOSSED WITH WIDE RICE NOODLES.

Sauce
1 tablespoon soy sauce
2 teaspoons white vinegar
2 teaspoons sugar
1 teaspoon oyster sauce
1 teaspoon mushroom soy sauce
2 teaspoons water

2 teaspoons vegetable oil
1 teaspoon minced garlic
1 teaspoon chili paste

4 ounces cooked ground chicken
2 teaspoons shredded black fungus
  mushroom
One 14-ounce package chow fun
  noodles
1 teaspoon sesame oil
1 teaspoon Sichuan preserved
  vegetables (found at Asian
  markets)
2 teaspoons minced green onions

1. Combine all the ingredients for the sauce in a bowl.
2. Heat a wok and add the vegetable oil.
3. Stir-fry the garlic and chili paste for about 10 seconds.
4. Add the ground chicken and continue to stir-fry 3 to 4 minutes.
5. Add the black fungus mushroom and the sauce to the chicken and stir-fry for about 10 seconds.
6. Separate the noodles and mix into the wok a little at a time.
7. Continue cooking for 2 to 4 minutes, until the noodles are hot.
8. Mix in the sesame oil before serving. Garnish with the Sichuan preserved vegetables and minced green onions.

Serves 2

Sichuan preserved vegetables are a salty-spicy medley of greens such as Napa cabbage, mustard, kohlrabi, and turnip, preserved with salt, Sichuan peppercorns, and chili powder.

PIZZA HUT

cavatini

TENDER NOODLES IN ASSORTED SHAPES TOPPED WITH A MEAT SAUCE AND CHEESE, THEN OVEN-BAKED.

4 tablespoons (½ stick) butter
1 large onion, diced
1 large green bell pepper, diced
1 teaspoon garlic powder
1 pound assorted pasta (wheels, shells, spirals, ziti)
One 16-ounce jar meat-flavored spaghetti sauce

8 ounces cooked ground beef
8 ounces cooked Italian sausage
8 ounces pepperoni, sliced thin and cut in half
2 cups shredded mozzarella cheese

1. Preheat the oven to 350°F.
2. Melt the butter in a skillet over medium-high heat. Add the onion, green pepper, and garlic powder. Sauté for about 4 minutes.
3. At the same time, cook the pasta according to the package directions.
4. Heat the spaghetti sauce and mix with the cooked ground beef and sausage.
5. Grease a 4-quart casserole. Place half of the cooked pasta in the dish, followed by half of the vegetables, half of the pepperoni, and half of the sauce. Repeat another layer.
6. Spread the mozzarella cheese over the top.
7. Bake for about 45 minutes, until the cheese is melted.

Serves 4 to 6

This is a great way to use up all those little leftover portions of various pastas!

Pizza Hut™ was founded in 1958 by brothers Frank and Dan Carney in Wichita, Kansas, with $600 borrowed from their mother; the first franchise store opened in Topeka in 1959. The menu includes pizzas, pastas, salads, and more.

PLANET HOLLYWOOD
cap'n crunch chicken

THIS UNIQUE DISH USES A CEREAL BREADING ON THE CHICKEN TO MAKE IT
TASTY AND CRUNCHY.

2 cups crushed Cap'n Crunch
  cereal
1½ cups crushed cornflakes
1 egg
1 cup milk
1 cup all-purpose flour

1 teaspoon onion powder
1 teaspoon garlic powder
½ teaspoon pepper
2 pounds boneless, skinless chicken
  breasts, cut into strips
Vegetable oil, for frying

1. Combine the cereals in a large bowl.
2. Beat the egg with the milk and set aside.
3. Stir together the flour, onion and garlic powders, and pepper. Set aside.
4. Dip the chicken strips into the seasoned flour. Move around to coat well,
   then shake off the excess flour. Dip into the egg mixture, coating well,
   then dip into the cereal mixture, coating well.
5. Heat the oil in a large, heavy skillet to 325°F.
6. Drop the coated chicken tenders carefully into 1 inch of hot oil and fry
   until golden brown and cooked through, 3 to 5 minutes, depending on
   size.
7. Drain on paper towels and serve.

Serves 6

Another great theme restaurant focusing on movie and Hollywood
memorabilia.

POPEYES

cajun rice

THE ZESTY FLAVOR OF CAJUN-SEASONED RICE AND BEEF COMPLEMENT THIS DISH.

I pound lean ground beef	I teaspoon Cajun seasoning
½ cup finely diced green bell pepper	¼ teaspoon red pepper flakes
⅓ cup diced green onions	4 cups cooked long-grain rice
½ teaspoon garlic powder	¼ to ⅓ cup water
½ teaspoon celery flakes	¼ teaspoon black pepper

1. In a skillet, combine the ground beef and green pepper and cook over medium-high heat until the beef loses its pink color and the pepper is soft.
2. Pour off the excess fat and reduce the heat to medium-low.
3. Add the remaining ingredients, then stir and cook together until the ground beef is completely cooked and the liquid is absorbed, 25 to 35 minutes.

Serves 4 to 6

For a serious bayou experience, add more Cajun seasoning and red pepper flakes.

To get the best results, use a good-quality rice for this recipe.

The Popeyes story began in Arabi, Louisiana, back in 1972, with Al Copeland's Chicken on the Run restaurant. Mild-tasting chicken just didn't have that Cajun spice that Louisiana is known for. So Copeland "turned up the heat" on his chicken recipe and changed the name to Popeyes. This spicier chicken was what the public wanted, and business began to boom. Perking up his chicken did the trick.

POPEYES
dirty rice

A COMBINATION OF BREAKFAST SAUSAGE AND RICE COOKED IN CHICKEN BROTH.
IT'S THE PERFECT SIDE DISH FOR FRIED CHICKEN.

I pound bulk spicy breakfast
sausage
One 14-ounce can chicken broth

½ cup long-grain rice
I teaspoon onion flakes

1. Brown the sausage in a skillet, stirring and crumbling with a fork, until the pink color disappears.
2. Stir in the broth, rice, and onion flakes.
3. Simmer gently, covered, for 18 to 20 minutes, or until the rice is tender and most of the broth is absorbed.

Serves 4

Use leftover rice. Just heat through.

RAINFOREST CAFE

blue mountain grilled chicken sandwich

TENDER GRILLED CHICKEN BREAST, CAJUN-SEASONED AND TOPPED WITH
BACON, SWISS CHEESE, ROASTED RED PEPPERS, AND LEAF LETTUCE. SERVED ON
A TOASTED BUN WITH SPICY RAINFOREST CAFE SAFARI SAUCE AND COLESLAW.

4 hamburger buns

4 boneless, skinless chicken breasts

1 tablespoon plus 1 teaspoon
Cajun seasoning

¼ cup teriyaki sauce

8 lettuce leaves

8 slices cooked bacon

8 slices Swiss cheese

One 8-ounce jar roasted red bell
peppers

Safari Sauce (page 182), for serving

2 cups coleslaw, for serving

1. Split and toast the hamburger buns.
2. Rub the chicken with the Cajun seasoning. Grill the chicken breasts
   until cooked through.
3. Brush with the teriyaki sauce after grilling.
4. Assemble each sandwich with 2 lettuce leaves, 2 bacon slices, 2 cheese
   slices, and ¼ cup of the roasted red pepper and serve with safari sauce
   and coleslaw.

Serves 4

Rainforest Cafe, a Wild Place to Shop and Eat, was founded in
1994 and is a dynamic restaurant and retail environment. Decor
that simulates a tropical rain forest allows customers to dine in
unique surroundings while enjoying a variety of dishes, many
inspired by tropical ingredients.

RAINFOREST CAFE
crab cakes

BROILED CRAB CAKES, MADE WITH LUMP CRABMEAT AND GARNISHED WITH
LEMON-BUTTER SAUCE.

Juice of ½ lemon
1 tablespoon Worcestershire sauce
3 egg yolks
½ teaspoon dry mustard
½ teaspoon black pepper
Pinch of red pepper flakes
Pinch of Old Bay seasoning

Pinch of salt
3 tablespoons mayonnaise
1 cup fresh bread crumbs
¼ cup finely chopped fresh parsley
1 pound lump crabmeat
Olive oil, for sautéing

1. Mix together the lemon juice, Worcestershire sauce, egg yolks, mustard, black pepper, red pepper flakes, Old Bay seasoning, salt, and mayonnaise in a large bowl.
2. Add the bread crumbs and parsley and mix well.
3. Pick over the crabmeat for any bits of shell. Add the crabmeat to the breading mixture and mix in lightly. Leave some chunks in the crabmeat.
4. Make into four 3-inch patties and sauté in the olive oil for 2 to 3 minutes on each side, until brown.

Makes 4 crab cakes

Use fresh crabmeat for the best flavor!

RAINFOREST CAFE
safari sauce

A WONDERFUL CREAMY MANGO CHUTNEY–BASED HONEY MUSTARD SAUCE TO COMPLEMENT YOUR SANDWICHES WITH A BIT OF A KICK.

One 8-ounce jar mango chutney
1 cup mayonnaise
½ cup yellow mustard

½ cup honey
2 teaspoons curry powder
Dash of Tabasco sauce

1. Spoon the chutney into a medium bowl and cut up any large chunks of fruit in the chutney.
2. With a wire whisk, blend in the mayonnaise. Add the mustard, honey, curry powder, and Tabasco sauce. Blend until thoroughly combined.
3. Spoon into three 8-ounce jars and seal with lids. Store the sauce in the refrigerator for up to 4 weeks.

Makes 3 cups

RED LOBSTER
batter-fried shrimp

SHRIMP COATED IN A MILDLY SEASONED BATTER AND DEEP-FRIED UNTIL GOLDEN.

Vegetable oil, for deep-frying
½ cup oil
1 egg, beaten
1 cup all-purpose flour
½ cup milk
¾ teaspoon seasoned salt
¼ teaspoon salt
1½ pounds medium shrimp, peeled
   and deveined

1. Preheat the oil to 350°F in a deep-fryer.
2. In a large bowl, combine the ½ cup oil and the egg; beat well.
3. Add the remaining ingredients except the shrimp and stir until well blended.
4. Dip the shrimp into the batter to coat. Drop the shrimp carefully into the hot oil and deep-fry for 30 to 60 seconds, until golden brown. Remove with a slotted spoon; drain on paper towels.

Serves 6

In 1968 Bill Darden opened the first Red Lobster in Lakeland, Florida. By the early 1970s, the company had expanded throughout the southeastern United States and was becoming a leader in seafood and casual dining. The chain continues to grow and today has more than 680 restaurants.

RED LOBSTER
caesar dressing

A PERFECT DRESSING—CREAMY WITH A ZESTY FLAVOR.

¼ cup mayonnaise
¼ cup Hidden Valley ranch
dressing
¼ cup Wish-Bone Italian dressing

1 tablespoon white vinegar
1 tablespoon water
1 teaspoon anchovy paste
2 tablespoons sour cream

1. Combine the mayonnaise, ranch and Italian dressings, vinegar, and water with a wire whisk until perfectly smooth and creamy.
2. Add the anchovy paste and the sour cream and whisk to blend.
3. Refrigerate the dressing tightly covered; it will keep for up to 1 month.

Serves 2 to 4

Anchovy paste is made primarily of anchovies, vinegar, spices, and water.

RED LOBSTER
cajun shrimp linguine

SPICY SHRIMP TOSSED IN A GARLIC-PARMESAN CREAM SAUCE, SERVED ON LINGUINE.

1 pound medium shrimp, peeled and deveined
⅛ teaspoon cayenne pepper
Salt and black pepper
½ teaspoon dried thyme (crushed)
1 pound linguine
2 tablespoons butter
2 tablespoons olive oil
1 medium white onion, chopped

4 cloves garlic, finely chopped
⅛ to ¼ teaspoon red pepper flakes
2 tablespoons tomato paste
½ cup heavy cream
¾ cup grated Parmesan cheese
Pinch of sugar
½ cup chopped fresh Italian parsley
Half a lemon

1. Place the shrimp in a small bowl. Dust with the cayenne, salt and black pepper, and thyme. Toss and let sit.
2. Boil the pasta in salted water until al dente. Drain, reserving some of the pasta water.
3. While the pasta is boiling, melt the butter in a large, heavy skillet with the olive oil over medium heat.
4. Sauté the onion until soft, 3 to 4 minutes.
5. Add the chopped garlic and red pepper flakes. Stir for 30 seconds and do not let the garlic burn.
6. Add the tomato paste, heavy cream, Parmesan, and a small pinch of sugar. Stir and continue to cook until blended.
7. Add the shrimp and cook for 2 minutes.
8. Add the pasta and toss; the reserved pasta water may be added to moisten if necessary.
9. Allow the shrimp to finish cooking another 1 to 2 minutes. Do not overcook. Add the parsley. Season to taste with additional salt and pepper, if desired. Remove from the heat, squeeze the lemon over, and serve.

Serves 4

RED LOBSTER
cheddar biscuits

LIGHT, AIRY, AND TASTY GARLIC-CHEESE BISCUITS.

2 cups biscuit mix
½ cup shredded mild Cheddar
  cheese
⅔ cup milk

4 tablespoons (½ stick) butter
¼ teaspoon garlic powder
Parsley flakes, for sprinkling

1. Preheat the oven to 450°F.
2. Stir together the biscuit mix, Cheddar, and milk until a soft dough forms. Beat with a wooden spoon for about 30 seconds.
3. Spoon onto a greased cookie sheet. Smooth down the tops to prevent hard points from forming.
4. Bake for 8 to 10 minutes, until the tops are brown.
5. While the biscuits are baking, melt the butter in a pan and stir in the garlic powder.
6. Once the biscuits are done, brush the butter on the tops, sprinkle with parsley flakes, and serve hot.

Makes 10 biscuits

RED LOBSTER
clam chowder

CLAMS AND POTATOES IN A THICK, CREAMY BROTH.

4 cups clam juice
1¾ cups chicken broth
1 cup nonfat dry milk
⅔ cup all-purpose flour
2 ribs celery, finely chopped
1 tablespoon onion flakes

One 10-ounce can clams, drained
Pinch of parsley flakes
2 medium baked potatoes, peeled
   and diced

Salt and pepper
½ cup heavy cream

1. In a blender, combine the clam juice, broth, dry milk, and flour.
2. Pour into a 2½-quart saucepan and simmer, stirring constantly, over medium-high heat until the mixture is thick and smooth.
3. Reduce the heat to low; stir in the celery, onion flakes, clams, parsley flakes, and potatoes.
4. Simmer for 15 to 20 minutes, until the potatoes are tender, then season with salt and pepper to taste. Add the cream and stir into the soup.

Serves 6

Leftover baked or steamed potatoes work well in this recipe.

RED LOBSTER
deep-fried catfish

CATFISH WITH A CORNMEAL COATING AND MILD SEASONINGS, DEEP-FRIED
UNTIL GOLDEN.

Four 8-ounce catfish fillets
1 cup milk
1/8 teaspoon salt
1/8 teaspoon pepper

1/8 teaspoon paprika
1 cup cornmeal
Vegetable oil

1. Rinse the catfish and pat dry.
2. In a shallow dish, mix together the milk, salt, pepper, and paprika.
3. Dip the fillets in the milk mixture. Roll the fish in the cornmeal and set the fillets on waxed paper.
4. Preheat almost 2 inches of the vegetable oil to 350°F in a heavy skillet.
5. Deep-fry the fish, turning once, until golden. Drain on paper towels.

Serves 4

Try this coating on other types of fish fillets.

RED LOBSTER
dungeness crab bisque

ALASKAN DUNGENESS CRABMEAT IN A CREAMY CHICKEN BROTH.

1 tablespoon minced onion
2 tablespoons butter or margarine
2 tablespoons all-purpose flour
2 cups chicken broth
2 cups half-and-half

1 pound Alaska Dungeness
  crabmeat
Salt and pepper
Chopped fresh parsley, for garnish

1. Sauté the onion in the butter until soft. Add the flour; cook, stirring, for 1 minute.
2. Slowly stir in the chicken broth and half-and-half; cook, stirring, for 5 minutes.
3. Break the crab into chunks; add to the broth.
4. Heat thoroughly and add salt and pepper to taste. Garnish with parsley.

Serves 4

Dungeness crab is high in protein and minerals and low in fat.

RED LOBSTER
fried chicken tenders

LIGHTLY FLOURED AND FRIED TO A GOLDEN BROWN. SERVE WITH HONEY MUSTARD.

Marinade
6 cloves garlic
2 cups buttermilk
1 ¼ teaspoons ground cumin
½ teaspoon salt
½ teaspoon black pepper
¼ teaspoon cayenne pepper
4 to 6 boneless, skinless chicken breasts, cut into strips

Coating
1 ½ cups all-purpose flour
1 ¾ teaspoons salt
1 ½ teaspoons black pepper
½ teaspoon ground cumin
1 teaspoon cayenne pepper

Safflower oil, for deep-frying

1. To marinate the chicken, smash and chop the garlic. Put the garlic in a medium bowl.
2. Add the buttermilk, cumin, salt, black pepper, and cayenne pepper and whisk.
3. Place the chicken strips in a 13 by 9-inch glass baking dish. Pour the buttermilk mixture over; turn the chicken to coat. Cover and refrigerate overnight, turning occasionally.
4. Place a rack over a baking sheet. Remove the chicken from the marinade and set on the rack. Drain for 10 minutes.
5. To coat the chicken, mix the flour, salt, black pepper, cumin, and cayenne pepper in a large bowl.
6. Toss the chicken strips in batches in the flour mixture, turning to coat; shake off the excess. Toss each piece again in the flour mixture; shake off the excess. Transfer the chicken to a rack on a baking sheet. Let stand for at least 15 minutes and up to 45 minutes.
7. Line the baking sheet with paper towels. Pour the oil into a large, heavy skillet to a depth of ¾ inch. Preheat the oil over high heat to 375°F.
8. Add the chicken strips to the skillet. Adjust the heat so that the oil

temperature remains between 340° and 350°F. Fry until the chicken is golden and cooked through, about 10 minutes.

9. Using tongs, transfer the chicken to the prepared sheet and drain. Transfer the chicken to a platter and serve.

Serves 4 to 6

Serve with mashed potatoes and broccoli for a complete kids' meal.

RED LOBSTER

grouper siciliano

BAKED GROUPER FILLETS COATED IN ITALIAN-STYLE BREAD CRUMBS.

2 pounds skinless grouper fillets

8 tablespoons (1 stick) butter

1 clove garlic, crushed

2 cups Italian bread crumbs

1. Preheat the oven to 450°F.
2. Cut the fillets into serving-sized pieces.
3. In a shallow saucepan, melt the butter; add the garlic.
4. Combine the garlic butter with the bread crumbs.
5. Dip the fish in the crumb mixture. Place on a baking sheet.
6. Bake for 10 minutes per inch of thickness or until the fish flakes easily when tested with a fork.

Serves 4 to 6

RED LOBSTER
hush puppies

A SOUTHERN FAVORITE—CORNMEAL HUSH PUPPIES, SIMPLY SEASONED AND DEEP-FRIED UNTIL GOLDEN.

1 cup cornmeal
2 teaspoons baking powder
½ teaspoon salt
¼ teaspoon black pepper
⅛ teaspoon white pepper

⅓ cup minced onion
1 egg, beaten
¼ cup milk
Vegetable oil, for deep-frying

1. Mix the cornmeal with the baking powder, salt, black pepper, white pepper, and onion.
2. Mix the egg with the milk and whisk into the cornmeal mixture.
3. Preheat the oil to 350°F in a deep-fryer.
4. Drop spoonfuls of the batter carefully into the hot oil and deep-fry the hush puppies until golden brown.

Serves 2

RED LOBSTER
lobster fondue

A CREAMY LOBSTER-CHEESE SAUCE TRADITIONALLY SERVED IN A WARM AND CRISPY SOURDOUGH BREAD BOWL. GREAT FOR DIPPING WITH SHRIMP, SWEET CRABMEAT, AND LOBSTER.

1 pound Velveeta, cubed
1/2 cup milk
1/2 teaspoon cayenne pepper
1/2 teaspoon paprika

Meat of 1 boiled lobster tail, shredded
1/2 cup chopped red bell pepper
2 tablespoons minced fresh parsley

1. Combine all the ingredients except the red pepper and parsley in a saucepan.
2. Heat over medium-low heat, stirring constantly, until the cheese has melted.
3. When ready to serve, garnish with the red pepper and parsley.

Serves 8

RED LOBSTER
shrimp diablo

BAKED SHRIMP INFUSED WITH THE SPICINESS OF BARBECUE SAUCE AND
TABASCO FOR THAT ADDED KICK.

3 pounds large shrimp, unpeeled	¼ cup Tabasco sauce
Milk for soaking	½ cup ketchup
One 18-ounce jar Kraft barbecue sauce (or your favorite brand)	1 tablespoon pepper

1. Wash the shrimp in cool water and remove the heads if needed.
2. Soak the shrimp in the milk overnight.
3. Mix the barbecue and Tabasco, ketchup, and pepper in a saucepan and stir until boiling.
4. Remove from the heat and refrigerate for at least 4 hours, for the flavors to meld.
5. Drain the milk from the shrimp, place the shrimp in a baking pan, and cover evenly with the chilled sauce. Let stand for 1 hour.
6. Preheat the oven to 450°F.
7. Bake the shrimp, uncovered, for 15 minutes (less time for smaller shrimp), until hot and bubbly.

Serves 6

This spicy meal goes great with your favorite pasta dish.
   Increase the amount of Tabasco sauce to your desired taste for an extra kick.

RED LOBSTER

south beach seafood paella

A SPANISH DISH OF SHRIMP, SAUSAGE, FISH, AND MUSSELS COMBINED WITH RICE AND VEGETABLES.

Vegetable Sauté (*Sofrito*)
3 tablespoons olive oil
1 cup minced onions
1 small red bell pepper, cut into ½-inch pieces
1 small green bell pepper, cut into ½-inch pieces
1 cup canned diced tomatoes, drained
1 tablespoon minced garlic
1 tablespoon minced fresh thyme

Seafood and Sausage
1 pound fish (grouper, scrod, haddock, halibut, or swordfish), skinless, cut into 1-inch chunks
12 large or jumbo shrimp, peeled and deveined, leaving tails intact

1 pound sea scallops
Sea salt and pepper
3 tablespoons olive oil
16 mussels, debearded and scrubbed
6 ounces andouille sausage, cut into ½-inch-thick pieces
½ cup dry white wine

3 cups long-grain rice
1 teaspoon saffron threads
3 cups hot chicken broth
3 cups hot clam juice
Sea salt and pepper
8 ounces sugar snap peas
1 medium red bell pepper, cut into long, ½-inch-wide strips
Chopped fresh parsley, for garnish

1. To make the *sofrito*, in a heavy 12-inch skillet, heat the olive oil over medium heat until hot.
2. Add the onions and red and green peppers, and cook, stirring, for 5 minutes, until the peppers are soft and the onions are translucent.
3. Add the tomatoes, garlic, and thyme. Cook, stirring, for 5 minutes more, until most of the liquid in the pan has evaporated and the mixture is thick.
4. Set the *sofrito* aside.
5. For the seafood and sausage, season the fish, shrimp, and scallops with salt and pepper.

6. In a skillet, heat the olive oil over medium-high heat until hot.
7. Add the fish, shrimp, and scallops, as well as the mussels, and sauté for 3 to 5 minutes.
8. Add the sausage and cook until light brown, about 3 minutes.
9. Transfer to a plate and deglaze the pan with the wine.
10. To assemble the paella, about 30 minutes before you plan to serve the paella, preheat the oven to 400°F.
11. In a 14-inch paella pan or a shallow casserole at least 14 inches in diameter, combine the *sofrito,* rice, and saffron.
12. Pour in the hot chicken broth and 2 cups of the hot clam juice. Stirring constantly, bring the mixture to a boil over high heat.
13. Remove the pan from the heat immediately and season with salt and pepper.
14. Arrange the seafood and sausage on top of the rice.
15. Set the pan on the lowest shelf in the oven and bake, uncovered, for 20 minutes. Do not stir the paella once it goes in the oven.
16. Sprinkle the sugar snap peas and the red pepper strips over the whole paella, and bake for 5 minutes more or until all of the liquid has been absorbed by the rice and the grains are tender but not too soft. If the rice needs to be softer, add the remaining 1 cup clam juice and bake for another 5 minutes.
17. Remove the paella from the oven and let stand for 5 minutes before serving. Garnish with parsley.

Serves 4 to 6

RED LOBSTER
trout veracruz

BAKED TROUT COVERED IN A MEDLEY OF OLIVES, ONION, BELL PEPPER, AND
TOMATOES IN AN OLIVE OIL–WINE MARINADE SAUCE.

Marinade
¼ cup sliced black olives
¼ cup sliced green olives
½ cup olive oil
½ cup white wine
1 teaspoon dried oregano
½ cup chopped onion

½ cup chopped green bell pepper
½ cup chopped tomato

2 trout fillets with skin on
4 tablespoons (½ stick) butter,
   melted
Salt and pepper

1. Preheat the oven to 350°F.
2. Mix together all the marinade ingredients and let sit for 10 minutes.
3. Brush the trout with the butter, season with salt and pepper, and place in
   a baking pan.
4. Pour the marinade over the fish and bake for 20 to 25 minutes, until the
   fish is lightly golden and flakes easily.

Serves 2

ROADHOUSE GRILL
roast beef and mashed potatoes

TENDER SLICES OF ROAST BEEF SMOTHERED IN A RICH GRAVY, SERVED WITH
MASHED POTATOES FLAVORED WITH A HINT OF GARLIC.

Mashed Potatoes
1⅓ pounds potatoes
1 cup low-fat milk, plus extra as
needed
2 tablespoons butter or margarine
3 cloves garlic, minced
Salt and pepper

Roast Beef and Gravy
One 10.25-ounce can beef gravy
1 teaspoon dried thyme
⅛ teaspoon pepper
12 ounces sliced deli roast beef

1. To make the mashed potatoes, pierce the potatoes with a fork; micro-wave on high for about 12 minutes, until the potatoes are tender.
2. When cool enough to handle, halve the potatoes lengthwise; scoop the pulp into a medium microwave-safe bowl. Mash the potatoes with a potato masher or beat with an electric hand-mixer; reserve.
3. Place the milk, butter, and garlic in a small microwave-safe bowl. Microwave on high for 2 minutes; thoroughly mix into the mashed potatoes.
4. Mix in additional milk, if necessary, to reach the desired consistency.
5. Season the mashed potatoes with salt and pepper to taste. Microwave on high for 1 to 2 minutes, until hot.
6. Meanwhile, prepare the roast beef and gravy. In a 2-quart saucepan, combine the gravy, thyme, and pepper; bring to a simmer over medium heat.
7. Add the beef slices and heat through. Serve the beef and gravy with the mashed potatoes.

Serves 2 to 4

Use instant mashed potatoes for this recipe. Slice leftover roast beef, add gravy, and freeze in portions for quick meals like this.

The Roadhouse Grill offers a fun, value-oriented dining experience that features premium-quality grilled entrées and friendly service consistent with the company's motto, "Good Food and a Smile . . . That's Roadhouse Style!" The first Roadhouse was opened in 1993 in Pembrooke Pines, Florida, by J. David Toole III and John Y. Brown, Jr.

RUBY TUESDAY
chicken quesadillas

GRILLED MARINATED CHICKEN TOPPED WITH CHEESE, TOMATO, PEPPER, AND
CAJUN SEASONING, FOLDED INTO A FLOUR TORTILLA.

6 ounces boneless, skinless chicken
breasts
Italian dressing, for coating
One 12-inch flour tortilla
Margarine, melted, for coating
1 cup shredded Monterey Jack or
Cheddar cheese
1 tablespoon diced tomato

1 tablespoon diced jalapeño
pepper
Cajun seasoning
Shredded lettuce
Diced tomato
Sour cream (regular or low-fat)
Salsa

1. Place the chicken in a bowl with enough Italian dressing to coat all sides;
   allow to marinate for 30 minutes in the refrigerator.
2. Grill the marinated chicken for 10 to 12 minutes, until no longer pink,
   on a lightly oiled griddle. Cut into ¾-inch cubes and set aside.
3. Brush one side of the tortilla with the melted margarine and place,
   brushed side down, in a skillet over medium heat.
4. In the following order, top one half of the tortilla with the cheese,
   tomato, pepper, and Cajun seasoning to taste. Spread evenly and then
   top with the cubed chicken. Fold over the empty tortilla side to close,
   then flip the quesadilla over in the pan so that the cheese is on top of the
   chicken. Cook until the cheese melts.
5. Remove the quesadilla from the pan to a serving plate and cut into
   6 equal wedges. Serve with lettuce, tomato, sour cream, and salsa on the
   side of the same plate.

Serves 3

Guacamole is another great topping for this recipe.

This restaurant was founded in 1972, when Sandy Beall and four of his fraternity buddies from the University of Tennessee opened the first Ruby Tuesday adjacent to the college campus in Knoxville. Today, the chain is one of three large public companies that dominate the bar-and-grill category of casual dining.

RUBY TUESDAY
shrimp pasta parmesan

A LITTLE ITALIAN AND A LOT DELICIOUS—PENNE PASTA IS PERFECT HERE WITH
A CREAMY SAUCE AND PLENTY OF SPICY SHRIMP.

2 tablespoons olive oil
1 teaspoon dried oregano
½ teaspoon salt
Black pepper
14 to 16 large shrimp, peeled and deveined
4 tablespoons (½ stick) butter
1 pound cremini mushrooms, sliced (optional)
1 large onion, finely chopped
¼ teaspoon red pepper flakes
1 tablespoon chopped fresh thyme
1 large tomato, chopped (skin the tomato, halve it, and squeeze the seeds out before chopping)

3 cloves garlic, minced
½ cup dry white wine
⅓ cup all-purpose flour
4 cups milk
1 cup heavy cream
1 cup chicken or vegetable broth
⅛ teaspoon ground nutmeg
One 16-ounce box pasta (penne, rigatoni, or fettuccine)
⅓ cup grated Parmigiano-Reggiano cheese

1. In a small bowl, mix together 1 tablespoon of the oil, the oregano, the ½ teaspoon salt, and black pepper to taste. Brush the mixture over the shrimp.
2. Preheat a griddle on medium-high. Add the shrimp and sear for about 2 minutes per side, until bright pink. Transfer to a medium bowl.
3. Melt 1 tablespoon of the butter in the remaining 1 tablespoon olive oil in a sauté pan. Add the mushrooms, if desired, and sauté over medium-high heat until the liquid from the mushrooms evaporates.
4. Add the onion, red pepper flakes, and thyme, and sauté until the onion is clear, about 8 minutes.
5. Add the chopped tomato and garlic, sauté for 2 minutes, then add the wine and simmer for 2 minutes more or until the liquid evaporates. Transfer the mushroom-tomato mixture to the bowl with the shrimp.

6. Melt the remaining 3 tablespoons butter in the same pan over medium-low heat. Using a wire whisk, add the flour and whisk for 2 minutes or until blended. Whisk in the milk, cream, broth, and nutmeg.
7. Increase the heat to high while stirring to prevent scorching. Reduce the heat to low and adjust the seasoning. Simmer, uncovered, whisking often, until the sauce thickens, about 15 minutes.
8. Meanwhile, cook the pasta until al dente. Drain and toss with the sauce. Remove the pasta with the sauce from the stove and add the shrimp mixture. Add the grated Parmigiano-Reggiano and toss before serving.

Serves 4 to 6

RUBY TUESDAY
sonoran chicken pasta

PASTA TOSSED IN A SPICY SOUTHWESTERN CHEESE SAUCE AND TOPPED WITH BAKED CHICKEN AND BLACK BEANS. ACCENTED WITH TOMATO AND GREEN ONION.

Sonoran Cheese Sauce

6 tablespoons (¾ stick) butter or margarine
½ cup finely chopped onion
1 small clove garlic, minced
1 jalapeño pepper, seeded and minced (use half for a less spicy dish)
⅓ cup all-purpose flour
1 cup hot water
1 tablespoon chicken bouillon powder
1 cup half-and-half
½ teaspoon salt
½ teaspoon sugar
¼ teaspoon Tabasco sauce

1 teaspoon lemon juice
¼ teaspoon cayenne pepper
¾ cup shredded Parmesan cheese
¾ cup Velveeta, cubed
¾ cup salsa
½ cup sour cream

10 ounces cooked penne pasta
6 ounces boneless, skinless chicken breasts, grilled and cut into ¼-inch-thick slices
⅓ cup prepared black beans (canned is fine)
¼ cup diced tomato
1 teaspoon chopped green onion

1. To make the Sonoran cheese sauce, melt the butter in a large saucepan and add the onion, garlic, and jalapeño.
2. Sauté until the onion is translucent.
3. Stir in the flour to make a roux and cook, stirring often, for 5 minutes.
4. Mix together the hot water, chicken bouillon powder, and half-and-half.
5. Add the mixture slowly to the roux, stirring constantly.
6. Allow the sauce to cook for about 5 minutes (it should have the consistency of honey). Add the salt, sugar, Tabasco sauce, lemon juice, cayenne pepper, and Parmesan cheese. Stir to blend. Do not allow to boil. Add the Velveeta and stir until melted. Add the salsa and sour cream and stir to blend.

7. To assemble the pasta, place the cooked penne in a medium bowl. Add ¾ cup of the cheese sauce and toss to coat evenly. Pour into a large serving bowl. Place the sliced chicken on top of the pasta, then ladle the black beans over. Sprinkle with the diced tomato and chopped green onion.

Serves 4

Using a ridge pasta such as penne or rigatoni will allow the sauce to stick to the surfaces of the pasta.

RUBY TUESDAY
super salad bar pasta

ROTINI SALAD WITH BROCCOLI, HAM, AND CHICKEN, TOSSED WITH A CREAMY
BLENDED RANCH DRESSING.

One 16-ounce box rotini pasta
3 cups diced cooked chicken
1 cup mayonnaise
One 10-ounce bag frozen broccoli
  florets, thawed
2 cups diced or shredded deli ham
½ cup regular or fat-free ranch
  dressing

1 cup regular or fat-free sour
  cream
2 teaspoons garlic salt
1 teaspoon pepper
Chopped fresh parsley, for
  garnish

1. Cook the pasta in a large pot over medium-high heat for 10 minutes or
   until tender. Drain and cool with running water. Place one half of the
   pasta in a large serving dish.
2. Add 1½ cups of the chicken to the pasta, and then add the mayonnaise,
   one half of the broccoli, 1 cup of the ham, and the ranch dressing. Stir
   well.
3. Place the remaining pasta in the dish and add the remaining 1½ cups
   chicken and 1 cup ham. Add the sour cream and the remaining broccoli.
   Stir in the garlic salt and pepper.
4. Toss the pasta until completely combined.
5. Add the parsley for garnish.

Serves 8

RUTH'S CHRIS STEAK HOUSE
barbecued shrimp

FLAVORED NEW ORLEANS–STYLE IN REDUCED WHITE WINE, BUTTER, GARLIC, AND ROSEMARY.

4 tablespoons (½ stick) butter, melted
1 tablespoon Tabasco sauce
2 cloves garlic, chopped
¼ teaspoon salt
½ teaspoon pepper
½ teaspoon finely chopped fresh parsley

Dash of dried rosemary
¼ cup white wine
6 extra-large shrimp, peeled and deveined, leaving tails intact
1 lemon

1. Preheat the oven to 400°F.
2. In a shallow baking dish, combine the melted butter, Tabasco sauce, garlic, salt, pepper, parsley, rosemary, wine, and shrimp. Stir until evenly combined.
3. Place the shrimp next to one another in the bottom of the dish and bake for about 8 minutes.
4. Immediately change the oven setting to broil and cook the shrimp for about 2 minutes more, until hot and bubbly.
5. Squeeze some fresh lemon juice over the shrimp and serve.

Serves 1 or 2

This restaurant is famous for its signature steaks—seared to perfection and topped with fresh butter so they sizzle all the way to your table.

SHONEY'S

marinated mushrooms

WHOLE AND SLICED FRESH MUSHROOMS MARINATED IN A BEEF BROTH–BASED, ITALIAN-SEASONED DRESSING.

1 pound mushrooms, whole
1 pound mushrooms, sliced
One 14-ounce can beef broth
½ cup store-bought Italian dressing

½ cup olive oil
2 teaspoons salt
1 teaspoon pepper

1. Combine the mushrooms, broth, Italian dressing, oil, salt, and pepper in a large bowl.
2. Cover with plastic wrap.
3. Refrigerate for 24 hours before serving.

Serves 4 to 6

You can replace the beef broth with ½ cup red wine vinegar.

Shoney's started as a drive-in restaurant called Parkette in Charleston, West Virginia, in 1947. It acquired a Big Boy franchise in 1951 and was renamed the Parkette Shoney's Big Boy in 1953. By 1972, Big Boy was dropped from the name.

SHONEY'S

pot roast

EASY TO PREPARE, AND EVEN KIDS LOVE IT!

3 pounds rump roast, trimmed of fat
2 tablespoons butter or margarine
2 ribs celery, chopped
1 large onion, chopped
3 cloves garlic, minced
1/2 teaspoon parsley flakes
1 1/2 teaspoons dried thyme
2 cups beef broth

20 peppercorns
1 bay leaf
1 1/2 teaspoons salt
2 medium carrots, sliced
2 medium potatoes, peeled and cubed
1/2 teaspoon salt
1/3 cup all-purpose flour

1. Preheat the oven to 325°F.
2. Brown the roast in the butter in an ovenproof Dutch oven, then remove the meat and set aside.
3. Sauté the celery, onion, garlic, parsley flakes, and thyme in the Dutch oven for 5 minutes, then return the meat to the pot.
4. Add 1 cup of the beef broth, the peppercorns, bay leaf, and salt to the Dutch oven and bake, covered, for 4 hours, basting every 30 minutes.
5. Remove the roast from the pot. Do not turn off the oven.
6. Strain the broth into a bowl and set aside; discard the vegetables.
7. Using two forks, shred the roast into bite-size pieces and return to the Dutch oven.
8. Pour the reserved broth over the beef, then add the carrots, potatoes, and salt.
9. Bake for 45 minutes. Remove from the oven.
10. Drain the broth from the Dutch oven into a saucepan. Add the remaining cup of beef broth. There should be 3 cups of stock. Transfer the meat and vegetables to a serving plate.
11. Whisk the flour into the broth in the saucepan and simmer until thick.
12. Pour the gravy over the meat and vegetables and serve.

Serves 8

Use a slow cooker for this recipe. Cook on low for 6 to 8 hours, or on high for 3 to 4 hours, until the meat is brown and tender.

SHONEY'S
tomato florentine soup

A TOMATO-CHICKEN SOUP WITH CHOPPED SPINACH.

Two 14-ounce cans chicken
broth
One 14.5-ounce can sliced
stewed tomatoes, with juice
1½ cups V8 juice
One 10.5-ounce can cream of
tomato soup

One 10-ounce box frozen
chopped spinach
1 tablespoon sugar
Pinch of ground nutmeg
½ teaspoon salt
½ teaspoon pepper

1. With a wire whisk, combine the broth, tomatoes, V8 juice, and soup in a saucepan over medium heat.
2. Add the remaining ingredients, without thawing the spinach.
3. Reduce the heat to medium-low and allow the soup to cook gently for 30 minutes or until the spinach is tender. Keep hot without letting the soup boil.

Serves 6

THE SOUP NAZI
crab bisque

A SLIGHTLY THICKENED HERB-INFUSED CRAB SOUP WITH POTATOES AND REFRIED BEANS.

4 pounds snow crab clusters (legs)
2 quarts water
2 quarts chicken broth
1 small onion, chopped
1½ ribs celery, chopped
2 cloves garlic, quartered
2 medium potatoes, peeled and chopped
¼ cup chopped fresh parsley
2 teaspoons dry mustard
1 tablespoon chopped canned pimiento

One 16-ounce can refried beans
½ teaspoon pepper
2 bay leaves
⅓ cup tomato sauce
¼ cup heavy cream
4 tablespoons (½ stick) butter
¼ teaspoon dried thyme
⅛ teaspoon dried basil
2 tablespoons Old Bay seasoning

1. Remove all the crabmeat from the shells and set it aside.
2. Discard one half of the shells and put the remainder into a large pot with the water and chicken broth over high heat. Add the onion, two thirds of the chopped celery, and the garlic, then bring the mixture to a boil. Continue to boil for 1 hour, stirring occasionally, then strain the broth. Discard the shells, onion, celery, and garlic, keeping only the broth.
3. Measure 3 quarts of the broth into a large saucepan or pot. Add water if there's not enough broth to measure 3 quarts.
4. Add the potatoes and bring the mixture to a boil; then add one half of the crabmeat and all the remaining ingredients, including the remainder of the chopped celery, to the saucepan and bring the mixture back to a boil. Reduce the heat and simmer, uncovered, for 4 hours or until the soup reduces by about half and starts to thicken. Add the remaining crabmeat and simmer for another hour or until the soup is very thick.

5. Refrigerate overnight—it's better the next day! Reheat and remove the bay leaves before serving.

Serves 4 to 6

Curly-leaf parsley and flat-leaf Italian parsley are used interchangeably in recipes.

You remember the rules: Pick the soup you want, have your money ready, and move to the extreme left after ordering, or else *no soup for you!* The Soup Nazi was a character made famous on the popular sitcom *Seinfeld.* The soup was said to be so good that customers were willing to follow the Soup Nazi's strict rules.

The original company—Soup Kitchen International, located in New York City—received a lot of publicity from the show. Its 1984 founder, Al Yeganeh, has now launched The Original SoupMan restaurants and is offering franchising opportunities worldwide.

THE SOUP NAZI

cream of sweet potato soup

A SPICY SOUP WITH SWEET POTATOES AND CASHEWS.

4 small sweet potatoes (about
  1 pound)
4 cups chicken broth
4 cups water
6 tablespoons melted butter
½ cup tomato sauce
3 tablespoons half-and-half
1 teaspoon salt
⅛ teaspoon pepper
2 tablespoons dried thyme
1 cup split cashews

¼ cup diced canned pimiento
1 jalapeño pepper, diced
¼ cup chopped fresh Italian
  parsley
2 teaspoons chili powder
2 teaspoons dried basil
2 teaspoons dried oregano
1 clove garlic, minced
2 teaspoons ground cumin
¼ teaspoon salt
Pinch of cayenne pepper

1. Preheat the oven to 375°F.
2. Bake the sweet potatoes for 45 minutes or until they are soft. Let the potatoes cool before handling.
3. Peel away the skins, then put the sweet potatoes into a large bowl. Mash the sweet potatoes for 15 to 20 seconds, until nearly smooth.
4. Spoon the mashed sweet potatoes into a large saucepan over medium-high heat, add the remaining ingredients, and stir to combine.
5. Once the soup begins to boil, reduce the heat and simmer for 1 hour or until the soup has thickened a bit. Serve and enjoy.

Serves 6 to 8

THE SOUP NAZI
indian mulligatawny soup

A SPICY VEGETABLE SOUP WITH PISTACHIOS AND ROASTED CASHEWS.

4 quarts water
6 cups chicken broth
2 medium potatoes, peeled and sliced
2 medium carrots, sliced
2 ribs celery, with tops
½ eggplant, peeled and diced
1 medium onion, chopped
1 cup frozen corn kernels
⅔ cup diced roasted red bell pepper
½ cup tomato sauce

½ cup shelled pistachios
½ cup salted roasted cashews
½ cup chopped fresh Italian parsley
¼ cup lemon juice
3 tablespoons sugar
½ teaspoon curry powder
½ teaspoon pepper
¼ teaspoon dried thyme
Pinch of dried marjoram
Pinch ground nutmeg
1 bay leaf

1. Using a food processor, puree all the ingredients except the bay leaf. It's okay if there are small chunks left. You can do this in batches.
2. Transfer the ingredients to a large pot over high heat.
3. Bring to a boil, add the bay leaf, then reduce the heat and simmer, uncovered, for 5 to 6 hours, until the soup has reduced by more than half and is thick. Stir several times throughout the cooking (and more frequently as it becomes thicker).
4. Refrigerate overnight and reheat before serving. Remove the bay leaf before serving.

Serves 4 to 6

Mulligatawny literally means "pepper water."

THE SOUP NAZI
mexican chicken chili

A THICK CHICKEN BROTH–BASED SOUP WITH CHICKEN BREAST FILLETS, VEGE-
TABLES, AND KIDNEY BEANS. COMBINE SOME CHOPPED ITALIAN PARSLEY WITH
SOUR CREAM TO SERVE AS A GARNISH.

1 tablespoon olive oil	½ cup tomato sauce
4 boneless, skinless chicken breasts	1 cup frozen corn kernels
1 medium potato, peeled and chopped	½ medium carrot, sliced
	1 rib celery, diced
1 small onion, diced	1 cup canned diced tomatoes
10 cups water	One 15-ounce can red kidney
2 cups chicken broth	beans, undrained

1. Pour the olive oil into a large pot and sauté the chicken in the olive oil over medium-high heat. Cook the chicken on both sides until done, about 8 minutes per side. Let the chicken cool until it can be handled. Do not rinse the pot.
2. Break the chicken up into small pieces by hand, placing the pieces back in the pot.
3. Add the remaining ingredients to the pot and bring the mixture to a boil over high heat. Reduce the heat and simmer, stirring often, for 4 to 5 hours (the longer, the better). The chili will thicken and get browner as it cooks.

Serves 4 to 6

STARBUCKS
chocolate fudge squares with mocha glaze

CHOCOLATE, COFFEE, NUTS—DELICIOUS!

Fudge Squares
8 tablespoons (1 stick) butter, softened
1 cup granulated sugar
1 egg
1 cup all-purpose flour
¼ teaspoon baking powder
2 ounces unsweetened chocolate, melted
½ cup milk
1 teaspoon vanilla extract
½ cup chopped walnuts

Glaze
1 heaped cup confectioners' sugar
1 tablespoon butter, softened
1 ounce unsweetened chocolate, melted
1 teaspoon vanilla extract
¼ cup brewed double-strength coffee, preferably made from dark-roasted beans

1. Preheat the oven to 350°F. Butter an 8-inch square baking pan.
2. To make the fudge squares, in a large bowl, cream the butter with the granulated sugar and egg.
3. In a small bowl, sift together the flour and baking powder. Add to the butter mixture, then add the melted chocolate. Do not overbeat. Stir in the milk, vanilla, and walnuts, just to blend.
4. Pour the batter into the prepared pan. Bake until the edges begin to pull away from the sides of the pan, about 30 minutes. Transfer the cake to a rack and let cool completely.
5. To make the glaze, in a medium bowl, combine the confectioners' sugar, butter, chocolate, and vanilla with a wire whisk. Stir in the coffee and whisk until smooth.
6. Refrigerate the glaze until cool, then pour over the top of the cake and cut the cake into squares.

Serves 4 to 6

Substitute milk for the coffee if you don't want a mocha-flavored glaze.

In 1971, the first Starbucks opened in Seattle's Pike Place Market. However, it wasn't until Howard Schultz was hired as the head of marketing that Starbucks became the powerhouse chain that it is today. Schultz had the groundbreaking idea to turn each coffeehouse in the United States into a community gathering place, much like the coffeehouses he experienced in Italy. The concept was a winner, and Starbucks soon became the largest coffeehouse company in the world.

STARBUCKS
gingerbread loaf

TRADITIONAL SPICE CAKE TOPPED OFF WITH A DELECTABLE ORANGE-FLAVORED CREAM CHEESE ICING, AND CROWNED WITH CANDIED ORANGE PEEL OR GINGER.

Cake
1½ cups all-purpose flour
2 teaspoons ground cinnamon
1 teaspoon ground cloves
2¼ teaspoons ground ginger
1 teaspoon salt
8 tablespoons (½ stick) butter, softened
1 cup granulated sugar
1 teaspoon orange extract
1 teaspoon baking soda
1 cup applesauce

Frosting
One 8-ounce package cream cheese, softened
1 teaspoon vanilla extract
½ teaspoon orange extract
2½ cups confectioners' sugar

Candied orange peel or candied ginger, for garnish

1. Preheat the oven to 350°F. Grease and flour a 9 by 5-inch loaf pan.
2. To make the cake, in a medium bowl, mix together the flour, cinnamon, cloves, ginger, and salt. Set aside.
3. In a large bowl, cream the butter and granulated sugar until fluffy. Stir in the orange extract.
4. Mix the baking soda into the applesauce and stir into the creamed butter mixture. Add the flour mixture. Mix until smooth in an electric mixer, 2 to 3 minutes.
5. Pour the batter into the prepared loaf pan.
6. Bake for 40 to 50 minutes, until a toothpick inserted in the center of the cake comes out clean. Transfer the cake to a rack and let cool completely.
7. To make the frosting, beat the cream cheese until fluffy. Beat in the vanilla and orange extracts. Slowly beat in the confectioners' sugar.
8. Once the cake has cooled, remove from the pan by placing a large cake plate over the pan and flipping it over. Spread the frosting evenly on top. Decorate with chopped candied orange peel or candied ginger.

Makes 1 loaf

SUBWAY

sweet onion sauce

USE THIS IN A SUB TO DRESS TERIYAKI CHICKEN STRIPS, ALONG WITH LETTUCE, TOMATO, RED ONION, GREEN PEPPER, AND OLIVES.

½ cup light corn syrup
1 tablespoon minced white onion
1 tablespoon red wine vinegar
2 teaspoons white vinegar
1 teaspoon balsamic vinegar
1 teaspoon dark brown sugar

1 teaspoon buttermilk powder
¼ teaspoon lemon juice
⅛ teaspoon poppy seeds
⅛ teaspoon salt
Pinch of cracked pepper
Pinch of garlic powder

1. Combine all the ingredients in a saucepan.
2. Cook, uncovered, over medium-high heat for about 2 minutes, until the mixture comes to a boil.
3. Whisk well and remove from the heat. Cover and let cool. Refrigerate for 30 minutes before serving.

Makes about 1 cup

This tastes great on sandwiches. Store in the refrigerator for up to a month.

Subway is the world's largest submarine-sandwich chain, with more than 30,000 restaurants in 87 countries.

TACO BELL
beef chalupa supreme

A CRISPY, CHEWY CHALUPA SHELL FILLED WITH SEASONED GROUND BEEF, SOUR CREAM, SHREDDED LETTUCE, CHEDDAR AND JACK CHEESE, AND DICED RIPE TOMATO. SERVE WITH RICE AND BEANS.

1 tablespoon onion flakes
½ cup water
1 pound ground beef
¼ cup all-purpose flour
1 tablespoon chili powder
1 teaspoon paprika
1 teaspoon salt
6 round flatbreads (pita bread is fine)

Vegetable oil, for deep-frying
1 cup sour cream
1 cup shredded lettuce
1 cup shredded Cheddar-Jack cheese blend
¼ cup diced tomato
Tabasco sauce or salsa

1. Mix the onion flakes with the water in a small bowl and let sit for 5 minutes.
2. Combine the ground beef, flour, chili powder, paprika, and salt, then stir in the onion and water mixture. In a skillet over medium-high heat, cook the beef. Stir often while cooking, to prevent large chunks from forming; it should be like a paste.
3. Remove from the heat, but keep warm.
4. Preheat 1 inch of oil to 450°F in a deep-fryer or skillet.
5. Deep-fry the breads for 30 seconds. Let drain on paper towels.
6. Assemble the chalupas starting with the meat, then the sour cream, lettuce, cheese, and tomato in that order. Top with Tabasco sauce or salsa, to taste.

Serves 4 to 6

You can easily substitute chicken, turkey, or steak in this recipe.

In 1946, Glen Bell opened a hot dog stand in San Bernardino, California. In 1952 he sold his stand and set about building an improved version. His new menu consisted of hamburgers and hot dogs, and then later, tacos. After choosing a location in a Hispanic neighborhood of San Bernardino, Bell began selling a chili dog from which he eventually developed his traditional taco sauce. He also developed taco shells that could be easily and quickly fried and later stuffed with ingredients. In 1962 this concept officially became the first Taco Bell.

TACO BELL
burrito supreme

A WARM SOFT TORTILLA WRAPPED AROUND SEASONED GROUND BEEF, HEARTY BEANS, TANGY RED SAUCE, SHREDDED LETTUCE, CHEDDAR CHEESE, DICED ONION, DICED TOMATO, AND SOUR CREAM. SERVE WITH SALSA, PICO DE GALLO, OR GUACAMOLE.

1 pound lean ground beef
¼ cup all-purpose flour
1 tablespoon chili powder
1 teaspoon salt
½ teaspoon onion flakes
½ teaspoon paprika
¼ teaspoon onion powder
Dash of garlic powder
½ cup water
One 16-ounce can refried beans

Eight 10-inch flour tortillas
½ cup store-bought enchilada
  sauce
¾ cup sour cream
2 cups shredded lettuce
2 cups shredded Cheddar
  cheese
1 medium tomato, diced
½ cup diced yellow onion

1. In a medium bowl, combine the beef, flour, chili powder, salt, onion flakes, paprika, onion powder, and garlic powder. Thoroughly massage the dry ingredients into the ground beef using your hands.
2. Add the seasoned beef, along with the water, to a skillet over medium heat. Mix well with a wooden spoon or spatula, breaking up the meat as it cooks. Cook for 5 to 6 minutes, until browned.
3. Microwave the refried beans in a microwave-safe container on high for 90 seconds.
4. Place the flour tortillas on a plate and cover with plastic wrap. Heat the tortillas for 30 to 45 seconds in the microwave on high.
5. Assemble each burrito by first spreading about ¼ cup of the refried beans on the center of a heated flour tortilla. Spread one eighth of the meat mixture over the beans, then pour about 1 tablespoon of the enchilada sauce over the meat.
6. Stir the sour cream, then spread about 1½ tablespoons onto the burrito.

Arrange the desired amount of lettuce, cheese, tomato, and onion on the tortilla.

7. Fold the end of the tortilla closest to you over the filling ingredients. Fold either the left or right end over next. Then fold the top edge over the filling, leaving one end of the burrito open and unfolded. Repeat with the remaining ingredients and serve immediately.

Serves 8

Refried beans are a Mexican specialty consisting of cooked pinto beans that are mashed, then fried.

TACO BELL
enchirito

A WARM SOFT FLOUR TORTILLA WRAPPED AROUND SEASONED GROUND BEEF AND REFRIED BEANS, TOPPED WITH ENCHILADA SAUCE, CHEDDAR CHEESE, AND SLICED OLIVES.

I pound ground beef
¼ teaspoon seasoned salt
I teaspoon chili powder
I ½ teaspoons onion flakes
One 16-ounce can refried beans
Six 10- or 12-inch flour tortillas

¼ cup diced onion
One 10-ounce can enchilada sauce
I ½ cups shredded Cheddar cheese
One 2-ounce can sliced black olives

1. Slowly brown the ground beef in a skillet, using a wooden spoon or spatula to separate the beef into tiny pieces. Add the seasoned salt, chili powder, and onion flakes.
2. Using a potato masher, mash the refried beans until smooth. Heat the beans as directed on the product label.
3. Spoon 3 tablespoons of the beef into the center of each tortilla. Sprinkle on 3 teaspoons of the diced onion. Add ⅓ cup of the refried beans.
4. Fold the sides of each tortilla over the beans. Place the tortilla on a plate. Spoon 3 tablespoon of the enchilada sauce over the top of the tortilla.
5. Sprinkle ¼ cup of the shredded cheese onto the folded tortilla.
6. Microwave on high for 45 seconds or until the cheese is melted. Top with a few olive slices.

Serves 6

TACO BELL
mexican pizza

CRISP FRIED TORTILLAS STACKED WITH SEASONED GROUND BEEF AND HEARTY
BEANS. TOPPED WITH ENCHILADA SAUCE AND MELTED CHEESE.

8 ounces ground beef
3 tablespoons taco seasoning
2 tablespoons water
Vegetable oil, for frying
Eight 6-inch flour tortillas
1 cup refried beans
⅔ cup store-bought enchilada
sauce

¼ cup chopped tomato
1 cup shredded Cheddar-Jack
cheese blend
¼ cup chopped green onions
¼ cup sliced black olives

1. Using your hands, mix together the beef, taco seasoning, and water.
2. Brown the beef mixture in a skillet over medium-high heat for 5 to
   6 minutes, using a wooden spoon or spatula to break up the meat as
   it cooks; set aside.
3. Preheat the oven to 375°F.
4. Preheat 1 inch of oil to 375°F. Fry the tortillas for 30 to 45 seconds per
   side, until golden brown. When frying each tortilla, be sure to pop any
   bubbles that form so that the tortilla lies flat in the oil. Drain the tortillas
   on brown paper bags or paper towels.
5. Assemble each pizza by first spreading ¼ cup of the refried beans on a
   tortilla, then spread with ¼ to ⅓ cup of the meat. Top with a second
   tortilla. Spread that tortilla with 2 tablespoons of the enchilada sauce.
   Top with 1 tablespoon of the tomato and ¼ cup of the cheese, then
   1 tablespoon each of the green onions and olives.
6. Bake the pizzas in the oven until the cheese has melted. Serve and enjoy.

Serves 4

T.G.I. FRIDAY'S
baked potato skins

TWICE-BAKED POTATO SKINS TOPPED WITH FRESH CHIVES, CRISP BACON, AND
CHEDDAR CHEESE; SERVED WITH SOUR CREAM.

5 baked potatoes, halved and flesh
scooped out (save for another
use)
1 tablespoon butter, melted
Seasoned salt

¾ cup shredded Cheddar cheese
½ cup diced bacon, fried crispy
(about 5 slices)
1 tablespoon snipped fresh chives
1 cup sour cream

1. Preheat the oven to 375°F.
2. Brush the potato shells with the melted butter and sprinkle with seasoned salt to taste.
3. Bake for 15 to 20 minutes, until crisp but not dry or hard. Remove from
   the oven and sprinkle with the cheese, bacon, and chives. Place back in
   the oven until the cheese is melted.
4. Serve with the sour cream.

Serves 5

T.G.I. Friday's, one of the first American casual dining chains, is a
dining experience that has become the favorite pastime of millions
since 1965. The first T.G.I. Friday's was located at First Avenue and
Sixty-third Street in New York City. The restaurant's focus is on
providing a comfortable, relaxing environment where patrons can
enjoy quality food and have a good time.

T.G.I. FRIDAY'S
broccoli-cheese soup

A CREAMY MIXTURE OF BROCCOLI SIMMERED IN A MILD CHEESE SOUP.

4 cups water
2 cups potato, peeled and diced
2 chicken bouillon cubes
I cup diced onion
Two 10-ounce packages frozen
  chopped broccoli, or I bunch
  fresh broccoli, chopped

Two 10.75-ounce cans cream of
  chicken soup
I pound Velveeta, cubed

1. Combine the water, potato, bouillon cubes, onion, and broccoli in a large, heavy saucepan. Cook over medium heat for 20 minutes, or until the potato and broccoli are tender.
2. Add the canned soup and the cheese, stirring until the cheese is melted and smooth. Simmer for 15 minutes; the soup should thicken.

Serves 4

T.G.I. FRIDAY'S
honey mustard dressing

A CREAMY HONEY MUSTARD DRESSING. THIS DRESSING IS GREAT ON MIXED SALAD GREENS AND AS A DIPPING SAUCE FOR CHICKEN FINGERS.

¼ cup honey
2 tablespoons mustard
1 tablespoon white vinegar

½ cup mayonnaise
½ cup sour cream

1. Combine the honey, mustard, vinegar, mayonnaise, and sour cream in a bowl and mix using a wire whisk.
2. Serve immediately or refrigerate.

Makes about 1½ cups

T.G.I. FRIDAY'S
jack daniel's dipping sauce

A SWEET AND MILDLY SPICY SAUCE GREAT FOR DIPPING MEAT, POULTRY, OR FISH.

⅓ cup diced red onion
½ teaspoon finely minced garlic
½ cup water
½ cup packed dark brown sugar
⅓ cup teriyaki sauce

¼ cup soy sauce
⅓ cup white grape juice
½ cup Jack Daniel's Tennessee whiskey
½ teaspoon Tabasco sauce

1. Combine all the ingredients in a saucepan in the order listed, mixing and stirring after each addition.
2. Place over medium heat and stir until the mixture comes to a boil.
3. Reduce the heat until the mixture is slowly simmering.
4. Cook the sauce for 35 to 45 minutes, until thick and bubbling.

Makes about 3 cups

T.G.I. FRIDAY'S
orange cream

THIS SIGNATURE T.G.I. FRIDAY'S COCKTAIL IS SERVED WITH A PINEAPPLE SLICE
AND A MARASCHINO CHERRY.

¾ cup orange juice
2 teaspoons grenadine
1 scoop vanilla ice cream
¼ cup crushed ice

Garnish
1 pineapple slice
1 maraschino cherry

1. Combine the orange juice, grenadine, ice cream, and ice in a blender.
2. Blend at high speed for 1 to 2 minutes.
3. Serve in a tall glass and garnish with the pineapple slice and cherry.

Serves 1

T.G.I. FRIDAY'S
shrimp marinara

A PLATEFUL OF PLUMP SHRIMP SAUTÉED IN A TANGY MARINARA SAUCE. SERVED
HOT OVER ANGEL HAIR PASTA.

3 tablespoons garlic butter
(combine 3 tablespoons softened
butter with ½ teaspoon finely
minced garlic)
6 medium shrimp, peeled and
deveined

¾ cup marinara sauce
4 ounces angel hair pasta,
cooked
I teaspoon chopped fresh parsley
2 slices French bread

1. Heat a sauté pan over medium heat.
2. Add 2 tablespoons of the garlic butter and heat for 30 seconds.
3. Add the shrimp and sauté until they turn pink.
4. Flip the shrimp once and cook for 1 to 2 minutes more.
5. Add the marinara sauce and stir to mix the ingredients.
6. Place the hot pasta in the center of a bowl and top with the sauce,
   distributing the shrimp evenly. Garnish with the chopped parsley.
7. Toast the French bread slices and brush with the remaining tablespoon
   garlic butter.

Serves 1

T.G.I. FRIDAY'S
sizzling chicken and cheese

A SIZZLING SKILLET OF ONION AND PEPPERS TOGETHER WITH GARLIC-
MARINATED CHICKEN BREASTS OVER MELTED MEXICAN AND AMERICAN CHEESES
ON A BED OF CREAMY MASHED POTATOES.

Two 4-ounce boneless, skinless
chicken breasts

Marinade
2 tablespoons chopped garlic
¼ cup olive oil
1 teaspoon red pepper flakes
¼ teaspoon black pepper
¼ teaspoon salt

Pepper and Onion Medley
1 green bell pepper, cut into thin
strips

1 red bell pepper, cut into thin
strips
1 yellow onion, cut into thin strips
¼ cup olive oil
1 teaspoon chopped garlic
Salt and black pepper

2 tablespoons olive oil
2 cups mashed potatoes
½ cup shredded Chihuahua cheese
2 slices American cheese
2 tablespoons chopped fresh parsley

1. Trim the fat and pound the chicken breasts until thin.
2. Combine all the marinade ingredients. Put the chicken in the marinade
   and refrigerate for 3 hours.
3. Sauté the peppers and onion and in the olive oil for 2 minutes. Then add
   the chopped garlic and continue to sauté for 2 to 3 minutes more.
   Season with salt and pepper to taste.
4. Sauté the chicken breast on all sides in the olive oil over medium heat.
5. Heat a cast-iron skillet over medium heat until very hot, then remove
   from the burner.
6. Place the mashed potatoes on the bottom of the skillet. Cover with the
   pepper and onion medley, then the cheeses. Top the cheeses with the
   chicken.
7. Sprinkle with the chopped parsley. Serve directly from the skillet.

Serves 2

Chihuahua cheese is a soft white Mexican cheese.

UNION PACIFIC
apple pancakes

TENDER PANCAKES SWEETENED WITH APPLESAUCE. SERVE WITH HOT MAPLE
SYRUP AND BUTTER.

1 cup all-purpose flour	1 egg, beaten
¼ teaspoon salt	½ teaspoon vanilla extract
1 ½ teaspoons baking powder	1 ¼ cups applesauce
1 tablespoon butter, melted	
½ cup milk	

1. Sift together the flour, salt, and baking powder into a medium bowl.
2. Combine the butter, milk, and egg. Stir into the flour mixture.
3. Add the vanilla and applesauce. Beat well.
4. Spoon the batter onto a hot, well-greased griddle, allowing enough batter to make 4-inch cakes. When the edges are slightly browned, turn the pancakes and cook on the other side.

Serves 2

UNION PACIFIC
grilled white pekin duck breast

CITRUS JUICE AND MINT COMBINED WITH SOY SAUCE IS THE SECRET MARINADE FOR GRILLED DUCK BREAST THAT IS SERVED OVER GREENS AND GARNISHED WITH ORANGE SECTIONS AND GRAPES.

4 navel oranges
1 tablespoon sesame oil
1 tablespoon soy sauce
2 tablespoons minced fresh mint
1 tablespoon sugar
1 medium red onion, sliced into thin rings
Salt and pepper

4 boneless, skinless Pekin duckling breasts
1 small bunch green seedless grapes, stemmed
1 head escarole, cored and chopped into 1-inch pieces
6 ounces baby red romaine leaves
1 tablespoon grapeseed oil

1. Juice three of the oranges.
2. Combine the orange juice with the sesame oil, soy sauce, mint, sugar, and red onion. Mix well, and season with salt and pepper to taste.
3. Marinate the duck breasts in this mixture for about 30 minutes. Remove the duck and save the marinade.
4. In a small saucepan, boil the leftover marinade for 1 minute. Season if necessary. Set aside and let cool.
5. Segment the remaining orange by slicing off the top and bottom. Setting the orange on a flat side, carefully cut away the skin and all of the pith. Then slide the knife between the sections and release the fruit into a bowl. Add the grapes to the orange sections, and set aside.
6. Preheat the grill.
7. Pat the duck breasts dry; season on both sides with salt and pepper.
8. Place the duck breasts on the grill and cook for about 8 minutes for medium. Remove from the grill and keep warm.
9. In a large bowl, lightly toss the escarole and romaine leaves with half of the reserved marinade.
10. Divide the greens equally among 4 plates.

11. Slice the duck breasts on an angle, and place on top of the salad. Scatter the citrus segments and grapes over each plateful.
12. In a bowl, mix the grapeseed oil into the remaining marinade. Drizzle the remaining marinade over the top of each serving.

Serves 4

Grapeseed oil is used in salad dressings, marinades, and flavored oils and for deep-frying and baking.

MEASUREMENTS

Pinch or dash	Less than ⅛ teaspoon
3 teaspoons	1 tablespoon
4 tablespoons	¼ cup
8 tablespoons	½ cup
12 tablespoons	¾ cup
16 tablespoons	1 cup
2 cups	1 pint
4 cups	1 quart
4 quarts	1 gallon
8 quarts	1 peck
4 pecks	1 bushel
16 ounces	1 pound
1 fluid ounce	2 tablespoons
8 fluid ounces	1 cup
16 fluid ounces	1 pint
32 fluid ounces	1 quart

Use standard measuring cups and spoons. All measurements are level.

RECIPES BY CATEGORY

Appetizers

Bahama Breeze™ Jamaican Jerk Grilled Chicken Wings   21
Bennigan's™ Broccoli Bites   26
The Cheesecake Factory™ Avocado Egg Rolls   49
The Cheesecake Factory™ Crab Cakes   54
Chili's™ Salsa   70
Chili's™ Southwestern Egg Rolls   72
Hooters™ Buffalo Shrimp   98
Hooters™ Buffalo Wings   100
Houston's™ Spinach and Artichoke Dip   102
Joe's Crab Shack™ Crab Cakes   109
Joe's Crab Shack™ Seafood-Stuffed Mushrooms   112
KFC™ Buttermilk Biscuits   118
KFC™ Honey Barbecue Wings   119
Macaroni Grill™ Focaccia   125
Olive Garden™ Bruschetta al Pomodoro   137
Olive Garden™ Fried Mozzarella   148
Outback Steakhouse™ Honey-Wheat Bushman Bread   161
P.F. Chang's™ Chicken-Lettuce Wrap   172
Rainforest Cafe™ Crab Cakes   181
Red Lobster™ Cheddar Biscuits   186
Ruby Tuesday™ Chicken Quesadillas   201
T.G.I. Friday's™ Baked Potato Skins   227

Breakfast

IHOP™ Banana-Nut Pancakes   103
IHOP™ Colorado Omelet   105
IHOP™ Cream of Wheat Pancakes   106
IHOP™ Pancakes   107
IHOP™ Swedish Pancakes   108

Perkins Restaurant and Bakery™ Pancakes 171
Union Pacific™ Apple Pancakes 234

Desserts

Applebee's™ Walnut Blondie with Maple Butter Sauce 15
Arby's™ Apple Turnovers 16
Baskin-Robbins™ Cheesecake Ice Cream 23
The Cheesecake Factory™ Banana Cream Cheesecake 51
The Cheesecake Factory™ Oreo Cheesecake 56
The Cheesecake Factory™ Pumpkin Cheesecake 58
Chili's™ Chocolate Chip Paradise Pie 68
Cracker Barrel™ Banana Pudding 78
Cracker Barrel™ Cherry-Chocolate Cobbler 79
Dairy Queen™ Heath Blizzard 81
Dairy Queen™ Ice Cream 82
Dollywood™ Dipped Chocolate Chip Cookies 86
Hardee's™ Cinnamon "Flake" Biscuits 96
Junior's™ Famous No. 1 Cheesecake 116
Macaroni Grill™ Chocolate Cake with Fudge Sauce 123
Macaroni Grill™ Reese's Peanut Butter Cake 129
Olive Garden™ Chocolate Lasagna 142
Olive Garden™ Lemon Cream Cake 149
Olive Garden™ Tiramisù 157
Outback Steakhouse™ Key Lime Pie 162
Starbucks™ Chocolate Fudge Squares with Mocha Glaze 217
Starbucks™ Gingerbread Loaf 219

Entrées

Applebee's™ Baby Back Ribs 1
Applebee's™ Chicken Quesadilla Grande 4
Applebee's™ Crispy Orange Chicken Skillet 5
Applebee's™ Fiesta Lime Chicken 7
Applebee's™ Low-Fat Grilled Tilapia with Mango Salsa 9
Applebee's™ Santa Fe Chicken 10
Applebee's™ Spinach Pizza 12
Arthur Treacher's™ Fried Fish 19

Recipes by Category

Benihana™ Hibachi Steak	24
Bennigan's™ Linguine Diablo	29
Boston Market™ Meat Loaf	37
Brooklyn Cafe™ Sun-Dried Tomato Seared Scallops	41
Bullfish Grill™ Shrimp and Cheese Grits	43
California Pizza Kitchen™ BBQ Chicken Pizza	45
California Pizza Kitchen™ Chicken-Tequila Fettuccine	46
Carrabba's Italian Grill™ Meatballs	47
The Cheesecake Factory™ Cajun Jambalaya Pasta	52
The Cheesecake Factory™ Chicken Fettuccine	53
Chi-Chi's™ Baked Chicken Chimichangas	60
Chi-Chi's™ Pork Tenderloin with Bourbon Sauce	61
Chi-Chi's™ Salsa Verde Chicken Kabobs	62
Chi-Chi's™ Steak and Mushroom Quesadillas	63
Chili's™ Baby Back Ribs	65
Chili's™ Beef Fajitas	66
Chili's™ Margarita Grilled Chicken	69
Chili's™ Southwestern Chicken Chili	71
Church's™ Fried Chicken	75
Denny's™ Country Fried Steak	84
El Pollo Loco™ Pollo Asada	88
Hard Rock Cafe™ BBQ Ribs	92
Hard Rock Cafe™ Pulled Pork	94
Hard Rock Cafe™ Shrimp Fajitas	95
Joe's Crab Shack™ Étouffée	110
Joe's Crab Shack™ Stuffed Shrimp en Brochette	114
Johnny Carino's™ Five-Cheese Chicken Fettuccine	115
KFC™ Original Recipe Fried Chicken	120
Macaroni Grill™ Insalata Florentine	126
Macaroni Grill™ Pasta Gamberetti e Pinoli	127
Macaroni Grill™ Sesame Shrimp	132
Macaroni Grill™ Shrimp Portofino	133
Olive Garden™ Beef Fillets in Balsamic Sauce	135
Olive Garden™ Chicken Crostina	138
Olive Garden™ Chicken San Marco	140

Recipes by Category

Olive Garden™ Fettuccine Alfredo	144
Olive Garden™ Fettuccine Assortito	145
Olive Garden™ Five-Cheese Lasagna	146
Olive Garden™ Pasta e Fagioli	152
Olive Garden™ Pizza Bianco	153
Olive Garden™ Pork Filettino	154
Outback Steakhouse™ Cyclone Pasta	160
Outback Steakhouse™ Marinated Steak	163
Panda Express™ Orange-Flavored Chicken	165
Pat's King of Steaks™ Philly Cheesesteak	169
P.F. Chang's™ Chicken with Black Bean Sauce	174
P.F. Chang's™ Sichuan Chicken Chow Fun	175
Pizza Hut™ Cavatini	176
Planet Hollywood™ Cap'n Crunch Chicken	177
Rainforest Cafe™ Blue Mountain Grilled Chicken Sandwich	180
Red Lobster™ Batter-Fried Shrimp	183
Red Lobster™ Cajun Shrimp Linguine	185
Red Lobster™ Deep-Fried Catfish	188
Red Lobster™ Fried Chicken Tenders	190
Red Lobster™ Grouper Siciliano	192
Red Lobster™ Lobster Fondue	194
Red Lobster™ Shrimp Diablo	195
Red Lobster™ South Beach Seafood Paella	196
Red Lobster™ Trout Veracruz	198
Roadhouse Grill™ Roast Beef and Mashed Potatoes	199
Ruby Tuesday™ Shrimp Pasta Parmesan	203
Ruby Tuesday™ Sonoran Chicken Pasta	205
Ruby Tuesday™ Super Salad Bar Pasta	207
Ruth's Chris™ Steak House Barbecued Shrimp	208
Shoney's™ Pot Roast	210
Taco Bell™ Beef Chalupa Supreme	221
Taco Bell™ Burrito Supreme	223
Taco Bell™ Enchirito	225
Taco Bell™ Mexican Pizza	226
T.G.I. Friday's™ Shrimp Marinara	232

T.G.I. Friday's™ Sizzling Chicken and Cheese   233
Union Pacific™ Grilled White Pekin Duck Breast   235

Salads

Bennigan's™ Honey Mustard Dressing   27
Bennigan's™ Hot Bacon Dressing   28
Boston Market™ Cucumber Salad   34
Houston's™ Buttermilk-Garlic Dressing   101
Luby's™ Cafeteria Spaghetti Salad   122
Macaroni Grill™ Roasted Garlic–Lemon Vinaigrette   131
Olive Garden™ Salad Dressing   155
Panera Bread™ Asian Sesame-Chicken Salad   167
Red Lobster™ Caesar Dressing   184
T.G.I. Friday's™ Honey Mustard Dressing   229

Side Dishes

Applebee's™ Bacon–Green Onion Mashed Potatoes   3
Applebee's™ Garlic Mashed Potatoes   8
Benihana™ Japanese Fried Rice   25
Boston Market™ Creamed Spinach   32
Boston Market™ Dill Potato Wedges   35
Boston Market™ Macaroni and Cheese   36
Boston Market™ Spicy Rice   38
Boston Market™ Squash Casserole   39
Boston Market™ Stuffing   40
Cracker Barrel™ Baby Limas   77
Cracker Barrel™ Fried Apples   80
Dairy Queen™ Onion Rings   83
El Pollo Loco™ Beans   87
Hard Rock Cafe™ BBQ Beans   91
Joe's Crab Shack™ Rice Pilaf   111
Olive Garden™ Bread Sticks   136
Olive Garden™ Oven-Roasted Potatoes   151
Popeyes™ Cajun Rice   178
Popeyes™ Dirty Rice   179

Red Lobster™ Hush Puppies 193
Shoney's™ Marinated Mushrooms 209

Soups
Applebee's™ Tomato-Basil Soup 14
Bennigan's™ Onion Soup 31
Chili's™ Chicken Enchilada Soup 67
Chili's™ Southwestern Vegetable Soup 74
Hard Rock Cafe™ Baked Potato Soup 89
Hard Rock Cafe™ Homemade Chicken Noodle Soup 93
Olive Garden™ Angel Hair and Three-Onion Soup 134
Olive Garden™ Zuppa Toscana 159
Outback Steakhouse™ Walkabout Soup 164
Panera Bread™ Broccoli-Cheese Soup 168
Red Lobster™ Clam Chowder 187
Red Lobster™ Dungeness Crab Bisque 189
Shoney's™ Tomato Florentine Soup 211
The Soup Nazi™ Crab Bisque 212
The Soup Nazi™ Cream of Sweet Potato Soup 214
The Soup Nazi™ Indian Mulligatawny Soup 215
The Soup Nazi™ Mexican Chicken Chili 216
T.G.I. Friday's™ Broccoli-Cheese Soup 238

Miscellaneous
Arby's™ Barbecue Sauce 18
Carrabba's Italian Grill™ Italian Butter 47
Denny's™ Country Gravy 85
Joe's Crab Shack™ Seafood Stuffing 113
Olive Garden™ Sangria 156
Olive Garden™ Tuscan Tea 158
Rainforest Cafe™ Safari Sauce 182
Subway™ Sweet Onion Sauce 220
T.G.I. Friday's™ Jack Daniel's Dipping Sauce 230
T.G.I. Friday's™ Orange Cream 231

TRADEMARKS

- Applebee's is a registered trademark of Applebee's International, Inc.
- Arby's is a registered trademark of Arby's Restaurant Group, Inc.
- Arthur Treacher's is a registered trademark of PAT Franchise Systems, Inc.
- Bahama Breeze is a registered trademark of Darden Concepts, Inc.
- Baskin-Robbins is a registered trademark of Baskin-Robbins.
- Benihana is a registered trademark of Benihana, Inc.
- Bennigan's is a registered trademark of Metromedia Restaurant Group.
- Boston Market is a registered trademark of Boston Market Corporation, which is a wholly owned subsidiary of McDonald's Corporation.
- Brooklyn Cafe is a registered trademark of Brooklyn Cafe.
- Bullfish Grill is a registered trademark of Bullfish Grill.
- California Pizza Kitchen is a registered trademark of California Pizza Kitchen, Inc.
- Carrabba's is a registered trademark of OSI Restaurant Partners, LLC.
- The Cheesecake Factory is a registered trademark of The Cheesecake Factory, Inc.
- Chi-Chi's is a registered trademark of Chi-Chi's, Inc., and Prandium, Inc.
- Chili's is a registered trademark of Brinker International.
- Church's is a registered trademark of Cajun Operating Company.
- Cracker Barrel is a registered trademark of CBOCS Properties, Inc.
- Dairy Queen is a registered trademark of International Dairy Queen, Inc., and Berkshire Hathaway, Inc.
- Denny's is a registered trademark of DFO, LLC.
- Dollywood is a registered trademark of The Dollywood Company.
- El Pollo Loco is a registered trademark of El Pollo Loco, Inc.

- Hard Rock Cafe is a registered trademark of Hard Rock America, Inc.
- Hardee's is a registered trademark of Hardee's Food Systems, Inc.
- Hooters is a registered trademark of Hooters of America.
- Houston's is a registered trademark of Bandera Restaurants.
- IHOP and International House of Pancakes are registered trademarks of International House of Pancakes, Inc.
- Joe's Crab Shack is a registered trademark of Landry's Seafood Restaurants, Inc.
- Johnny Carino's is a registered trademark of Fired Up, Inc.
- Junior's is a registered trademark of Junior's Cheesecake, Inc.
- KFC is a registered trademark of Yum! Brands, Inc.
- Luby's Cafeteria is a registered trademark of Luby's, Inc.
- Macaroni Grill is a registered trademark of Brinker International.
- Olive Garden is a registered trademark of Darden Restaurants, Inc.
- Outback Steakhouse is a registered trademark of Outback Steakhouse, Inc.
- Panda Express is a registered trademark of Panda Restaurant Group, Inc.
- Panera Bread is a registered trademark of Panera Bread.
- Pat's King of Steaks is a registered trademark of Pat's King of Steaks.
- Perkins Restaurant and Bakery is a registered trademark of The Restaurant Company of Minnesota.
- P.F. Chang's is a registered trademark of P.F. Chang's China Bistro, Inc.
- Pizza Hut is a registered trademark of Yum! Brands, Inc.
- Planet Hollywood is a registered trademark of Planet Hollywood, Inc.
- Popeyes is a registered trademark of AFC Enterprises, Inc.
- Rainforest Cafe is a registered trademark of Landry's Restaurants, Inc.
- Red Lobster is a registered trademark of Darden Restaurants, Inc.
- Roadhouse Grill is a registered trademark of Roadhouse Grill, Inc.
- Ruby Tuesday is a registered trademark of Morrison Restaurants, Inc.
- Ruth's Chris Steak House is a registered trademark of Ruth's Hospitality Group, Inc.

Trademarks

- Shoney's is a registered trademark of Shoney's, Inc.
- The Soup Nazi is a registered trademark of Soup Kitchen International.
- Starbucks is a registered trademark of Starbucks Corporation.
- Subway is a registered trademark of Doctor's Associates, Inc.
- Taco Bell is a registered trademark of Yum! Brands, Inc.
- T.G.I. Friday's is a registered trademark of T.G.I. Friday's, Inc.

RESTAURANT WEB SITES

To find a restaurant near you, please visit:

Applebee's	www.applebees.com
Arby's	www.arbys.com
Arthur Treacher's	www.arthurtreachers.com
Bahama Breeze	www.bahamabreeze.com
Baskin-Robbins	www.baskinrobbins.com
Benihana	www.benihana.com
Bennigan's	www.bennigans.com
Boston Market	www.bostonmarket.com
Brooklyn Cafe	www.brooklyncafe.com
Bullfish Grill	www.bullfishgrill.com
California Pizza Kitchen	www.cpk.com
Carrabba's Italian Grill	www.carrabbas.com
The Cheesecake Factory	www.thecheesecakefactory.com
Chi-Chi's	www.chichis.com
Chili's	www.chilis.com
Church's	www.churchs.com
Cracker Barrel	www.crackerbarrel.com
Dairy Queen	www.dairyqueen.com
Denny's	www.dennys.com
Dollywood	www.dollywood.com
El Pollo Loco	www.elpolloloco.com
Hard Rock Cafe	www.hardrock.com
Hardee's	www.hardees.com
Hooters	www.hooters.com
Houston's	www.hillstone.com
IHOP	www.ihop.com
Joe's Crab Shack	www.joescrabshack.com
Johnny Carino's	www.carinos.com

Junior's	www.juniorscheesecake.com
KFC	www.kfc.com
Luby's Cafeteria	www.lubys.com
Macaroni Grill	www.macaronigrill.com
Olive Garden	www.olivegarden.com
Outback Steakhouse	www.outback.com
Panda Express	www.pandaexpress.com
Panera Bread	www.panerabread.com
Pat's King of Steaks	www.patskingofsteaks.com
Perkins Restaurant and Bakery	www.perkinsrestaurants.com
P.F. Chang's	www.pfchangs.com
Pizza Hut	www.pizzahut.com
Planet Hollywood	www.planethollywood.com
Popeyes	www.popeyes.com
Rainforest Cafe	www.rainforestcafe.com
Red Lobster	www.redlobster.com
Roadhouse Grill	www.originalroadhousegrill.com
Ruby Tuesday	www.rubytuesday.com
Ruth's Chris Steak House	www.ruthschris.com
Shoney's	www.shoneys.com
The Soup Nazi	www.originalsoupman.com
Starbucks	www.starbucks.com
Subway	www.subway.com
Taco Bell	www.tacobell.com
T.G.I. Friday's	www.fridays.com

INDEX

Alfredo (sauce):
  Cyclone Pasta, Outback Steakhouse, 160
  Fettuccine, Olive Garden, 144
  Five-Cheese Chicken Fettuccine, Johnny
    Carino's, 115
  Seafood-Stuffed Mushrooms, Joe's Crab
    Shack, 112
American cheese:
  Macaroni and Cheese, Boston Market,
    36
  Sizzling Chicken and Cheese, T.G.I.
    Friday's, 233
andouille sausage, in Red Lobster South
  Beach Seafood Paella, 196–97
angel hair pasta, 128
  Gamberetti e Pinoli, Macaroni Grill,
    127–28
  Shrimp Marinara, T.G.I. Friday's, 232
  and Three-Onion Soup, Olive Garden,
    134
appetizers:
  Avocado Egg Rolls, The Cheesecake
    Factory, 49–50
  Broccoli Bites, Bennigan's, 26
  Bruschetta al Pomodoro, Olive Garden,
    137
  Buttermilk Biscuits, KFC, 118
  Cheddar Biscuits, Red Lobster, 186
  Chicken-Lettuce Wrap, P.F. Chang's,
    172–73
  Crab Cakes, The Cheesecake Factory,
    54–55
  Crab Cakes, Joe's Crab Shack, 109
  Crab Cakes, Rainforest Cafe, 181
  Egg Rolls, Southwestern, Chili's, 72–73
  Focaccia, Macaroni Grill, 125
  Honey-Wheat Bushman Bread, Outback
    Steakhouse, 161
  Mozzarella, Fried, Olive Garden, 148
  Potato Skins, Baked, T.G.I. Friday's, 227
  Salsa, Chili's, 70
  Seafood-Stuffed Mushrooms, Joe's Crab
    Shack, 112

Shrimp, Buffalo, Hooters, 98
Spinach and Artichoke Dip, Houston's,
  102
Wings, Buffalo, Hooters, 100
Wings, Honey Barbecue, KFC, 119
Wings, Jamaican Jerk Grilled, Bahama
  Breeze, 21–22
apple(s):
  Fried, Cracker Barrel, 80
  Pancakes, Union Pacific, 234
  Turnovers, Arby's, 16–17
artichoke(s):
  buying, xxv
  hearts, in Macaroni Grill Shrimp
    Portofino, 133
  and Spinach Dip, Houston's, 102
Asiago cheese, 115
  Five-Cheese Chicken Fettuccine, Johnny
    Carino's, 115
  Spinach Pizza, Applebee's, 12–13
Asian:
  Hibachi Steak, Benihana, 24
  Japanese Fried Rice, Benihana, 25
  Sesame-Chicken Salad, Panera Bread,
    167
  see also Chinese
asparagus, buying, xxv
au gratin, xxiii
au jus, xxiii
Avocado Egg Rolls, The Cheesecake
  Factory, 49–50

baby back ribs:
  Applebee's, 1–2
  Chili's, 65
Baby Limas, Cracker Barrel, 77
bacon:
  Baked Potato Skins, T.G.I. Friday's, 227
  Baked Potato Soup, Hard Rock Cafe,
    89–90
  bits, in Bennigan's Broccoli Bites, 26
  Blue Mountain Grilled Chicken
    Sandwich, Rainforest Cafe, 180

Index

bacon (*cont.*)
Colorado Omelet, IHOP, 105
Dressing, Hot, Bennigan's, 28
drippings, in Cracker Barrel Fried
Apples, 80
Green Onion Mashed Potatoes,
Applebee's, 3
Zuppa Toscana, Olive Garden, 159
baked:
Chicken Chimichangas, Chi-Chi's, 60
Potato Skins, T.G.I. Friday's, 227
Potato Soup, Hard Rock Cafe, 89–90
baking pans:
dusting with flour, xxi
glass, oven temperature and, xx
greasing, xx
Balsamic Sauce, Beef Fillets in, Olive
Garden, 135
banana(s):
buying, xxvi
Cream Cheesecake, The Cheesecake
Factory, 51
Nut Pancakes, IHOP, 103
overripe, saving for baking, xx
Pudding, Cracker Barrel, 78
Syrup, IHOP, 103
barbecue(d):
Honey Wings, KFC, 119
Shrimp, Ruth's Chris Steak House, 208
see also BBQ
barbecue sauces:
Arby's, 18
Chili's, 65
Hard Rock Cafe, 92
basil, xxvii
Bruschetta al Pomodoro, Olive Garden,
137
Tomato Soup, Applebee's, 14
basting, xxiii
Batter-Fried Shrimp, Red Lobster, 183
bay leaves, xxvii
BBQ:
Beans, Hard Rock Cafe, 91
Chicken Pizza, California Pizza Kitchen,
45
Ribs, Hard Rock Cafe, 92
see also barbecue(d)
beans:
Baby Limas, Cracker Barrel, 77
BBQ, Hard Rock Cafe, 91
black, in Chili's Southwestern Egg Rolls,
72–73

buying, xxv
El Pollo Loco, 87
green, in Chili's Southwestern Vegetable
Soup, 74
making easier to digest, xix
Mexican Chicken Chili, The Soup Nazi,
216
Pasta e Fagioli, Olive Garden, 152
Southwestern Chicken Chili, Chili's, 71
Southwestern Vegetable Soup, Chili's, 74
see also refried beans
bean sprouts:
Hibachi Steak, Benihana, 24
storing, xix
beef:
Burrito Supreme, Taco Bell, 223–24
Cajun Rice, Popeyes, 178
Cavatini, Pizza Hut, 176
Chalupa Supreme, Taco Bell, 221
cooking tips for, xx, xxi
Country Fried Steak, Denny's, 84–85
Enchirito, Taco Bell, 225
Fajitas, Chili's, 66
Fillets in Balsamic Sauce, Olive Garden,
135
ground, healthier alternatives for, xv
hamburgers, cooking tip for, xxi
Hibachi Steak, Benihana, 24
Marinated Steak, Outback Steakhouse,
163
Meat Loaf, Boston Market, 37
Mexican Pizza, Taco Bell, 226
Pasta e Fagioli, Olive Garden, 152
Philly Cheesesteak, Pat's King of Steaks,
169
Pot Roast, Shoney's, 210
Roast, and Mashed Potatoes, Roadhouse
Grill, 199–200
roast, in IHOP Colorado Omelet, 105
roasts, bone-in vs. boneless, xxi
Steak and Mushroom Quesadillas, Chi-
Chi's, 63–64
berries, buying, xxvi
beverages:
Orange Cream, T.G.I. Friday's, 231
Sangria, Olive Garden, 156
tips for, xix
Tuscan Tea, Olive Garden, 158
biscuits:
Buttermilk, KFC, 118
Cheddar, Red Lobster, 186
Cinnamon "Flake," Hardee's, 96–97

Index

bisques, xxiii
  Crab, The Soup Nazi, 212–13
  Dungeness Crab, Red Lobster, 189
black beans, in Chili's Southwestern Egg
  Rolls, 72–73
Black Bean Sauce, Chicken with, P.F.
  Chang's, 174
blackberries, buying, xxvi
blanching, xxiii
Blondie, Walnut, with Maple Butter Sauce,
  Applebee's, 15
blue cheese, in Boston Market Macaroni
  and Cheese, 36
Blue Mountain Grilled Chicken Sandwich,
  Rainforest Cafe, 180
boiling vegetables, xix
Bourbon Sauce, Pork Tenderloin with, Chi-
  Chi's, 61
bran, in Hardee's Cinnamon "Flake"
  Biscuits, 96–97
bread:
  Bruschetta al Pomodoro, Olive Garden,
   137
  cooking tips for, xx–xxi
  crumbs, making, xxi
  Focaccia, Macaroni Grill, 125
  Honey-Wheat Bushman, Outback
   Steakhouse, 161
  Sticks, Olive Garden, 136
  white, healthier alternatives for, xv
breakfast:
  Colorado Omelet, IHOP, 105
  see also pancakes
broccoli:
  Bites, Bennigan's, 26
  buying, xxv
  Cheese Soup, Panera Bread, 168
  Cheese Soup, T.G.I. Friday's, 228
  Chicken San Marco, Olive Garden,
   140–41
  Fettuccine Assortito, Olive Garden,
   145
  Super Salad Bar Pasta, Ruby Tuesday,
   207
Bruschetta al Pomodoro, Olive Garden,
  137
brussels sprouts, buying, xxv
Buffalo:
  Sauce, Hooters, 98
  Shrimp, Hooters, 98
  Wings, Hooters, 100
burgers, cooking tip for, xxi

Burrito Supreme, Taco Bell, 223–24
butter:
  Garlic-Lemon, Bennigan's, 29
  healthier alternatives for, xiv
  Italian, Carrabba's Italian Grill, 47
  Maple Sauce, Applebee's, 15
Buttercream Icing, Olive Garden, 142
Butterfinger Blizzard, Dairy Queen
  (variation), 81
buttermilk:
  Biscuits, KFC, 118
  Cinnamon "Flake" Biscuits, Hardee's,
   96–97
  Garlic Dressing, Houston's, 101
  making your own, 97
  Pancakes, IHOP, 107

cabbage:
  buying, xxv
  cooking tips for, xix, xxi
Caesar Dressing, Red Lobster, 184
Cajun:
  Blue Mountain Grilled Chicken
   Sandwich, Rainforest Cafe, 180
  Jambalaya Pasta, The Cheesecake
   Factory, 52
  Rice, Popeyes, 178
  Shrimp Linguine, Red Lobster, 185
cake flour, 143
cakes:
  Chocolate, with Fudge Sauce, Macaroni
   Grill, 123
  Chocolate Lasagna, Olive Garden,
   142–43
  Gingerbread Loaf, Starbucks, 219
  Lemon Cream, Olive Garden, 149–50
  Reese's Peanut Butter, Macaroni Grill,
   129–30
  Tiramisù, Olive Garden, 157
  see also cheesecake
cantaloupes, buying, xxvi
Cap'n Crunch Chicken, Planet Hollywood,
  177
caraway, xxvii
carrots:
  Broccoli-Cheese Soup, Panera Bread,
   168
  Chicken San Marco, Olive Garden,
   140–41
  Fettuccine Assortito, Olive Garden,
   145
  Stuffing, Boston Market, 40

cashews:
 Cream of Sweet Potato Soup, The Soup
  Nazi, 214
 Dipping Sauce, The Cheesecake Factory,
  49
 Indian Mulligatawny Soup, The Soup
  Nazi, 215
casseroles:
 Baked Chicken Chimichangas, Chi-
  Chi's, 60
 Cavatini, Pizza Hut, 176
 Squash, Boston Market, 39
Catfish, Deep-Fried, Red Lobster, 188
cauliflower:
 buying, xxv
 cooking tips for, xix, xxi
Cavatini, Pizza Hut, 176
celery:
 bean digestibility and, xix
 keeping crisp, xxi
Chalupa Supreme, Beef, Taco Bell, 221
Cheddar cheese:
 Baked Potato Skins, T.G.I. Friday's,
  227
 Baked Potato Soup, Hard Rock Cafe,
  89–90
 Beef Chalupa Supreme, Taco Bell, 221
 Biscuits, Red Lobster, 186
 Broccoli-Cheese Soup, Panera Bread,
  168
 Burrito Supreme, Taco Bell, 223–24
 Chicken Quesadilla Grande,
  Applebee's, 4
 Chicken Quesadillas, Ruby Tuesday, 201
 Colorado Omelet, IHOP, 105
 Enchirito, Taco Bell, 225
 Macaroni and Cheese, Boston Market,
  36
 Mexican Pizza, Taco Bell, 226
 Shrimp and Cheese Grits, Bullfish Grill,
  43–44
 Spinach and Artichoke Dip, Houston's,
  102
 Squash Casserole, Boston Market, 39
 Walkabout Soup, Outback Steakhouse,
  164
cheese:
 Broccoli Soup, Panera Bread, 168
 Broccoli Soup, T.G.I. Friday's, 228
 Five-, Chicken Fettuccine, Johnny
  Carino's, 115
 Five-, Lasagna, Olive Garden, 146–47
 grating, tip for, xix
 Grits, Shrimp and, Bullfish Grill, 43–44
 Lobster Fondue, Red Lobster, 194
 Macaroni and, Boston Market, 36
 Pecorino Romano, in Houston's Spinach
  and Artichoke Dip, 102
 Pizza Bianco, Olive Garden, 153
 Sauce, Sonoran, Ruby Tuesday, 205–6
 Sizzling Chicken and, T.G.I. Friday's,
  233
 see also Cheddar cheese; Fontina cheese;
  Jack cheese; Monterey Jack cheese;
  mozzarella cheese; Parmesan cheese;
  Romano cheese; Velveeta
cheesecake:
 Banana Cream, The Cheesecake Factory,
  51
 Ice Cream, Baskin-Robbins, 23
 Junior's Famous No. 1, 116–17
 Oreo, The Cheesecake Factory, 56–57
 Pumpkin, The Cheesecake Factory,
  58–59
Cheesesteak, Philly, Pat's King of Steaks,
 169
Cheez Whiz, in Pat's King of Steaks Philly
 Cheesesteak, 169
Cherry-Chocolate Cobbler, Cracker Barrel,
 79
chicken:
 BBQ, Pizza, California Pizza Kitchen, 45
 with Black Bean Sauce, P.F. Chang's, 174
 Broccoli-Cheese Soup, T.G.I. Friday's,
  228
 Cajun Jambalaya Pasta, The Cheesecake
  Factory, 52
 Cap'n Crunch, Planet Hollywood, 177
 Chili, Mexican, The Soup Nazi, 216
 Chili, Southwestern, Chili's, 71
 Chimichangas, Baked, Chi-Chi's, 60
 Chow Fun, Sichuan, P.F. Chang's, 175
 cooking tips for, xx, xxii
 Country Fried, Denny's (variation),
  84–85
 Crispy Orange, Skillet, Applebee's, 5–6
 Crostina, Olive Garden, 138–39
 Cyclone Pasta, Outback Steakhouse, 160
 Enchilada Soup, Chili's, 67
 Étouffée, Joe's Crab Shack, 110
 Fettuccine, The Cheesecake Factory, 53
 Fiesta Lime, Applebee's, 7
 fingers, T.G.I. Friday's Honey Mustard
  Dressing as dip for, 229

Five-Cheese Fettuccine, Johnny Carino's, 115
Fried, Arthur Treacher's (variation), 19
Fried, Church's, 75
Fried, KFC Original Recipe, 120–21
Grilled, Sandwich, Blue Mountain, Rainforest Cafe, 180
Insalata Florentine, Macaroni Grill, 126
Kabobs, Salsa Verde, Chi-Chi's, 62
Lettuce Wrap, P.F. Chang's, 172–73
Margarita Grilled, Chili's, 69
and Mushroom Quesadillas, Chi-Chi's (variation), 63–64
Noodle Soup, Homemade, Hard Rock Cafe, 93
Orange-Flavored, Panda Express, 165–66
Pasta, Sonoran, Ruby Tuesday, 205–6
Pollo Asada, El Pollo Loco, 88
Quesadilla Grande, Applebee's, 4
Quesadillas, Ruby Tuesday, 201
San Marco, Olive Garden, 140–41
Santa Fe, Applebee's, 10–11
Sesame, Salad, Panera Bread, 167
Sizzling, and Cheese, T.G.I. Friday's, 233
Southwestern Egg Rolls, Chili's, 72–73
Super Salad Bar Pasta, Ruby Tuesday, 207
Tenders, Fried, Red Lobster, 190–91
Tequila Fettuccine, California Pizza Kitchen, 46
Tomato Florentine Soup, Shoney's, 211
Wings, Buffalo, Hooters, 100
Wings, Honey Barbecue, KFC, 119
Wings, Jamaican Jerk Grilled, Bahama Breeze, 21–22
Chihuahua cheese, in T.G.I. Friday's Sizzling Chicken and Cheese, 233
chili:
Chicken, Mexican, The Soup Nazi, 216
Chicken, Southwestern, Chili's, 71
Chimichangas, Baked Chicken, Chi-Chi's, 60
Chinese:
Avocado Egg Rolls, The Cheesecake Factory, 49–50
Chicken-Lettuce Wrap, P.F. Chang's, 172–73
Chicken with Black Bean Sauce, P.F. Chang's, 174
Orange-Flavored Chicken, Panda Express, 165–66

Sichuan Chicken Chow Fun, P.F. Chang's, 175
chives, xxvii
chocolate:
Cake with Fudge Sauce, Macaroni Grill, 123
Cherry Cobbler, Cracker Barrel, 79
Chip Cookies, Dipped, Dollywood, 86
Chip Paradise Pie, Chili's, 68
Fudge Squares with Mocha Glaze, Starbucks, 217
fudge topping, in Dairy Queen Heath Blizzard, 81
Glaze, Macaroni Grill, 129–30
Lasagna, Olive Garden, 142–43
Chowder, Clam, Red Lobster, 187
Chow Fun, Sichuan Chicken, P.F. Chang's, 175
chutney, mango, in Rainforest Cafe Safari Sauce, 182
cilantro, xxvii
Cinnamon "Flake" Biscuits, Hardee's, 96–97
clam(s):
Chowder, Red Lobster, 187
Linguine Diablo, Bennigan's, 29–30
Cobbler, Cherry-Chocolate, Cracker Barrel, 79
coconut, in Chili's Chocolate Chip Paradise Pie, 68
coffee:
Mocha Glaze, Starbucks, 217
storing, xix
Tiramisù, Olive Garden, 157
Colby cheese, in Bennigan's Broccoli Bites, 26
Colorado Omelet, IHOP, 105
Cookies, Dipped Chocolate Chip, Dollywood, 86
cooking terms, xxiii–xxiv
corn:
bread, in Boston Market Squash Casserole, 39
cooking tip for, xxi
Grits, Cheese, Shrimp and, Bullfish Grill, 43–44
masa harina, in Chili's Chicken Enchilada Soup, 67
Southwestern Egg Rolls, Chili's, 72–73
Southwestern Vegetable Soup, Chili's, 74
cornmeal, in Red Lobster Hush Puppies, 193

Country Fried Steak, Denny's, 84–85
crab(meat):
    Bisque, The Soup Nazi, 212–13
    Cakes, The Cheesecake Factory, 54–55
    Cakes, Joe's Crab Shack, 109
    Cakes, Rainforest Cafe, 181
    Dungeness, Bisque, Red Lobster, 189
    Seafood Stuffing, Joe's Crab Shack, 113
cranberry juice, in Olive Garden Sangria,
    156
crawfish, in Joe's Crab Shack Étouffée, 110
Creamed Spinach, Boston Market, 32–33
creaming, xxiii
Cream of Sweet Potato Soup, The Soup
    Nazi, 214
Cream of Wheat Pancakes, IHOP, 106
crimping, xxiii
Crispy Orange Chicken Skillet, Applebee's,
    5–6
crucifers, reducing cooking odors from,
    xix
crudités, xxiii
crusts:
    Graham Cracker, The Cheesecake
        Factory, 58
    Graham Cracker, Chili's, 68
    Oreo Cookie, 56
    Vanilla Sandwich Cookie, 51
cucumber(s):
    buying, xxv
    Salad, Boston Market, 34
curry powder, xxvii
Cyclone Pasta, Outback Steakhouse, 160

deep-fried, see fried
degreasing, xxiii
desserts:
    Apple Turnovers, Arby's, 16–17
    Banana Pudding, Cracker Barrel, 78
    Cherry-Chocolate Cobbler, Cracker
        Barrel, 79
    Chocolate Chip Paradise Pie, Chili's, 68
    Chocolate Fudge Squares with Mocha
        Glaze, Starbucks, 217
    Cinnamon "Flake" Biscuits, Hardee's,
        96–97
    Dipped Chocolate Chip Cookies,
        Dollywood, 86
    Heath Blizzard, Dairy Queen, 81
    Ice Cream, Dairy Queen, 82
    Key Lime Pie, Outback Steakhouse,
        162

Swedish Pancakes, IHOP, 108
Walnut Blondie with Maple Butter
    Sauce, Applebee's, 15
see also cakes; cheesecake; ice cream
dill, xxvii
    Potato Wedges, Boston Market, 35
Dipped Chocolate Chip Cookies,
    Dollywood, 86
dips and dipping sauces:
    Bread Sticks for, Olive Garden, 136
    The Cheesecake Factory Dipping Sauce,
        49
    Chocolate Dip, Dollywood, 86
    Honey Mustard Dressing, Bennigan's,
        27
    Honey Mustard Dressing, T.G.I. Friday's,
        229
    Jack Daniel's Dipping Sauce, T.G.I.
        Friday's, 230
    Lobster Fondue, Red Lobster, 194
    Salsa, Chili's, 70
    Spinach and Artichoke Dip, Houston's,
        102
Dirty Rice, Popeyes, 179
dredging, xxiii
dressings:
    Applebee's, 7
    Asian Sesame, Panera Bread, 167
    Buttermilk-Garlic, Houston's, 101
    Caesar, Red Lobster, 184
    healthier alternatives for, xv
    Honey Mustard, Bennigan's, 27
    Honey Mustard, T.G.I. Friday's, 229
    Hot Bacon, Bennigan's, 28
    Olive Garden, 155
    Roasted Garlic-Lemon Vinaigrette,
        Macaroni Grill, 131
Duck Breast, Grilled White Pekin, Union
    Pacific, 235–36
Dungeness Crab Bisque, Red Lobster,
    189

egg rolls:
    Avocado, The Cheesecake Factory,
        49–50
    Southwestern, Chili's, 72–73
eggs:
    Colorado Omelet, IHOP, 105
    determining freshness of, xxi
    hard-boiled, peeling, xix
    healthier alternatives for, xv
Enchilada Soup, Chicken, Chili's, 67

Index

Enchirito, Taco Bell, 225
entrées, xxiii
  Étouffée, Joe's Crab Shack, 110
  Insalata Florentine, Macaroni Grill, 126
  Meatballs, Carrabba's Italian Grill, 48
  Meat Loaf, Boston Market, 37
  see also beef; chicken; fish; pasta; pizza;
    pork; seafood; shrimp
Étouffée, Joe's Crab Shack, 110
extracts, shelf life of, xxix

fajitas:
  Beef, Chili's, 66
  Shrimp, Hard Rock Cafe, 95
fat, reducing intake of:
  ingredient substutions and, xiv-xv
  meat cuts and, xix
  see also low-fat
fennel, xxvii
fettuccine:
  Alfredo, Olive Garden, 144
  Assortito, Olive Garden, 145
  Chicken, The Cheesecake Factory, 53
  Chicken Crostina, Olive Garden
    (variation), 138–39
  Chicken San Marco, Olive Garden,
    140–41
  Chicken-Tequila, California Pizza
    Kitchen, 46
  Five-Cheese Chicken, Johnny Carino's,
    115
Fiesta Lime Chicken, Applebee's, 7
fillings:
  Lemon, Olive Garden, 149
  Peanut Butter, Macaroni Grill, 129
fish:
  Catfish, Deep-Fried, Red Lobster, 188
  cooking tips for, xx
  Fried, Arthur Treacher's, 19
  Grouper Siciliano, Red Lobster, 192
  Seafood Stuffing, Joe's Crab Shack,
    113
  South Beach Seafood Paella, Red
    Lobster, 196–97
  Tilapia, Low-Fat Grilled, with Mango
    Salsa, Applebee's, 9
  Trout Veracruz, Red Lobster, 198
  see also crab(meat); seafood; shrimp
five-cheese:
  Chicken Fettuccine, Johnny Carino's,
    115
  Lasagna, Olive Garden, 146–47

flour:
  all-purpose, healthier alternatives for,
    xiv
  cake, 143
  dusting baking pans and work surfaces
    with, xxi
  self-rising, mixing your own, xx
  sifting before measuring, xx
  Wondra, 141
Focaccia, Macaroni Grill, 125
folding, xxiii
Fondue, Lobster, Red Lobster, 194
Fontina cheese, 147
  Five-Cheese Lasagna, Olive Garden,
    146–47
  Pizza Bianco, Olive Garden, 153
  Sauce, Olive Garden, 145
fried:
  Apples, Cracker Barrel, 80
  Avocado Egg Rolls, The Cheesecake
    Factory, 49–50
  Catfish, Red Lobster, 188
  Chicken, Cap'n Crunch, Planet
    Hollywood, 177
  Chicken, Church's, 75
  Chicken, KFC Original Recipe, 120–21
  Chicken, Orange-Flavored, Panda
    Express, 165–66
  Chicken Skillet, Crispy Orange,
    Applebee's, 5–6
  Chicken Tenders, Red Lobster, 190–91
  Chicken Wings, Buffalo, Hooters, 100
  Chicken Wings, Honey Barbecue, KFC,
    119
  Crab Cakes, Joe's Crab Shack, 109
  Egg Rolls, Southwestern, Chili's, 72–73
  Fish, Arthur Treacher's, 19
  Hush Puppies, Red Lobster, 193
  Mozzarella, Olive Garden, 148
  Onion Rings, Dairy Queen, 83
  Rice, Japanese, Benihana, 25
  Shrimp, Batter-Fried, Red Lobster,
    183
  Shrimp, Buffalo, Hooters, 98
  Shrimp, Stuffed, en Brochette, Joe's Crab
    Shack, 114
  Steak, Country, Denny's, 84–85
frostings, *see* icings
fruits, buying, guidelines for, xxvi
frying:
  meat, tip for, xx
  testing oil temperature for, 19

Index

fudge:
  Chocolate, Squares with Mocha Glaze, Starbucks, 217
  Sauce, Macaroni Grill, 123
  topping, in Dairy Queen Heath Blizzard, 81

garlic:
  Buttermilk Dressing, Houston's, 101
  Lemon Butter, Bennigan's, 29
  Mashed Potatoes, Applebee's, 8
  Roasted, Lemon Vinaigrette, Macaroni Grill, 131
ginger, xxvii
Gingerbread Loaf, Starbucks, 219
glass baking pans, oven temperature and, xx
glazes, xxiii
  Chocolate, Macaroni Grill, 129–30
  Mocha, Starbucks, 217
  Orange, Applebee's, 5–6
Gouda cheese, smoked, in California Pizza Kitchen BBQ Chicken Pizza, 45
graham cracker crusts:
  The Cheesecake Factory, 58
  Chili's, 68
grapefruit, buying, xxvi
grapes, in Union Pacific Grilled White Pekin Duck Breast, 235–36
grapeseed oil, 236
gravy:
  Country, Denny's, 85
  oversalted, tip for, xxii
  Roast Beef and, Roadhouse Grill, 199–200
greasing pans, xx
green beans, in Chili's Southwestern Vegetable Soup, 74
Green Onion-Bacon Mashed Potatoes, Applebee's, 3
greens:
  cooking tips for, xix
  see also lettuce; spinach
Grenadine, in T.G.I. Friday's Orange Cream, 231
grilled:
  Baby Back Ribs, Chili's, 65
  Chicken, Fiesta Lime, Applebee's, 7
  Chicken, Margarita, Chili's, 69
  Chicken, Santa Fe, Applebee's, 10–11
  Chicken Kabobs, Salsa Verde, Chi-Chi's, 62
  Chicken Quesadillas, Ruby Tuesday, 201

Chicken Sandwich, Blue Mountain, Rainforest Cafe, 180
Chicken Wings, Jamaican Jerk, Bahama Breeze, 21–22
Duck Breast, White Pekin, Union Pacific, 235–36
Pollo Asada, El Pollo Loco, 88
Ribs, BBQ, Hard Rock Cafe, 92
Steak, Hibachi, Benihana, 24
Steak, Marinated, Outback Steakhouse, 163
Steak and Mushroom Quesadillas, Chi-Chi's, 63–64
Tilapia with Mango Salsa, Low-Fat, Applebee's, 9
Grits, Cheese, Shrimp and, Bullfish Grill, 43–44
Grouper Siciliano, Red Lobster, 192

ham:
  Colorado Omelet, IHOP, 105
  Cyclone Pasta, Outback Steakhouse, 160
  Fettuccine Assortito, Olive Garden, 145
  Super Salad Bar Pasta, Ruby Tuesday, 207
hamburgers, cooking tip for, xxi
health concerns, ingredient substitutions and, xiv–xv
Heath Blizzard, Dairy Queen, 81
herbs, xxvii–xxviii
  storing, xxix
Hibachi Steak, Benihana, 24
hoisin sauce, 6
  Orange Glaze, Applebee's, 5–6
honey:
  Barbecue Wings, KFC, 119
  Mustard Dressing, Bennigan's, 27
  Mustard Dressing, T.G.I. Friday's, 229
  Safari Sauce, Rainforest Cafe, 182
  Wheat Bushman Bread, Outback Steakhouse, 161
honeydews, buying, xxvi
Hot Bacon Dressing, Bennigan's, 28
Hush Puppies, Red Lobster, 193

ice cream:
  Cheesecake, Baskin-Robbins, 23
  Dairy Queen, 82
  Heath Blizzard, Dairy Queen, 81
icings:
  Buttercream, Olive Garden, 142
  Hardee's, 96–97

Orange-Flavored Cream Cheese, Starbucks, 219
Indian Mulligatawny Soup, The Soup Nazi, 215
Insalata Florentine, Macaroni Grill, 126
Italian:
  Angel Hair and Three-Onion Soup, Olive Garden, 134
  Beef Fillets in Balsamic Sauce, Olive Garden, 135
  Bread Sticks, Olive Garden, 136
  Bruschetta al Pomodoro, Olive Garden, 137
  Butter, Carrabba's Italian Grill, 47
  Chicken Crostina, Olive Garden, 138–39
  Chicken San Marco, Olive Garden, 140–41
  Chocolate Lasagna, Olive Garden, 142–43
  Focaccia, Macaroni Grill, 125
  Fried Mozzarella, Olive Garden, 148
  Grouper Siciliano, Red Lobster, 192
  Insalata Florentine, Macaroni Grill, 126
  Marinated Mushrooms, Shoney's, 209
  Meatballs, Carrabba's Italian Grill, 48
  Oven-Roasted Potatoes, Olive Garden, 151
  Pork Filettino, Olive Garden, 154
  Salad Dressing, Olive Garden, 155
  Tiramisù, Olive Garden, 157
  Zuppa Toscana, Olive Garden, 159
  see also pasta; pizza

Jack cheese:
  Beef Chalupa Supreme, Taco Bell, 221
  Chicken Quesadilla Grande, Applebee's, 4
  Fiesta Lime Chicken, Applebee's, 7
  Mexican Pizza, Taco Bell, 226
  see also Monterey Jack cheese
Jack Daniel's Dipping Sauce, T.G.I. Friday's, 230
Jamaican Jerk Grilled Chicken Wings, Bahama Breeze, 21–22
Jambalaya Pasta, Cajun, The Cheesecake Factory, 52
Japanese:
  Fried Rice, Benihana, 25
  Hibachi Steak, Benihana, 24
Jerk Grilled Chicken Wings, Jamaican, Bahama Breeze, 21–22

jicama, storing, xix
julienning, xxiii

Kabobs, Salsa Verde Chicken, Chi-Chi's, 62
kale, in Olive Garden Zuppa Toscana, 159
Key Lime Pie, Outback Steakhouse, 162
kidney beans:
  Mexican Chicken Chili, The Soup Nazi, 216
  Pasta e Fagioli, Olive Garden, 152
  Southwestern Chicken Chili, Chili's, 71
  Southwestern Vegetable Soup, Chili's, 74

Lasagna, Five-Cheese, Olive Garden, 146–47
lemon(s):
  buying, xxvi
  Cream Cake, Olive Garden, 149–50
  -Flavored Syrup, Olive Garden, 158
  Garlic Butter, Bennigan's, 29
  juice, perking up soggy lettuce with, xix
  juice, removing odors with, xix
  Roasted Garlic Vinaigrette, Macaroni Grill, 131
lettuce:
  buying, xxv
  Chicken Wrap, P.F. Chang's, 172–73
  soggy, perking up, xix
  storing, xxi
  washing, xxi
lima beans:
  Baby, Cracker Barrel, 77
  buying, xxv
lime:
  Chicken, Fiesta, Applebee's, 7
  Key, Pie, Outback Steakhouse, 162
lingonberry sauce, in IHOP Swedish Pancakes, 108
linguine:
  Cajun Jambalaya Pasta, The Cheesecake Factory, 52
  Cajun Shrimp, Red Lobster, 185
  Chicken Crostina, Olive Garden, 138–39
  Diablo, Bennigan's, 29–30
Lobster Fondue, Red Lobster, 194
low-fat:
  Grilled Tilapia with Mango Salsa, Applebee's, 9
  see also fat, reducing intake of

Macaroni and Cheese, Boston Market, 36
mango:
    chutney, in Rainforest Cafe Safari Sauce,
      182
    Salsa, Applebee's, 9
Maple Butter Sauce, Applebee's, 15
margarine, healthier alternatives for, xiv
Margarita Grilled Chicken, Chili's, 69
marinades:
    Bahama Breeze (Jamaican, for chicken),
      21
    Chi-Chi's (for pork), 61
    Chi-Chi's (for steak), 63
    El Pollo Loco (for chicken), 88
    Red Lobster (for chicken), 190
    Red Lobster (for trout), 198
    T.G.I. Friday's (for chicken), 233
marinara:
    Sauce, Bennigan's, 29
    Shrimp, T.G.I. Friday's, 232
marinated:
    Mushrooms, Shoney's, 209
    Steak, Outback Steakhouse, 163
marinating, xxiii
    meat, tip for, xx
marjoram, xxvii
masa harina, in Chili's Chicken Enchilada
    Soup, 67
mascarpone cheese:
    Cheesecake, Junior's Famous No. 1
      (variation), 116–17
    Tiramisù, Olive Garden, 157
mashed potatoes:
    Bacon-Green Onion, Applebee's, 3
    Garlic, Applebee's, 8
    Roast Beef and, Roadhouse Grill, 199–
      200
    Sizzling Chicken and Cheese, T.G.I.
      Friday's, 233
mayonnaise, healthier alternatives for, xv
meat:
    cooking tips for, xix–xx
    Loaf, Boston Market, 37
    see also bacon; beef; ham; pork; sausage
meatballs:
    Carrabba's Italian Grill, 48
    cooked, storing, xxi
melons, buying, xxvi
Mexican and Tex-Mex:
    Baked Chicken Chimichangas, Chi-
      Chi's, 60
    Beans, El Pollo Loco, 87

Beef Chalupa Supreme, Taco Bell, 221
Beef Fajitas, Chili's, 66
Burrito Supreme, Taco Bell, 223–24
Chicken Chili, The Soup Nazi, 216
Chicken Enchilada Soup, Chili's, 67
Chicken Quesadilla Grande,
    Applebee's, 4
Chicken Quesadillas, Ruby Tuesday, 201
Enchirito, Taco Bell, 225
Margarita Grilled Chicken, Chili's, 69
Mexican Pizza, Taco Bell, 226
Pollo Asada, El Pollo Loco, 88
Shrimp Fajitas, Hard Rock Cafe, 95
Steak and Mushroom Quesadillas, Chi-
    Chi's, 63–64
Trout Veracruz, Red Lobster, 198
see also Southwestern
microwaving chicken, tip for, xx
milk, healthier alternatives for, xv
mincing, xxiii
mint, xxvii
Mocha Glaze, Starbucks, 217
Monterey Jack cheese:
    Broccoli Bites, Bennigan's, 26
    Chicken Quesadillas, Ruby Tuesday, 201
    Santa Fe Chicken, Applebee's, 10–11
    Seafood-Stuffed Mushrooms, Joe's Crab
      Shack, 112
    Southwestern Egg Rolls, Chili's, 72–73
    Stuffed Shrimp en Brochette, Joe's Crab
      Shack, 114
mozzarella cheese:
    BBQ Chicken Pizza, California Pizza
      Kitchen, 45
    Cavatini, Pizza Hut, 176
    Five-Cheese Chicken Fettuccine, Johnny
      Carino's, 115
    Five-Cheese Lasagna, Olive Garden,
      146–47
    Fried, Olive Garden, 148
    Onion Soup, Bennigan's, 31
    Pizza Bianco, Olive Garden, 153
Mulligatawny Soup, Indian, The Soup
    Nazi, 215
mushroom(s):
    buying, xxi, xxv
    Hibachi Steak, Benihana, 24
    Marinated, Shoney's, 209
    Seafood-Stuffed, Joe's Crab Shack, 112
    Shrimp Portofino, Macaroni Grill, 133
    Spinach Pizza, Applebee's, 12–13
    and Steak Quesadillas, Chi-Chi's, 63–64

Stuffing, Boston Market, 40
  see also shiitake mushrooms
mussels, in Red Lobster South Beach
  Seafood Paella, 196–97
mustard:
  Honey Dressing, Bennigan's, 27
  Honey Dressing, T.G.I. Friday's, 229
  Safari Sauce, Rainforest Cafe, 182

New Orleans-style: Barbecued Shrimp,
  Ruth's Chris Steak House, 208
noodle(s):
  Chicken, Soup, Homemade, Hard Rock
    Cafe, 93
  Sichuan Chicken Chow Fun, P.F.
    Chang's, 175
  see also pasta
nut(s):
  Banana Pancakes, IHOP, 103
  Reese's Peanut Butter Cake, Macaroni
    Grill, 129–30
  storing, xix
  Walnut Blondie with Maple Butter
    Sauce, Applebee's, 15

oil:
  grapeseed, 236
  healthier alternatives for, xiv
  testing temperature of, 19
olives:
  Pizza Bianco, Olive Garden, 153
  Trout Veracruz, Red Lobster, 198
Omelet, Colorado, IHOP, 105
onion(s):
  Green, Bacon Mashed Potatoes,
    Applebee's, 3
  and Pepper Medley, T.G.I. Friday's,
    233
  removing odor of, xix
  Rings, Dairy Queen, 83
  Sauce, Sweet, Subway, 220
  Soup, Bennigan's, 31
  Three-, and Angel Hair Soup, Olive
    Garden, 134
  Walkabout Soup, Outback Steakhouse,
    164
orange(s):
  buying, xxvi
  Chicken Skillet, Crispy, Applebee's, 5–6
  Cream, T.G.I. Friday's, 231
  -Flavored Chicken, Panda Express,
    165–66

Grilled White Pekin Duck Breast, Union
  Pacific, 235–36
oregano, xxviii
Oreo:
  Blizzard, Dairy Queen (variation), 81
  Cheesecake, The Cheesecake Factory,
    56–57
orzo:
  Insalata Florentine, Macaroni Grill, 126
  Spicy Rice, Boston Market, 38
Oven-Roasted Potatoes, Olive Garden, 151

pancakes:
  Apple, Union Pacific, 234
  Banana-Nut, IHOP, 103
  Cream of Wheat, IHOP, 106
  IHOP, 107
  Perkins Restaurant and Bakery, 171
  Swedish, IHOP, 108
paprika, xxviii
parboiling, xxiv
paring, xxiv
Parmesan cheese:
  Cajun Shrimp Linguine, Red Lobster,
    185
  Fettuccine Alfredo, Olive Garden, 144
  Five-Cheese Chicken Fettuccine, Johnny
    Carino's, 115
  Five-Cheese Lasagna, Olive Garden,
    146–47
  Pizza Bianco, Olive Garden, 153
  Potato Crust, Chicken Crostina with,
    Olive Garden, 138–39
  Shrimp Pasta, Ruby Tuesday, 203–4
  Sonoran Chicken Pasta, Ruby Tuesday,
    205–6
  Spinach Pizza, Applebee's, 12–13
parsley, xxviii
  flat-leaf Italian and curly-leaf, 213
pasta:
  Angel Hair and Three-Onion Soup,
    Olive Garden, 134
  Cajun Jambalaya, The Cheesecake
    Factory, 52
  Cavatini, Pizza Hut, 176
  Chicken, Sonoran, Ruby Tuesday, 205–6
  Chicken Crostina, Olive Garden,
    138–39
  Chicken Fettuccine, The Cheesecake
    Factory, 53
  Chicken San Marco, Olive Garden,
    140–41

Index

pasta (*cont.*)
Chicken-Tequila Fettuccine, California Pizza Kitchen, 46
cooking al dente, 36
Cyclone, Outback Steakhouse, 160
enriched, healthier alternatives for, xv
e Fagioli, Olive Garden, 152
Fettuccine Alfredo, Olive Garden, 144
Fettuccine Assortito, Olive Garden, 145
Five-Cheese Chicken Fettuccine, Johnny Carino's, 115
Five-Cheese Lasagna, Olive Garden, 146–47
Gamberetti e Pinoli, Macaroni Grill, 127–28
Linguine Diablo, Bennigan's, 29–30
Macaroni and Cheese, Boston Market, 36
orzo, in Boston Market Spicy Rice, 38
orzo, in Macaroni Grill Insalata Florentine, 126
Sesame Shrimp, Macaroni Grill, 132
Shrimp, Parmesan, Ruby Tuesday, 203–4
Shrimp Linguine, Cajun, Red Lobster, 185
Shrimp Marinara, T.G.I. Friday's, 232
Shrimp Portofino, Macaroni Grill, 133
Spaghetti Salad, Luby's Cafeteria, 122
Super Salad Bar, Ruby Tuesday, 207
Peanut Butter Cake, Reese's, Macaroni Grill, 129–30
Pear Turnovers, Arby's (variation), 16–17
peas, buying, xxv
pecans, in IHOP Banana-Nut Pancakes, 103
Pecorino Romano cheese:
Five-Cheese Chicken Fettuccine, Johnny Carino's, 115
Spinach and Artichoke Dip, Houston's, 102
Pekin Duck Breast, Grilled White, Union Pacific, 235–36
Peking Stir-fry Sauce, P.F. Chang's, 174
penne:
Cyclone Pasta, Outback Steakhouse, 160
Shrimp Pasta Parmesan, Ruby Tuesday, 203–4
Sonoran Chicken Pasta, Ruby Tuesday, 205–6
pepper(s) (bell):
Chicken San Marco, Olive Garden, 140–41

Fettuccine Assortito, Olive Garden, 145
and Onion Medley, T.G.I. Friday's, 233
Oven-Roasted Potatoes, Olive Garden, 151
roasted red, in Rainforest Cafe Blue Mountain Grilled Chicken Sandwich, 180
pepperoni, in Pizza Hut Cavatini, 176
Philly Cheesesteak, Pat's King of Steaks, 169
pies:
Chocolate Chip Paradise, Chili's, 68
Key Lime, Outback Steakhouse, 162
see also crusts
Pilaf, Rice, Joe's Crab Shack, 111
pine nuts:
Pasta Gamberetti e Pinoli, Macaroni Grill, 127–28
toasting, 128
pinto beans:
BBQ, Hard Rock Cafe, 91
El Pollo Loco, 87
see also refried beans
pistachios, in The Soup Nazi Indian Mulligatawny Soup, 215
pizza:
BBQ Chicken, California Pizza Kitchen, 45
Bianco, Olive Garden, 153
Mexican, Taco Bell, 226
Spinach, Applebee's, 12–13
poaching, xxiv
pollack, in Joe's Crab Shack Seafood Stuffing, 113
Pollo Asada, El Pollo Loco, 88
pork:
Baby Back Ribs, Applebee's, 1–2
Baby Back Ribs, Chili's, 65
BBQ Ribs, Hard Rock Cafe, 92
Filettino, Olive Garden, 154
Pulled, Hard Rock Cafe, 94
Tenderloin with Bourbon Sauce, Chi-Chi's, 61
see also bacon; ham; sausage
potato(es):
Bacon-Green Onion Mashed, Applebee's, 3
Baked, Soup, Hard Rock Cafe, 89–90
cooking tips for, xxi
Dill, Wedges, Boston Market, 35
Garlic Mashed, Applebee's, 8
instant, as thickener for stews, xix

mashed, in T.G.I. Friday's Sizzling
  Chicken and Cheese, 233
Mashed, Roast Beef and, Roadhouse
  Grill, 199–200
Oven-Roasted, Olive Garden, 151
Parmesan Crust, Chicken Crostina with,
  Olive Garden, 138–39
Skins, Baked, T.G.I. Friday's, 227
Zuppa Toscana, Olive Garden, 159
Pot Roast, Shoney's, 210
poultry, cooking tips for, xx
provolone cheese, in Johnny Carino's Five-
  Cheese Chicken Fettuccine, 115
Pudding, Banana, Cracker Barrel, 78
Pulled Pork, Hard Rock Cafe, 94
pumpkin:
  Cheesecake, The Cheesecake Factory,
    58–59
  spice, making your own, 59

quesadillas:
  Chicken, Grande, Applebee's, 4
  Chicken, Ruby Tuesday, 201
  Steak and Mushroom, Chi-Chi's, 63–64

raspberries, buying, xxvi
Reese's (peanut butter cups):
  Blizzard, Dairy Queen (variation), 81
  Peanut Butter Cake, Macaroni Grill,
    129–30
refried beans, 224
  Baked Chicken Chimichangas, Chi-
    Chi's, 60
  Burrito Supreme, Taco Bell, 223–24
  Crab Bisque, The Soup Nazi, 212–13
  Enchirito, Taco Bell, 225
  Mexican Pizza, Taco Bell, 226
ribs:
  Baby Back, Applebee's, 1–2
  Baby Back, Chili's, 65
  BBQ, Hard Rock Cafe, 92
rice:
  Cajun, Popeyes, 178
  Dirty, Popeyes, 179
  Japanese Fried, Japanese, Benihana,
    25
  Pilaf, Joe's Crab Shack, 111
  South Beach Seafood Paella, Red
    Lobster, 196–97
  Spicy, Boston Market, 38
  white, healthier alternatives for, xv
rice wine vinegar, 22

ricotta cheese:
  Five-Cheese Lasagna, Olive Garden,
    146–47
  Pizza Bianco, Olive Garden, 153
  see also pizza
roast(s):
  Beef and Mashed Potatoes, Roadhouse
    Grill, 199–200
  bone-in vs. boneless, xxi
  tenderizing with tomato, xx
Roasted Garlic-Lemon Vinaigrette,
  Macaroni Grill, 131
Romano cheese:
  Fettuccine Alfredo, Olive Garden,
    144
  Five-Cheese Lasagna, Olive Garden,
    146–47
  Oven-Roasted Potatoes, Olive Garden,
    151
rosemary, xxviii
rotini pasta:
  Macaroni and Cheese, Boston Market,
    36
  Super Salad Bar Pasta, Ruby Tuesday,
    207

Safari Sauce, Rainforest Cafe, 182
saffron, xxviii
sage, xxviii
salad(s):
  Bar Pasta, Super, Ruby Tuesday, 207
  Cucumber, Boston Market, 34
  Insalata Florentine, Macaroni Grill,
    126
  Sesame-Chicken, Panera Bread, 167
  Spaghetti, Luby's Cafeteria, 122
  see also dressings
salad bowls, xxi
salsa:
  Chili's, 70
  Mango, Applebee's, 9
  Verde Chicken Kabobs, Chi-Chi's, 62
salt, healthier alternatives for, xv
sandwiches:
  Barbecue Sauce for, Arby's, 18
  Grilled Chicken, Blue Mountain,
    Rainforest Cafe, 180
  Safari Sauce for, Rainforest Cafe, 182
  Sweet Onion Sauce for, Subway, 220
  see also quesadillas
Sangria, Olive Garden, 156
San Marco Sauce, Olive Garden, 140–41

Index

Santa Fe Chicken, Applebee's, 10–11
sauces:
  Banana Syrup, IHOP, 103
  Buffalo, Hooters, 98
  Cheese, Sonoran, Ruby Tuesday, 205–6
  Cooking, P.F. Chang's, 172
  Fontina Cheese, Olive Garden, 145
  Fudge, Macaroni Grill, 123
  Jack Daniel's Dipping, T.G.I. Friday's, 230
  Lobster Fondue, Red Lobster, 194
  Maple Butter, Applebee's, 15
  Marinara, Bennigan's, 29
  Onion, Sweet, Subway, 220
  Orange, Panda Express, 165
  Peking Stir-fry, P.F. Chang's, 174
  Safari, Rainforest Cafe, 182
  San Marco, Olive Garden, 140–41
  see also barbecue sauces; dressings; glazes
sausage:
  andouille, in Red Lobster South Beach Seafood Paella, 196–97
  Cavatini, Pizza Hut, 176
  Colorado Omelet, IHOP, 105
  Dirty Rice, Popeyes, 179
  Zuppa Toscana, Olive Garden, 159
sautéing, xxiv
saving money, cooking at home and, xi–xiii
scallops:
  Linguine Diablo, Bennigan's, 29–30
  South Beach Seafood Paella, Red Lobster, 196–97
  Stuffed, en Brochette, Joe's Crab Shack, 114
  Sun-Dried Tomato Seared, Brooklyn Cafe, 41–42
seafood:
  Clam Chowder, Red Lobster, 187
  Étouffée, Joe's Crab Shack, 110
  Linguine Diablo, Bennigan's, 29–30
  Lobster Fondue, Red Lobster, 194
  Paella, South Beach, Red Lobster, 196–97
  -Stuffed Mushrooms, Joe's Crab Shack, 112
  Stuffing, Joe's Crab Shack, 113
  see also crab(meat); scallops; shrimp
seeds, storing, xix
sesame (seeds):
  Chicken Salad, Panera Bread, 167
  Shrimp, Macaroni Grill, 132
  toasting, 132

shiitake mushrooms:
  Chicken-Lettuce Wrap, P.F. Chang's, 172–73
  Cyclone Pasta, Outback Steakhouse, 160
  Pasta Gamberetti e Pinoli, Macaroni Grill, 127–28
shortening:
  greasing pans with, xx
  healthier alternatives for, xiv
shrimp:
  Barbecued, Ruth's Chris Steak House, 208
  Batter-Fried, Red Lobster, 183
  Buffalo, Hooters, 98
  Cajun Jambalaya Pasta, The Cheesecake Factory, 52
  and Cheese Grits, Bullfish Grill, 43–44
  Diablo, Red Lobster, 195
  Étouffée, Joe's Crab Shack, 110
  Fajitas, Hard Rock Cafe, 95
  Linguine, Cajun, Red Lobster, 185
  Linguine Diablo, Bennigan's, 29–30
  Marinara, T.G.I. Friday's, 232
  Pasta Gamberetti e Pinoli, Macaroni Grill, 127–28
  Pasta Parmesan, Ruby Tuesday, 203–4
  Portofino, Macaroni Grill, 133
  Seafood Stuffing, Joe's Crab Shack, 113
  Sesame, Macaroni Grill, 132
  South Beach Seafood Paella, Red Lobster, 196–97
  Stuffed, en Brochette, Joe's Crab Shack, 114
Sichuan Chicken Chow Fun, P.F. Chang's, 175
side dishes:
  Apples, Fried, Cracker Barrel, 80
  Beans, BBQ, Hard Rock Cafe, 91
  Beans, El Pollo Loco, 87
  Bread Sticks, Olive Garden, 136
  Buttermilk Biscuits, KFC, 118
  Honey-Wheat Bushman Bread, Outback Steakhouse, 161
  Hush Puppies, Red Lobster, 193
  Limas, Baby, Cracker Barrel, 77
  Macaroni and Cheese, Boston Market, 36
  Onion Rings, Dairy Queen, 83
  Spinach, Creamed, Boston Market, 32–33
  Squash Casserole, Boston Market, 39

Stuffing, Boston Market, 40
see also potato(es); rice
simmering, xxiv
Sizzling Chicken and Cheese, T.G.I.
   Friday's, 233
slow cooker, recipes adapted for:
   Baby Back Ribs, Chili's, 65
   Pot Roast, Shoney's, 210
   Pulled Pork, Hard Rock Cafe, 94
Sofrito (Vegetable Sauté), Red Lobster, 196
Sonoran Chicken Pasta, Ruby Tuesday,
   205–6
soups:
   Angel Hair and Three-Onion, Olive
     Garden, 134
   Baked Potato, Hard Rock Cafe, 89–90
   Broccoli-Cheese, Panera Bread, 168
   Broccoli-Cheese, T.G.I. Friday's, 228
   Chicken Enchilada, Chili's, 67
   Chicken Noodle, Homemade, Hard
     Rock Cafe, 93
   Clam Chowder, Red Lobster, 187
   Crab Bisque, The Soup Nazi, 212–13
   Cream of Sweet Potato, The Soup Nazi,
     214
   Dungeness Crab Bisque, Red Lobster,
     189
   Indian Mulligatawny, The Soup Nazi,
     215
   Onion, Bennigan's, 31
   Pasta e Fagioli, Olive Garden, 152
   Tomato-Basil, Applebee's, 14
   Tomato Florentine, Shoney's, 211
   Vegetable, Southwestern, Chili's, 74
   Walkabout, Outback Steakhouse, 164
   Zuppa Toscana, Olive Garden, 159
sour cream, healthier alternatives for, xv
South Beach Seafood Paella, Red Lobster,
   196–97
Southwestern:
   Chicken Chili, Chili's, 71
   Egg Rolls, Chili's, 72–73
   Santa Fe Chicken, Applebee's, 10–11
   Sonoran Chicken Pasta, Ruby Tuesday,
     205–6
   Vegetable Soup, Chili's, 74
   see also Mexican and Tex-Mex
Spaghetti Salad, Luby's Cafeteria, 122
Spanish:
   Sangria, Olive Garden, 156
   South Beach Seafood Paella, Red
     Lobster, 196–97

spices, xxvi–xxviii
   storing, xxix
Spicy Rice, Boston Market, 38
spinach:
   and Artichoke Dip, Houston's, 102
   Creamed, Boston Market, 32–33
   Hot Bacon Dressing for, Bennigan's, 28
   Insalata Florentine, Macaroni Grill, 126
   Pasta Gamberetti e Pinoli, Macaroni
     Grill, 127–28
   Pizza, Applebee's, 12–13
   Southwestern Egg Rolls, Chili's, 72–73
   Tomato Florentine Soup, Shoney's, 211
Squash Casserole, Boston Market, 39
steak:
   Beef Fajitas, Chili's, 66
   Country Fried, Denny's, 84–85
   Hibachi, Benihana, 24
   Marinated, Outback Steakhouse, 163
   and Mushroom Quesadillas, Chi-Chi's,
     63–64
   Philly Cheesesteak, Pat's King of Steaks,
     169
steeping, xxiv
stews, thickener for, xix
stir-fries:
   Chicken-Lettuce Wrap, P.F. Chang's,
     172–73
   Chicken with Black Bean Sauce, P.F.
     Chang's, 174
   Cooking Sauce for, P.F. Chang's, 172
   Peking Stir-fry Sauce for, P.F. Chang's,
     174
   Sichuan Chicken Chow Fun, P.F.
     Chang's, 175
storing:
   bean sprouts and jicama, xix
   celery, xxi
   coffee, xix
   cooked meatballs, xxi
   herbs and spices, xxix
   lettuce, xxi
   poultry, xx
   seeds and nuts, xix
strawberries, buying, xxvi
Stuffed Shrimp en Brochette, Joe's Crab
   Shack, 114
stuffings:
   Boston Market, 40
   Seafood, Joe's Crab Shack, 113
substitutions, healthier alternatives and,
   xiv–xv

Sun-Dried Tomato Seared Scallops, Brooklyn Cafe, 41–42
Super Salad Bar Pasta, Ruby Tuesday, 207
Swedish Pancakes, IHOP, 108
Sweet Onion Sauce, Subway, 220
Sweet Potato Soup, Cream of, The Soup Nazi, 214
Swiss cheese:
    Blue Mountain Grilled Chicken Sandwich, Rainforest Cafe, 180
    Onion Soup, Bennigan's, 31
symbols, guide to, xxx–xxxi
syrups:
    Banana, IHOP, 103
    Lemon-Flavored, Olive Garden, 158

tamarind, in The Cheesecake Factory Dipping Sauce, 49
tarragon, xxviii
Tea, Tuscan, Olive Garden, 158
tequila:
    Chicken Fettuccine, California Pizza Kitchen, 46
    Margarita Grilled Chicken, Chili's, 69
Tex-Mex, see Mexican and Tex-Mex
thawing meat, xx
thyme, xxviii
Tilapia, Low-Fat Grilled, with Mango Salsa, Applebee's, 9
Tiramisù, Olive Garden, 157
tomato(es):
    Basil Soup, Applebee's, 14
    Bruschetta al Pomodoro, Olive Garden, 137
    Chicken Enchilada Soup, Chili's, 67
    Florentine Soup, Shoney's, 211
    Mango Salsa, Applebee's, 9
    Marinara Sauce, Bennigan's, 29
    ripening, xxi
    Salsa, Chili's, 70
    sun-dried, in Outback Steakhouse Cyclone Pasta, 160
    Sun-Dried, Seared Scallops, Brooklyn Cafe, 41–42
    tenderizing roasts with, xx
tortilla(s):
    Baked Chicken Chimichangas, Chi-Chi's, 60
    Beef Fajitas, Chili's, 66
    Burrito Supreme, Taco Bell, 223–24
    Chicken Quesadilla Grande, Applebee's, 4

Chicken Quesadillas, Ruby Tuesday, 201
chips, Houston's Spinach and Artichoke Dip for, 102
Enchirito, Taco Bell, 225
Mexican Pizza, Taco Bell, 226
Pollo Asada, El Pollo Loco, 88
Shrimp Fajitas, Hard Rock Cafe, 95
Southwestern Egg Rolls, Chili's, 72–73
Steak and Mushroom Quesadillas, Chi-Chi's, 63–64
tossing, xxiv
Trout Veracruz, Red Lobster, 198
turkey:
    Colorado Omelet, IHOP (variation), 105
    Meat Loaf, Boston Market (variation), 37
Turnovers, Apple, Arby's, 16–17
Tuscan:
    Tea, Olive Garden, 158
    Zuppa Toscana, Olive Garden, 159

vanilla ice cream:
    Dairy Queen, 82
    Heath Blizzard, Dairy Queen, 81
    Orange Cream, T.G.I. Friday's, 231
vegetable(s):
    buying, guidelines for, xxv
    cooking tips for, xix, xxii
    Indian Mulligatawny Soup, The Soup Nazi, 215
    Sauté (Sofrito), Red Lobster, 196
    Soup, Southwestern, Chili's, 74
    see also side dishes; specific vegetables
Velveeta:
    Broccoli-Cheese Soup, T.G.I. Friday's, 228
    Chicken Enchilada Soup, Chili's, 67
    Lobster Fondue, Red Lobster, 194
    Sonoran Chicken Pasta, Ruby Tuesday, 205–6
vinaigrettes:
    Roasted Garlic-Lemon, Macaroni Grill, 131
    see also dressings
vinegar:
    Balsamic Sauce, Beef Fillets in, Olive Garden, 135
    cooking odors and, xix
    rice wine, 22

Index

Walkabout Soup, Outback Steakhouse, 164
walnut(s):
    Blondie with Maple Butter Sauce,
        Applebee's, 15
    Chocolate Chip Paradise Pie, Chili's, 68
watermelons, buying, xxvi
whipping, xxiv
whiskey, in T.G.I. Friday's Jack Daniel's
    Dipping Sauce, 230
white beans:
    Pasta e Fagioli, Olive Garden, 152
    Southwestern Chicken Chili, Chili's, 71
whole wheat:
    Honey-Wheat Bushman Bread, Outback
        Steakhouse, 161
    Pancakes, IHOP (variation), 107
wine:
    Balsamic Sauce, Beef Fillets in, Olive
        Garden, 135
    Sangria, Olive Garden, 156

Wondra flour, 141
Wrap, Chicken-Lettuce, P.F. Chang's,
    172–73

yeast, testing temperature for, xx
yellow squash:
    Chicken San Marco, Olive Garden,
        140–41
    Fettuccine Assortito, Olive Garden,
        145
    Squash Casserole, Boston Market,
        39

zucchini:
    Chicken San Marco, Olive Garden,
        140–41
    Fettuccine Assortito, Olive Garden,
        145
    Squash Casserole, Boston Market, 39
Zuppa Toscana, Olive Garden, 159